Accelerated Spanish

Volume 2: Basic Fluency

Accelerated Spanish

Learn fluent Spanish with a proven accelerated learning system.
Volume 2: Basic Fluency

CREATED BY TIMOTHY MOSER

with Josiah Moser and Samuel Moser

Kamel Press, LLC

Visit SpanishIn1Month.com for an abundance of materials that accompany this book, including video, audio, and quizzes, as well as further volumes in the series.

Published by Kamel Press.

Library of Congress 2016950770

ISBN: 9781624870668

Book design and cover design by Timothy Moser.

PRINTED IN THE UNITED STATES OF AMERICA

Contents

Dedication   1
Introduction: Are You Ready To Accelerate?   3

Lesson 7   **6**
    Theory: Think in Spanish   9
    Vocabulary: Yol   15
    Application: Polishing Syntax   43

Lesson 8   **62**
    Theory: Build Your Own Sentences   65
    Vocabulary: Hacer, Poder, and Querer   73
    Application: Verb Contractions   93

Lesson 9   **110**
    Theory: Leverage Essential Vocabulary   113
    Vocabulary: Adverbs and Adjectives   119
    Application: Descriptiveness   155

Lesson 10   **170**
    Theory: Listen Well   173
    Vocabulary: Irregular Verbs   179
    Application: Idioms   205

Lesson 11   **218**
    Theory: Practice Right   221
    Vocabulary: Nouns!   229
    Application: Labels   255

Lesson 12   **272**
    Theory: Have Adventures   275
    Vocabulary: Regular Verbs   283
    Application: Verb Fluency   309

Appendix: Dialogues   **335**

Dedication

This book is especially dedicated to the kickstarter contributors.

A million thanks for supporting the future of accelerated language learning.

And a million apologies for the time it's taken me to finish this book.

- Giuseppe Todaro
- Andrea Mielke Schroer
- Kevin Lee
- Astra Morris
- Elizabeth Bartson
- Ziva Lynn
- Kathleen Spracklen
- James Small
- Carter Brownrigg
- Sean Mathews
- Rhett Connelly
- Andrew Peoples
- Heather Arling
- Kermit Jones Jr.
- Douglas Provencher
- Vinod Krishnan

- Cassandra Sanford
- William Moffatt
- Jessica Seebauer
- Paul Stefan Ort
- Katherine Kaneko
- Patrick Radtke
- Graham Gilmour
- Donald Bruce
- Anthony N. Semones
- Robert Love
- Matthew Smith
- Britton Miller
- Martin McNamara
- Tom Los
- Jared King
- Debby Chlebana

- Lee Culbertson Gonzalez
- Melinda Ring
- Aadam Quraishi
- Kate Rahimzadeh
- Thomas Heiman
- Stephanie Albertson
- Gina Rubio
- Gunter Heiss
- "Kekekabic" Dubinsky
- Osvaldo Muñoz Jiménez
- Sheila Breeden
- Brandon
- Elizabeth Thompson
- Nanda
- Travis Paul Grether

"I have a decent time with vocabulary, but struggle with conjugation and speaking correctly. It gets very frustrating."
— Jessalyn

"My biggest frustration has always been getting overwhelmed. Should I write down every new word I hear each day? Work through a textbook? Watch a TV show? Study characters? Read a novel? Of course, you just end up spinning."
— Ken

"I am frustrated with being overwhelmed and not seeing a system that links everything together so that you can find the patterns quickly."
— Sylvia

Introduction:

Are You Ready To Accelerate?

*We're about to jump to light speed. Make sure your seat
is bolted down and your safety belt is secured.*

THE THREE STUDENTS quoted on the facing page had one thing in common: They were trying to learn Spanish, but without following a clear accelerated learning protocol.

Fortunately, Accelerated Spanish, so far, has given you a clear protocol to follow!

But are you really where you need to be right now?

Up to this point, we've been trudging through the extremely important fundamentals of syntax and working with a limited vocabulary of 100 words. We've been exclusively focused on making those mechanics second-nature.

Here's the good news: Your efforts get rewarded now. By the end of this book and with proper practice, you should reach a basic level of fluency.

But here's the reality check: You're going to be tempted to lose direction if you take off too fast, without the proper precautions.

If you are confident in your mastery of the first volume, volume two will move a lot faster. But fluency is not to be taken lightly, and there are all kinds of pitfalls and traps to avoid along the way. So before you proceed, let's make sure you have reached an appropriate comfort level.

Hopefully, you left Volume 1 with the capability of carrying conversations like this:

- *¿Dónde estás ahora?*

- *Estoy en casa. ¿Vas a estar aquí?*

- *Sí, voy a estar ahí. Y tengo que tener esa cosa.*

- *¿La cosa que tengo yo? Bueno, está bien, la vas a tener.*

- *Muy bien. ¡Hasta esta noche!*

3

Some would say that this is fairly simple Spanish. But the immeasurable value here is our mastery of Spanish **syntax** (the way that Spanish sentences work).

Most students have one of these reactions after finishing volume 1:

(1) "I feel awesome. I know 50% of the Spanish language, and I've mastered most of the grammar that I need in order to be fluent."

(2) "Man, I hope the pace picks up soon. I only really know 100 words. How am I supposed to be talking like this?"

Yes, Volume 1 taught a small amount of vocabulary. But that was for a reason. We focused mostly on theory and grammar, two elements that are essential to the accelerated process.

But now that that's done, it's time to build on the foundation we've laid, using the same principles but at a much faster rate.

See, one of the most common comments we get about Volume 1 is that it moves slowly. We focus on theory for a long time, and we only learn about 100 total words.

But Volume 2 is the opposite: 500 words are taught, and the lessons move at a very rapid pace.

If you're comfortable with the simple vocabulary but complex grammar of Volume 1, you're now ready to work toward conversation that sounds more like this:

- ¿Siquiera sabes dónde está?

- No, pero la voy a buscar.

- ¿Y conoces a alguien que sepa cómo entrar?

- No, no conozco a nadie que haya entrado.

And you'll be ready for sentences that are this complex:

- Es que para que todo volviera a ser lo que era, había que encontrar el agua y llevarla lejos.

- Quizá olvides algo que no parecía importante pero lo era, y cuanto más buscas más encuentras.

Believe it or not, our goal is to make these sentence structures second nature by the end of this book.

Don't be intimidated; we've already laid the foundation. Volume 1 has primed you for everything to come. Those first six lessons carved out the two primary elements of accelerated language learning:

(1) Learn vocabulary by function.

(2) Learn phrases in natural dialogues.

Building on that, we'll be able to take your Spanish learning all the way to fluency.

And then Volume 3 will be presented entirely in Spanish.

If you're sure you've mastered Volume 1, proceed with cautious confidence.

LESSON 7

Think in Spanish

To speak Spanish, you have to <u>think</u> Spanish.

You already have enough words to express most of your thoughts in Spanish. In this lesson, you're going to train yourself to think in Spanish by changing your habits.

Let's start forcing our minds to turn English thoughts into Spanish thoughts.

Lesson 7 Theory:
Think in Spanish

"You can never understand one language until you understand at least two."

- Geoffrey Willans

"Listen to your heart, listen to the rain, listen to the voices in your brain."

- Becky and Joe

NOW THAT you have mastered Lessons 1-6 of this course, you might be congratulating yourself: "I know 50% of Spanish! I'm on my way to becoming a true Spanish speaker."

But "knowing" Spanish words isn't the same thing as <u>thinking</u> in Spanish. Don't get too comfortable yet; you are now faced with the difficult task of helping your mind make the switch.

Right away, let's try two quick tests to see what your current level is of thinking in Spanish.

(1) Can you say this phrase out loud and think the meaning, without thinking about English?

Mis cosas están en tu casa.

This is pretty easy to translate, word by word; it means "my things are at your house".

But when you say this sentence, do you translate each word one by one? Or do you actually know what it means, in your mind, in Spanish… without translating the words into English?

"Mis cosas están en tu casa."

Say it several times, thinking about the heart of what each word means, but not thinking about the English versions of those words.

(2) Next, try this sentence:

Para entonces, se habrán ido.

Wow, that's a lot harder.

In English, the sentence means "By that time, they will have left." Sorry, but you can't translate it word by word! If you try, you get something like "for then, themselves they will have gone"… nope, doesn't work.

"Para entonces, se habrán ido." Say this several times, and make sure you know what you're saying. This is the only way to genuine fluency: Starting to think in Spanish phrases.

True Spanish speakers know exactly what *para entonces* means as soon as they hear it. They don't translate word by word and figure it out.

This isn't unique to Spanish, of course; English is the same: If I say "he's here <u>as well</u>", you aren't going to puzzle over these two words: "as… well? Why are these two words being used together?" Instead, you immediately know that this phrase means "also" ("he's here also").

And that's for a simple reason: If you're a native English speaker, you've been using the phrase "as well" your entire life. It's like its own word, one you've used every day.

You never even think about it; "as well" and "also" are used interchangeably. In your conscious mind, the thought behind the phrase "as well" is more important than the individual words you use to put that meaning into your sentence.

So that's our goal with Spanish. You need to be able to THINK Spanish, using idiomatic phrases without consciously puzzling through the individual words.

The sooner you do this, the sooner you'll be able to jump into even the most advanced Spanish conversations.

Labels vs. Syntax

Imagine that you accidentally stumble into a classroom where you don't belong.

You're a first-year medical student, and you happen to enter a forum where two surgeons are describing the analgesic protocols for use during atlantoaxial stabilization procedures.

If you're like me, you'll probably walk out of the room in a daze, saying, "That was all Greek to me."

What's funny is that they weren't speaking Greek; they were speaking English. But they were using a lot of words you don't know: Specifically, words we call <u>labels</u>.

Labels are different from syntax. Those doctors were speaking with completely English syntax that you would understand; their articles ("the", "a", "an"), pronouns ("it", "they", "their"), prepositions ("of", "at", "with"), and other essential connectors are all entirely within your comfortable vocabulary. It was just the labels, certain big nouns, verbs, etc., that you couldn't understand. The syntax itself was English.

"So what?" you might ask. "I still didn't understand a thing."

Well, that's because you weren't participating in the conversation. If you had asked a few questions, you might have clarified what some of those labels meant.

This would be easy for you to do if you're fluent in English syntax. Once you were talking with them, it would be very clear that you and they were essentially speaking the same language, just with some labels that you would have to clarify.

How does the difference between labels and syntax help you with thinking in Spanish?

Let's imagine that you have this English thought:

"My suitcase is very full, and I'm not sure if I can carry it."

There are plenty of words in there that you probably don't know yet in Spanish, such as "suitcase" and "carry". But you can still work out the syntax of this sentence:

"*Mi* suitcase *está muy* full, *y no estoy* sure *si lo* I can carry."

That's a Spanish sentence. It just happens to be missing a few labels. But if you can think that sentence, you're still thinking in Spanish.

Once you're thinking that way, and speaking that way, you'll very soon be able to participate in Spanish conversations, no matter how advanced they are. At that point, Spanish conversation on ANY topic will be very much like English conversation where you simply don't know some of the labels.

Using your Spanish syntax, you could even jump into the conversation with the surgeons! Or into any other conversation. You would just

have to be willing to ask questions; you'd have to be humble and admit that although you CAN speak Spanish, you don't know everything.

Imagine that you're working in an office in Chile, and you know all the syntax that is necessary for conversation, but you're missing some important labels for your everyday office work.

One day the printer runs out of ink, and you need to let the techs know what the problem is so they can fix it. At first, you'll be confronted with unfamiliar words like *impresora* and *amarillo* and *cian*, but once you learn those few new labels, it will start to make sense. Since you understand the syntax, all you'll need to clarify are a few labels. And at any point, if you need to indicate something that you don't know the label for, you can improvise with terms like *esta cosa* and *cuando esté mejor*.

Let's look at some practical ways to make this a part of your life.

The Spanish Zone

Remember, you've arrived at 50%. That means that at this point, you really have a lot of things you can say that are entirely in Spanish.

De verdad, ya tienes muchas cosas que son sólo de español.

Wait, what did I just do?

I took this sentence: "At this point, you really have a lot of things you can say that are entirely in Spanish."

And then I modified it to simpler, more accessible terms: "Really, now you have many things that are only of Spanish:" *De verdad, ya tienes muchas cosas que son sólo de español.*

Theoretically, you could do this with every single thought that you have! But that would get tiring very quickly. So let's implement The Spanish Zone.

Choose a place in your house, or maybe an hour of the day, to be your Spanish Zone where you must force yourself to think in Spanish. There's just one rule: While in The Spanish Zone, all of your English thoughts must turn into Spanish thoughts.

It's a three-step process:

(1) Express the thought clearly, using English words. (Maybe even write it down.)

(2) Rephrase it and translate it into a Spanish sentence.

(3) *Think* that thought again, this time using your Spanish sentence.

(4) Bonus: Now write down the Spanish version (and, ideally, send it to a native Spanish teacher to see if you're on the right track).

To make this work, it's important that you start with your English thoughts and then translate those into Spanish. The English has to come first. If you start with the Spanish words, you will probably gravitate towards topics and structures that you're already familiar with. In real life, if you're in a situation where you need to speak Spanish, it's likely that what you need to express won't fit naturally within the patterns you've practiced. They'll require some creative thinking to get the ideas across.

Imagine that you're sitting at your desk and this phrase occurs to you: "I want to get up and get some coffee."

You don't have the words for "want", "get up", or "coffee", so let's modify this. Simply point at the coffee and change your sentence to "I don't have that": *Yo no tengo eso.*

Or maybe even "There is something that I don't have": *Ahí está algo que no tengo.*

Another phrase that

might commonly occur to you is "I'm bored; I want to go do something else." We can change this to "I have to leave; I have to have something else now." *Yo me tengo que ir, tengo que tener algo más ahora.*

But then you might tell yourself, "But I can't leave; I have to be here." *Pero no hay que ir, tengo que estar aquí.*

Sure, these sentences don't perfectly express your thoughts. But they're getting close. You're turning your English thoughts into Spanish thoughts.

And at the same time, you're giving yourself extensive practice with Spanish grammar. Instead of creating simple sentences, you'll be forced to turn complex English sentences (the type that you think all the time) into complex Spanish sentences.

There will still be a lot of English sentence structures that you have difficulty converting into Spanish, but fortunately, the vocabulary and grammar that we're about to learn in Lesson 7 will greatly expand your capabilities.

LANGUAGE IS DIVIDED BETWEEN LABELS AND SYNTAX. PERFECT THE SYNTAX, AND THE LANGUAGE WILL BE YOURS.

Lesson 7 Vocabulary:

Yol
(Joel's World)

THIS LESSON'S vocabulary will involve a survey of Joel's entire world, besides verbs. We'll review the words that we've learned in previous lessons, and we'll add words to those same scenes (because these new words are used in similar ways).

Fruit Amusement

Joel comes to the amusement park extremely early on a Monday morning, just before the sun comes up.

Of course, Joel likes the light. We've

seen before that he feels like he belongs to the "day". So when he picks a ride in the early morning, he wants to pick the ride that looks closest to the rising sun.

To help him with this task, he uses a piece of fruit that he found in the marketplace. This fruit's colors look a lot like the colors of the rising sun. As Joel stands next to the park binoculars, he compares the different parts of the sky with the fruit he's holding, insisting, "I want to go where the dawn is", or "I want to go *donde* the dawn is".

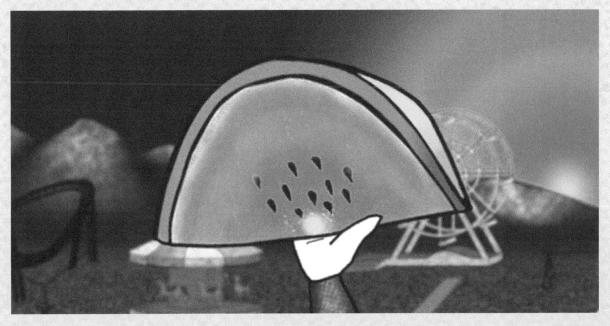

The word *donde* means "where" as a conjunction. You'll notice that this is similar to a word in the marketplace, but there it had an accent mark (*dónde*), whereas now it doesn't. ("It's not in the market, so don't mark it.") Instead of asking questions, this word *donde* is used to join phrases, just like other conjunctions. So we'll leave this little slice of "dawn-day melon" next to the binoculars, along with the *pero* pear and the *porque* pig.

There's another new item here at the conjunction paths. Joel realizes that he has spent a lot of money at this amusement park. He is a wealthy bee, but it seems that his wealth is being partly redistributed to the people who own the different rides. As he sits at the intersection pondering this, he starts placing Yen bills on the different branches of the path, based on how many times he has gone to each ride in the last week, trying to determine who has gotten the most money from him.

When he sees the most money on the path that goes to the *por* water slide, Joel concludes, "The water slide owner is the one who has the most Yen!"

To rephrase this, he says "The water slide owner is the one *quien* has the most Yen!"

As you can see, the word *quien* is a lot like the word *que*. In fact, in Joel's sentence, we could have used *que* instead ("the person *que* has the most Yen"). But sometimes when Joel is referring to a person, he chooses *quien* instead.

This word is pronounced exactly like the word *quién*, which we learned in the swamp as a question, with the stress on "Yen". But this version without an accent is used to connect phrases in a statement, like the word *donde* and other conjunctions.

Let's go to the rides. Joel concludes that he wants to ride the ferris wheel, but he makes a mistake and follows the path to the carousel. Now that he's walked all the way to the carousel, he doesn't want to go all the way back up the path. So he tries to take a shortcut.

But he realizes that there's a good reason for those paths.

The ground in the amusement park is treacherously rough and deceptive. Joel is hungry, and since he doesn't have the energy to fly, he is forced to crawl along this horribly unreliable ground on his hands and feet.

When he finally reaches the ferris wheel, he asks the operator how much time has passed. "I started crawling here on Monday morning," he tells him.

The ride operator replies, "It's Friday afternoon now."

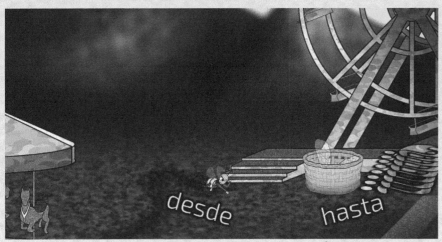

Wow! Joel has been crawling for days, since Monday! How grueling.

To say "I have been crawling since Monday", Joel uses a preposition with the stressed syllable "days": "I have been crawling *desde* Monday."

The ride operator is surprised. "Where did you crawl here from?" he asks.

"I crawled *desde* the carousel *hasta* the ferris wheel."

The literal meaning of the word desde is "since", but it doesn't just refer to time. It's used when you're traveling "from / since" one point "to / until" another point, whether in time or in space. So as you can see, *desde* is related to *hasta*, but as the opposite. Compare these two examples:

- "I crawled *desde* Monday *hasta* Friday."

- "I crawled *desde* the carousel *hasta* the ferris wheel."

For English speakers, this takes some getting used to. Note that in the second example, the word *de* could also be used, but native speakers would more likely use *desde* in situations that go along with *hasta*. For this reason, we're officially storing the word *desde* at the ferris wheel, near *hasta*.

Stay, All of You

After leaving the amusement park, Joel tries to rush past the shepherd and the sheep. He has big plans for shopping in the marketplace today and doesn't want to be distracted.

The shepherd can tell that Joel is in a hurry. "What's your rush?" he asks.

Joel angrily responds, "I have plans today. Big important plans. But what would you know about it, sitting here all day with your sheep?"

In Joel's estimation, the shepherd is a small-minded person. He and his sheep just stay in one place all day,

doing nothing interesting except dancing once in a while. Meanwhile, Joel and his friends the pandas have all kinds of adventures throughout Yol.

Remember that Joel has names for each of the characters: The shepherd is *tú*, the main female sheep is *ella*, the main male sheep is *él*, Joel is *yo*, and Joel uses the word *nosotros* when he's talking about himself and the pandas ("we").

But when Joel is addressing the shepherd and his sheep, if he's speaking to them as a group, he calls them by a word whose stressed syllable is "stay": *ustedes*. This is the plural form of "you", as in "you all", or "All you people who just stay here all the time."

Joel contrasts the boring *ustedes* with the more exciting *nosotros*, Joel and the pandas. "We (*nosotros*) have adventures, but you all (*ustedes*) just stay here doing nothing."

The shepherd is offended by this. "I respectfully disagree," says the shepherd. "We have adventures too, you know."

"Like what?" asks Joel.

"Well, for one thing, all the sheep know how to dance," says the shepherd. He whistles, and suddenly all the sheep are dancing. "Heya! Look! See, all of them can dance!"

He points at the female sheep: "*Ellas* can all dance!" Then he points at the male sheep: "*Ellos* can dance too!"

Joel rolls his eyes. "So what if some boring sheep can dance? I bet any old sheep can do that. That's not special at all."

Pulling out his spray paint, Joel paints the word *unas* on one fence and *unos* on the other.

These words are a lot like *una* and *un*, but they apply to more than one sheep. For example, if a sheep is male, "a sheep" is "*un* sheep". But "some sheep" would be "*unos* sheep". Joel uses these words when he's emphasizing sheep (or any other objects) that aren't considered special. (For the nerds, these words are called "plural indefinite articles".)

As the shepherd looks around at all the "art" painted on his fences, Joel says, "Bye now. *Nosotros* are leaving *ustedes* alone. We have more important things to do than sit around staring at *unas* dancing sheep."

Before we leave this scene, I want to point out that the word *ustedes* confuses a lot of English speakers. In English, we just use the word "you", whether we're talking to one person or to several people. But for Joel, they're completely different things. *Tú* is used when there's just one person, but *ustedes* is used when there are more than one. This is something we'll get used to as we practice Spanish phrases.

Les

Today Joel rushes through the next scenes quickly, so it's hard to say exactly what he does in each place. Instead, let's talk about these three areas in a more general way.

Normally, Joel visits the "direct object" hill, the "indirect object" crossroads area, and the "reflexive" stream. In all three of these scenes, the words that we store are used right before a verb. For example, "I have it" is "*lo tengo*" (from the direct object scene). "I'm giving her a book" is "*le* I'm giving a book" (from the indirect object scene). "I seat myself" is "*me* I seat" (from the reflexive scene).

Each of these areas seems to store very similar items. The words *me*, *te*, and *nos* are in all three scenes, though they mean different things in each scene. But the word *lo*, stored in the direct object scene, transforms to *le* in the indirect object scene (for the sheep that "lay" down) and turns into *se* at the reflexive scene. And the word *la* goes through the same changes: *le* as

an indirect object and *se* as a reflexive object.

As you noticed in the sheep pasture scene today, the words *una* and *ella* can be made plural when you put an S at the end: *unas* and *ellas*. Similarly, the words *un* and *él* can be turned into *unos* and *ellos*.

This rule will work for some of our object pronouns as well. For example, let's try it at the direct object scene. If I have one house, I can say "I have it" by saying "*La tengo.*" But what if I have more than one house? To say "I have them", I say "*Las tengo.*"

So the words *la* and *lo*, at the direct object scene, can turn into *las* and *los*. But be careful! As always, it's very important to recognize that these words are completely different from the words *las* and *los* that we learned as articles in the sheep scene; those words mean "the", whereas these words mean "them". "*Los hombres*" means "the men" (sheep pasture scene), but "*los tengo*" means "I have them" (direct object scene).

When we move on to the indirect objects, we can do something very similar with the word *le*. Normally, you use *le* when one person receives something: "I'm giving him some books" is "*Le* I'm giving some books."

But what if you want to say "I'm giving them some books"? That would be "*Les* I'm giving some books."

The word *se*, meanwhile, doesn't change when there's more than one person. To say "she sees herself", you use "*se* she sees", and if it's more than one person, it's just "*se* they see". In other words, *se* can be either singular or plural, depending on the context.

Check out the three pictures of these scenes (on the previous page and this page). It's really important that you have all of these words stored where they belong. Also practice using them all in sentences; for example, for the direct object scene, use the sentence "*lo* they see", and then switch out *lo* for all the different options (*la* they see, *los* they see, *te* they see, etc.).

Our Panda Waste

When Joel gets to the woods today, he and the pandas begin to feel hungry. He looks inside the barrel that he's holding and sees that it still has some oats in it. He tosses a few of these dry oats into his mouth.

The pandas ask, "Can we have some of those oats too?"

Joel responds, "No, the barrel is mine!" To say this, he says, "The barrel is *mío*!"

The word *mío* means "mine". It's similar to *mi*, but it's used when it's not followed by a noun, just like the difference between "my" and "mine" in English: "It's my barrel" is "*Es mi* barrel," but "It's mine" is "*Es mío.*"

The pandas argue: "But you said that the oats were for all of us. Can't you share our oats?"

Joel doesn't like to share. Why should he <u>waste</u> the oats on the pandas when he can have them all to himself? He tells the pandas, "They're not <u>our</u> oats; that would be a waste. They're MY oats." As he says this, he accidentally

spills some of the oats on the forest floor, effectively wasting them so that nobody can eat them.

The word "our" in Spanish is *nuestro*, with the stress on "waste".

Quickly review what we've learned in this scene: Before a noun, you can use *mi*, *tu*, *su*, or *nuestro*. But when Joel says "It's mine," he uses a special word, *mío*. (This changes to *mía* when the noun is feminine.)

There are a couple of related words: *tuyo*, based on *tu*, means "yours" rather than "your". For example, if Joel wants to say "the house is yours", he says "*la casa es tuya.*" Similarly, the word *su* changes to *suyo*. "The house is theirs" would be "*la casa es suya*".

Plaza

When Joel first arrives at the plaza today, he almost runs into the fountain again. This is an episode he doesn't want to repeat, so he stops and looks carefully at the hole in the side, where we learned *hola*, *gracias*, and *oh*.

To remind himself never to run into this fountain again, he draws the most happy, positive image he can think of: An imitation of the trophy that's drawn on the side of his house. He tells himself, "All right, if you can avoid running into this fountain, you win!"

The word *bueno*, which we learned to mean "good" or "nice", is also used as an interjection or a filler word. Joel sometimes says "*Bueno…*" when he's thinking. It basically means "All right…", often before he starts a sentence. We've categorized this with other exclamations and filler words (*oh*, *gracias*, and *hola*).

Boo! Yes or No?

Joel looks up at the statue and sees something unexpected. Two chainsaws are sticking out of the statue's legs.

Perhaps some vandal came here during the night and tried to cut the statue down. One way or another, these "saws" are located halfway down the statue. In other words, they're positioned somewhere between *sí* ("yes") on the statue's head and *no* ("not") on the ground behind the statue.

So Joel uses the word *quizás* to mean "maybe" or "perhaps". It's halfway between "yes" and "no", and the stressed syllable sounds like "saws". Joel often shortens this word to *quizá* (stress on "saw"), which means the same thing.

Let's take an overall look at the statue before we move around the plaza. All the words on the statue are exchangeable with the word *sí* or *no*, and they can answer yes/no questions.

At the top, we have words that affirm a statement: *sí* ("yes" or "indeed"), *sólo* ("only"), *hasta* ("even"), and *también* ("also"). You could use any of these words before the statement "it's mine": "*Sí es mío*," "*Sólo es mío*," "*Hasta es mío*," or "*También es mío*."

Halfway down, we have *quizás* (or *quizá*), meaning "perhaps". In this case, we have to exchange the verb *es* for the subjunctive form, *sea*, which is the standard rule for chainsaws; after a "perhaps" or "maybe", we always use a subjunctive verb: "*Quizás sea mío*."

And then at the bottom, we have no, meaning "not": "*No es mío*."

All of these words fall into the category of <u>booleans</u>. Booleans are words that can answer a yes/no question or can be used at the beginning of a sentence to say whether it's true or not. To remember what "boolean" means, remember that this statue basically looks (and sometimes acts) like a ghost. Associate the statue with the word "boo!", and you'll remember that these words (*sí*, *no*, and everything in between) are booleans.

Más o Menos

At the steak stand, we previously learned *muy* ("very") and *tan* ("so"). These are degree adverbs. We'll learn two more today.

Joel notices that on the right side of the stand, there's a steak that's almost entirely covered with mold. This should be disgusting, but Joel thinks that this mold is "moss", which he finds oddly beautiful (because it's the substance that covers his blue car).

We learned on Joel's driveway that the word for "more" is *más*. That word is also located here at the butcher's stand, because it can be used as an adverb, in place of *muy* and *tan*. For example, something can be *muy bueno*, *tan bueno*, or *más bueno*.

Of course, the opposite of "more" is "less". On the left side of the stand is a steak with much less mold on it, and it's shaped like a lion's mane. Joel's word for "less" is *menos*. So "less good" is *menos bueno*.

menos   más

Oil and Tar

Joel proceeds to the baker's stand.

Quickly review what we learned here previously: *ya* and *ahora* refer to the present moment; *siempre* ("always") surrounds the stand and refers to all time; *nunca* is behind the stand and means "never"; *entonces* ("then") is scattered all over the stand and can refer to any moment in the past, present, or future; and *antes*, drawn on the front of the stand, means "first" or "beforehand".

Remember that the baker calls out "aunts before uncles!" Well, the baker has drawn the uncles lined up behind the aunts, and he insists that they must wait in "this place". The word *después* means "afterwards", and it's the opposite of *antes*.

Joel examines this picture closely. It looks like the uncles are taking turns standing on a scale. "Why are the uncles being weighed?" he asks.

The baker responds, "Because they're overweight. They can't eat bread while they're on a diet. The have to wait until later, after they've lost some weight."

The word for "later" is *luego*, with the stress on "weigh". Apparently the baker wants to serve the aunts "beforehand" (*antes*), but he wants to serve the uncles "afterwards" (*después*), which is going to end up being much "later" (*luego*).

On top of the grain stand, Joel notices a long baguette that is broken into a V shape. Joel recognizes this loaf, because it's been there for months. "Why haven't you sold that long piece

of bread yet?" he asks. "Why do you still have it?"

"Because it's not for sale!" says the baker. "I own that piece of bread."

Joel's word for "still" is *aún*, which sounds kind of like "own". It's important to point out that this loaf is in the middle of the stand, because it represents the present moment (just like *ya* and *ahora*), but it stretches into the past and the future. Whereas *ya* (represented by the knife) means that something has changed ("anymore"), *aún* represents that nothing has changed ("still").

To the right, a little bit of tar is dripping down from the edge of the stand, slightly covering part of the baker's artwork. Apparently this tar was used to assemble the stand, but it starts to drip when the sun gets hot, late in the day. The word *tarde* means "late".

The loaves of bread on the front of the baker's stand have names. The one in the middle is extremely oily, and it's called *hoy*. The crescent-shaped loaf to the right looks like a banana that's yawning, and it's called *mañana*.

These loaves represent days. *Hoy* means "today", and it's related to *ahora* (now). But *mañana* means "tomorrow", which is why it's placed after *hoy*.

As you can see, Joel uses a lot of adverbs related to time. Make sure you can remember all of these before moving on to the fruit stand.

Spiders

Today at the fruit stand, Joel once again refrains from buying fruit, because the fruit merchant still has a spider problem.

We learned the word *aquí* to mean "here", in the middle of the fruit basket. The word *ahí* means "there", represented by a spider standing on the edge of the basket by the fruit merchant's face.

In Spanish, there's another word for "there", represented by a second spider. This one is on the edge of the basket, not close to Joel or the fruit merchant. When Joel was scared, he yelled "*Ahí!*" loudly because of the spider by the fruit merchant's face. But this time, the spider is further away, and so Joel says very clearly: "*Allí.*"

This word (pronounced like "ah-YEE") means "there", but it's different from *ahí*. Joel normally uses *ahí* to refer to the place of the person he's speaking to; for example, if Joel is at home talking on the phone and the lizard is in the plaza, Joel might say "I'll go there", referring to the plaza: "*Voy ahí.*"

But *allí* refers to a third place. If Joel is at home and the lizard is in the plaza, and Joel is referring to the far-off mountain of Ría, his word for "there" will probably be *allí*.

So remember that *aquí* is close to Joel, *ahí* is close to the fruit merchant's face, and *allí* isn't close to either one of them.

Badly Mauled Vegetables

When Joel flies up to the farming monkey's stand, he's shocked to see some disgusting, smashed vegetables on the left side of the stand. They look like they've been badly mauled by clubs or dull knives.

"What happened here?" he asks.

"Oh," says the farmer, "I tried to chop up these vegetables, but I did it very badly."

Comparing the left end of the stand with the right end of the stand, Joel sees a huge contrast. On the right end is the can of money, which represents the word *bien*, meaning "well". But on the left end are these horribly mauled vegetables, representing the word *mal* (pronounced like "maul"), which means "badly".

"I don't want any smashed vegetables," says Joel. "Do you happen to have any mint tea that I could buy?"

"Sure!" says the monkey. "I keep that in the cubby under the stand. Open that door and you'll find the tea there."

Joel looks down, and sure enough, there's a door at the bottom of the front of the stand that he had never noticed before. He opens it, and to his shock, he sees the shepherd inside the cubby!

"Hello," says the shepherd. "Would you like to come and buy tea with me?"

"I'm not going anywhere with you!" says Joel. He's a bit freaked out to see the shepherd here; he's never seen him anywhere but in the countryside before.

To say "I don't want to shop for tea with you", Joel says "I don't want to shop for tea *contigo*. The stress is on "tea", and the word means "with you".

Meanwhile, the word for "with me" is *conmigo*: "I won't shop for tea *contigo*, and you can't shop for tea *conmigo*."

Disappointed that he's not bought anything, and still shaken at the sight of the shepherd in the plaza, Joel flies home.

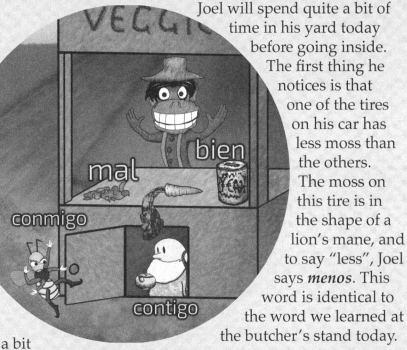

Compare: Moss or Mane?

Joel will spend quite a bit of time in his yard today before going inside. The first thing he notices is that one of the tires on his car has less moss than the others. The moss on this tire is in the shape of a lion's mane, and to say "less", Joel says *menos*. This word is identical to the word we learned at the butcher's stand today.

Using all three of the words that we've learned here, you could say that you have *más cosas*, *menos cosas*, or *mejores cosas*.

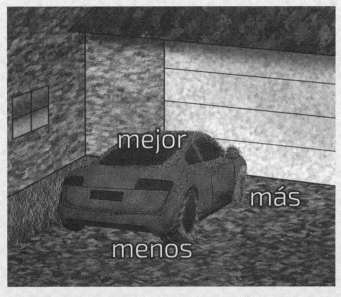

27

Indefinite Garage

Let's move around to the other side of the garage, where Joel keeps his other car.

The word for "other" is *otro*, and of course this is modified to *otra* for feminine nouns; for example, "other things" is *otras cosas*.

A similar word in the garage comes from the laundry in his washer. Although Joel put some yellow clothes in the laundry, they've now become completely red, like the tanned butcher from the marketplace. Apparently this is because he put so much laundry in that it burnt and became red. All because he tried to wash so much laundry at once.

Joel's word for "so much" is *tanto*. The stress is on "tan", just like the word from the butcher's stand, but it's used like the word *otro*: "so many things" is *tantas cosas*.

Behind the car, right in the doorway of the garage, a carrot is sticking straight out of the pavement. It stands very tall, and Joel wonders how such a thing can be: How is the carrot still standing there, in spite of the car and the garage door?

The word for "such" is *tal*, pronounced like "tall". "Such a thing" is *tal cosa*.

On the outer wall of his garage, someone has thrown a huge splotch of mud on the side of Joel's house. When Joel sees this, he's furious: "Who did this?!"

Although Joel never saw who threw mud on his wall, he assumes that it was "some goon", which is his default insult when he doesn't know whom he's insulting. Maybe it was more than one neighbor, in which case the insult is "some goons".

Joel's word for "some" or "several" is *algunos*. The stressed syllable is "goon", and it changes to *algunas* when it's feminine.

Between the driveway and the wall, a toad is hiding in the grass. This creature is just like the ones in Joel's bedroom: In fact, just like the toads up there, it says "moo" a lot. This annoys Joel, but he can never find this toad because it's hiding. This toad represents the words *todo* and *mucho*.

As you should remember, these words can be nouns. *Todo* means "all", as in "all the time" (*todo el tiempo*). *Mucho* means "much", or "a lot", as in "much of the time" (*mucho del tiempo*).

However, if the words are used right before a noun, they turn into adjectives. *Mucho* can mean "much" or "many"; for example, "many houses" would be *muchas casas*. The phrase *mucho tiempo* means "much time" (or "lots of time").

The word *todo*, as an adjective, actually means "every". For example, "every time" would be *toda vez*.

Near the toads is some money poking out of the grass. This represents the word *poco*, which, when used as an adjective, means "very little" or "very few". For example, *pocas cosas* means "very few things".

Quickly practice switching out *toda cosa*, *muchas cosas*, and *pocas cosas* to get used to these words.

While *todo* is the word for "every", there's a different word for "each". And it's a strange one, so it's located on Joel's roof.

A ball is rolling down the slope of Joel's roof. This is ominous, because if it rolls off right when Joel is pulling out with his *otro* car, the ball might fall on top of his car and damage it. But fortunately, there are some grooves in the roof, between shingles, and so the ball stops and gets caught each time it hits one of these grooves, temporarily delaying the impending fall.

Since the ball is getting caught in "each" crack, the word for "each" is *cada*. Remember the word "caught" as the stressed syllable.

Something strange about the word *cada* is that even though it ends with the letter A, it doesn't change when the noun is masculine. So "each thing" is *cada cosa*, and "each man" is *cada hombre*.

Take a final look at this scene. These words are all very similar: They're used right before nouns, and they are used instead of articles; you never use a word such as *una* or *los* when you use one of these adjectives.

The general term for these adjectives is indefinite adjectives. To remember this, it might help to keep in mind that the garage is an "indefinite" part of Joel's house: Does it count as indoors or outdoors? For Joel's purposes, the garage counts as part of the "outdoors", but he still refers to this part of his yard as an indefinite area.

Which Human?

Joel has strange opinions about humans.

Are they mammals? Technically they are, but he often tolerates them anyway. Actually, he has a curious fascination with this particular type of mammals, though he still tries to maintain his distance from them.

There are actually quite a few humans in Joel's neighborhood, particularly in the apartment complex right next to him. He sometimes goes out in his yard to observe them, and even to take notes about them.

He always knows who the newcomers in the neighborhood are. Neighbors who just moved in are excited at the sight of Joel: "Look! A talking bee who drinks tea! Hi there! What's your name?"

Only "new" neighbors greet Joel and wave at him constantly, which is something he hates. His word for "new" is *nuevo* (stress on "wave").

One of his favorite neighbors to watch is a girl who sits in her apartment all day, staring at a backwards mirror. This girl used to be friends with her own reflection, which Joel found very entertaining. But now the mirror is turned away from her, and she bitterly misses her old "friend", which of course is the same person as herself. Joel's word for "same" is *mismo* (stress on "miss").

These words, *nuevo* and *mismo*, are used before nouns, but unlike the indefinite adjectives, these words get articles before them. So "a new thing" is *una nueva cosa*, and "the same man" is *el mismo hombre*.

Watt Row

Let's go back to the part of the yard that Joel is most afraid of.

Joel is generally terrified of mammals. Remember that there's an area in his back yard where he once encountered two deer one night, and his number for two is *dos* because the deer were does.

When he saw the deer, he panicked. It was dark, and he wasn't sure which way to go to get back into his house. So he did the first thing that he could think of: He decided to make a decoy of himself, in case the evil mammals were chasing him to eat him.

His "decoy" idea wasn't the brightest. His original thought was that he could draw a picture of himself in the sand by his stream, but he's not very good at drawing when he's scared. So he lay down in the sand and tried to trace himself. But if you've ever tried to trace your own body in the sand, you know how hard it is. All that he managed to trace was the ends of his wings.

The image that he "traced" ended up looking like a number 3, not like Joel. It was a miserable failure. But now his word for 3 is *tres*.

Further along in the sand by this stream, there's a flagpole with light bulbs on it. After trying to trace himself, Joel climbed up the pole to turn these lights on.

But unfortunately these bulbs have a very low wattage, just four watts each, so their light didn't really help anything. The four bulbs on the flagpole also outline the shape of the number 4. The word *cuatro*, for four, has the stressed syllable "watt".

We'll continue the story about Joel's numbers later, but for now remember *uno*, *dos*, *tres*, and *cuatro*.

Safe in the Goo

The next part of the yard is where we find adjectives that are used with the verb Estar.

Outside Joel's giant dining room window, there's a huge puddle of something blue that Joel calls "goo". He often comes here when he's scared of animals, because he thinks it's a great place to hide. If he rolls around in the "goo", he's nearly invisible, and he feels very safe.

The pandas don't trust this plan. "You really think you're safe in the goo? Are you sure?"

"*Sí!*" says Joel. "*Estoy seguro.*"

The word *seguro*, with the stressed syllable "goo", means both "safe" and "sure". In the goo, Joel is *seguro* ("sure") that he is *seguro* ("safe").

A sandal sits next to the goo. It is a left-foot sandal, without a match. Normally, Joel is scared of shoes, but in this case he's not worried, because the sandal is all alone; it doesn't have a match, so Joel thinks that means it can't step on him.

The word *solo* means both "alone" and "lonely". It's a lot like the English word "solo", and it's represented by a sandal, which is the "sole" of a shoe.

Meanwhile, we have an unusual adjective represented by Joel's window. When the window is cloudy, Joel can't see anything in it. But sometimes the clouds clear, and Joel sees streaks on the window that look like claws.

If the window is cloudy, Joel sits still in the goo and does nothing. But when the clouds clear and he sees the "claws", Joel is very decisive: "It's very clear that we need to get out of here!"

The word *claro*, with the stressed syllable "claw", means "clear" in this sense. To say "it's clear that…", Joel says "*Está claro que…*"

Practice using these common adjectives with Estar: *solo* and *seguro* for how someone feels, and "*está claro*" for when something seems to be clearly true.

Clear Pool

Joel hardly ever swims in his front yard pool.

That may seem strange, because he's happy to splash around in the "goo" on the left side of the house. But there's something unsettling about the pool: Sharp "claws" are at the bottom, ready to harm anyone who dares to swim low.

When Joel bought the house, he didn't know about these claws. But he found out very quickly, because the water in the pool is very clear, and the claws can easily be seen.

The word *claro* means "clear" or "light". We already learned this, but it has two meanings: When it's used with Estar (at the side of the house), it refers to an idea being clear to the speaker (e.g. "it's clear that we should get out of here"). But when it's used with Ser, it refers to a physical object, such as a "clear" pool or "clear" glass.

Another adjective used to describe an object is *seguro*. Joel allows there to be "goo" next to the pool, and he spends time rolling in this goo. He tells the pandas, "The pool isn't safe, but the goo is."

The word *seguro*, when used with Ser, always means "safe" or "secure". It generally refers to a place: "This area *es seguro*," or "The house *es segura*."

Next to the pool, near the driveway, are some trees. Joel is particularly proud of the largest tree, which he thinks is very "grand" because it's so big. His word for "large" or "big" is *grande*.

All of these words are exchangeable with *bueno*, which is painted on the side of the house. Practice switching out these adjectives in this sentence structure, imagining a large, glass house that has a strong security system:

- *La casa es buena.*

- *La casa es clara.*

- *La casa es segura.*

- *La casa es grande.*

Next, let's enter Joel's own house. It may not be *clara*, but as you're about to see, it's very *grande* on the inside.

Hall "Things"

When we first enter Joel's house, we find a large hall. This entryway could take us either to his living room (to the left) or upstairs, but first let's look around here a little while. Joel's words for physical items are stored here.

You might be surprised to see that the carpet on the left side has a few *cosas* scattered over it. Didn't we already learn these in the kitchen, as an abstract noun?

Well, the word *cosa*, or "thing", can be either an abstract noun or a physical noun, just like in English. When I say "I have a few things in my pockets",

I'm referring to physical objects, which is why these *cosas* are in the hall here. But when I say "there are many things wrong with your plan", I'm probably referring to something abstract, which is why *cosa* can also be an abstract noun (stored in the kitchen).

Another physical object that might be in my pockets is money. On the right side of this hall, an arrow has struck the wall above the window. As you can see, this arrow was carrying a bag of money.

What happened here? Apparently, Robin Hood has paid Joel a visit. He very mistakenly thought that Joel was a poor man, and he decided to gift Joel with this bag of money, using an

arrow (as is Robin Hood's style). Joel is actually a wealthy bee, but he's not complaining; he'll take all the money he can get, even if it's delivered by arrow.

Joel's word for money is *dinero*.

Let's go through the door to our left and see who might be in Joel's living room.

Ma and Pa

Family is visiting today. Joel's parents are sitting on his couch, and he calls them "ma" and "pa".

Actually, he has two versions of words for his parents: The more formal sounding "mother" and "father" are *madre* and *padre*. But the less formal, equivalent to "mom" and "dad", are *mamá* and *papá*. In each case, the stressed syllables are "ma" and "pa".

Beneath Joel's mom's feet is a small bee girl. She's trying to fly away, but her mother's feet are holding her down. Of course, when a tiny bee is trying to fly, its wings always make a pathetic high-pitched buzzing noise that sounds like "eeeeehh!". The word for "daughter" is *hija* ("EEH-ha").

Sometimes Joel's dad tries to trap Joel under his feet too, in which case Joel would make the "eeehh!" buzzing sound as well. The word for "son" is *hijo* ("EEH-ho").

Notice that these words are organized by how they're positioned on the couch, with females to our left and males to our right. In Joel's household, children are ceremonially subjected to parents by being held under their feet.

When Joel wants to say "children", in the sense of "sons and daughters", the word he uses is *hijos*. To say "parents", he says *padres*. So technically speaking, we use the masculine plural even when it's a mixed group. To say "my parents", Joel says *mis padres*.

One more person is here in the living room: Joel's friend, the lizard. Joel's dad wonders what this lizard is doing in Joel's house. Joel responds, "Oh, he's my best friend. He goes with me wherever I go." To shorten this, his words "me" and "go" show up in the word *amigo*, which means friend.

Now let's turn to the stage for a moment and notice that in addition to the *hombre*, the *señor*, and the *uno*, there's a new guy. He's an odd-looking dude with a tea pot for a head, and Joel calls him a *tipo*, which means "guy" or "dude". In the play, this "tea pot guy" is skateboarding off the edge of the stage.

On the left side of the stage is a person who looks a lot like the *hombre*, but she has a lot more hair. This is how Joel knows she's a woman; he sometimes has trouble telling human males from human females, so he insists that in every stage production, the women must have much more hair

than the men. For this reason, his word for "woman" is *mujer*.

To the left of the stage, on the wall, is a poster advertising an upcoming play. This play will have all-new people, but Joel insists that they must be the people that he likes. He has drawn a picture on this poster of all the types of people he likes: Reptiles, birds, insects, and some humans. Joel says, "These are the people that I want in the play."

As you can see, this picture forms the image of a giant hen. Joel's word for "people" is *gente*.

We'll turn back around and continue through the house. Beyond the living room is a dining room, where Joel stores all his feelings. Today we don't have to learn any words here, so we'll just pass through on our way to the kitchen.

Kitchen "Things"

The way that Joel organizes his kitchen is extremely important for our use of abstract nouns.

We already learned that Joel's *cosas* are on the island in the middle of the room. This word can be used in many ways, and it's fairly intuitive because "things" is the same in Spanish as it is in English.

But we also learned that *favor* is on the counter behind the island. This counter is where we store things that you "do". For example, you can "do" a favor and you can "do" work.

Of course, Joel isn't a fan of doing work. Whenever Joel's chef needs extra help in the kitchen and asks Joel for assistance, perhaps in chopping up some food for dinner, Joel shouts, "Bah! Humbug! I would never do work."

Joel's word for work is *trabajo*, with the stress on "bah". We are using a sheep's leg to represent this, because Joel always refuses to chop up sheep legs (and he associates the sound "bah" with sheep).

Although these words on the counter are considered things you "do", the things in the cabinets above the counter are things that you "have"; for example, you can "have an idea" or "have a problem".

In the cabinets to the left, Joel keeps light bulbs. But these aren't for lighting his house. Instead, they're more like thinking caps: He shines these lights on his head when he's trying to come up with good ideas. The word *idea*, with the stressed syllable "day", shows that he always associates good ideas with "daylight" (even when that daylight comes from light bulbs).

He also has a painting of the sun on the back of these cabinets. But this is very inconvenient for the chef, because whenever the chef tries to put dishes here, Joel gets angry and says "don't block the sun!" If the chef asks Joel, "why does this painting of the sun have to be here?", Joel always says, "I have my reason."

The word for "reason" is *razón*. As we'll learn soon, this word is used for a lot of purposes in Spanish, largely in arguments. So make sure to associate *razón* (the stressed syllable sounds like "sun") with Joel insisting that he's won this argument about the painted sun.

On the right side of the cabinets is a chef's hat that has been burnt almost to ashes. The chef's hat caught fire during a strange experiment that Joel was conducting as the chef tried to cook. Of course, it was entirely Joel's fault, but Joel insisted on blaming the chef: "Your hat is on fire? That's not my problem! I blame you. It's your problem, not mine."

The word *problema* means "problem". It's obviously very similar to the English word, but in Spanish the stress is on the syllable that sounds like "blame".

Inside the freezer, we've learned the word *verdad* for truth. This word is often used after the word *de*; *de verdad* means "of truth" or "truly".

Another word that's used after de is the word *acuerdo*, whose stress sounds kind of like "weirdo". Joel and the chef often disagree with each other, and they insult each other all the time. But they agree on one thing: They're both "weirdos". This is the one subject on which they're in agreement.

In the door of the freezer, they've painted pictures of each other's faces, one on top of the other, in a very weird fashion. The phrase *de acuerdo* is an idiom that means "in agreement" (literally "of agreement"), just like *de verdad* is an idiom meaning "truly" (or "of truth").

Ballroom Auras

The first room we get to when we go up the stairs is the ballroom.

We've already learned the words *tiempo*, *día*, and *año* on the right side. To the left, we've learned *vez* and *noche*.

As you can see, although there are *años* hanging on the right side of the ceiling, there's something else on the left side of the ceiling: Colored lights. Joel likes to use special mood light in his dance parties, creating an individual "aura", as he says, based on what time it is. Each hour, the "aura" changes, and his word for "hour" is *hora*.

At the bottom of each window is a bunch of tar. This tar melts and drips down the wall when it's late in the day, and Joel's word for "afternoon" is *tarde*.

Between the big windows are some smaller windows that look like yawning mouths. Joel's parties often go extremely late, but he knows it's morning when the sun begins to shine through these yawning mouths. (He can also tell because some of his guests will start yawning.) The word for "morning" is *mañana*, which has the stressed syllable "yawn".

Mañana actually means both "morning" and "tomorrow", as we saw at the grain stand; this is because Joel thinks that "morning" and "tomorrow" arrive at the same time, when the sun shines through

the yawning mouths, so they mean basically the same thing: *mañana*.

On the right side of the ballroom, the floor has mint candies all over the place, one on each of the black squares. These mints make a small cracking sound each time someone steps on them, which happens very often, as you can imagine; if you were dancing in a strangely-lit room, you'd probably step on the mint candies on the floor pretty frequently. For Joel, when something happens this frequently, he says it happens "every moment", or *todo momento*. The word *momento*, with a stressed syllable that sounds like "mint", means "moment".

To avoid stepping on these mints, let's turn away from the ballroom and proceed to the library instead.

parte

lugar   mundo

Places and Places

In Lesson 5, the only thing that we looked at from the library was Joel's *casa*, the house-shaped bookshelf that cost a lot of money. This is on the left side of the room.

Above the *casa* is a big window that's divided into small parts, or panels. Joel likes to stain these parts different colors to represent individual places in his house. This window ends up looking like a map of his house, with the different rooms represented by different colors.

The word *parte* means "place", at least in one sense. Actually, Joel has a few different words for "place", but this one is generally used when he's referring to the different "parts" of a larger place. For example, if he's looking all over the window for the color yellow, he might say, "I looked at every part of the window, but I couldn't find yellow." To say "every part" or "every place", he says *toda parte*.

Another word for "place" can be found on the right side of the room. Joel has a giant atlas, and strangely enough, his atlas has a picture of his own blue car on the cover. There's a very personal reason for this: Joel likes to look through the atlas for places that he'd like to go some day. If the place is boring, he says he would go there in his "*otro* car". But if the place is really interesting, Joel draws a picture of his blue car on the page. He imagines that some day he might actually drive his beautiful blue car to that place if it's special enough.

So for Joel, if a place is special enough, he associates it with his blue car. Joel's general word for "place" is *lugar*.

Meanwhile, Joel also has a globe, but it's not a globe of Yol. This globe actually represents Planet Earth! However, the globe is constructed from a pale, doughy substance, so Joel's "planet earth" actually looks like the surface of the moon. This is due to bad education: In Yol, children are taught in schools that Planet Earth is made of "moon dough". This makes Earth sound very unattractive.

For this reason, Joel's word for "the world" is *el mundo*.

Bed Parts

As we enter Joel's bedroom, we encounter some small pieces of money on the floor, between the toads.

These little rolled-up Yen bills give Joel comfort every morning: When he puts on his slippers and gets out of bed, he wants the first thing he feels to be money. So this tiny bit of money pokes his feet through his slippers as he walks through his room.

Joel's word for "a little" is **un poco**. Just like the other words on the floor, this is a word that relates to an amount of something. If Joel has "all" of something, that's **todo**. If he has "much" or "a lot", that's **mucho**. But if he only has "a little", that's **un poco**.

Now take a look at Joel's blankets. On the left side of the bed, the blanket is divided

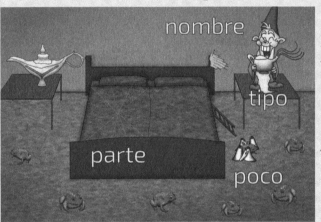

into small parts, like a pie. Joel sleeps under different parts of this blanket depending on what kind of dream he wants to have, and his word for "part" is **parte**. Of course, we already learned this word in the library as well; it can be used to mean either "part" or "place".

To the sides of Joel's bed are two nightstands. On the left, we already

learned the word **vida** for "life". But on the right side, there's a garden gnome holding a teapot.

This teapot functions as Joel's alarm clock. Every morning, he wakes up to the smell of tea brewing. And it's always a surprise, because he never knows what type of tea it's going to be.

The word for "type" is **tipo**. We also learned the word **tipo** on the stage to mean "guy" or "dude", which is a very informal word. But this word, **tipo** for "type", is quite standard and common.

Meanwhile, the gnome that holds the teapot doesn't have a name. Every time Joel asks the gnome, "What's your name?", it brays loudly, like the mule on the stage.

Joel's word for "name" is **nombre**, with the stressed syllable "gnome" plus "bray".

Before we leave Joel's room, take careful note of how these words are used. The words on the nightstands are <u>aspects</u> of something. Something can have a "name", a "life", and a "type". We'll learn more <u>aspect</u> words here, such as "number", "color", and "value". But **vida**, **nombre**, and **tipo** are the most common.

Lesson 7 Application:
Polishing Syntax

THERE ARE TWO things you should plan to learn from this section:

(1) Be able to use your new vocabulary in sentences, properly.

(2) Memorize some specific sentences that help you speak with flow.

We have a lot of sentence examples to cover, but remember that you should write out your own variations on these phrases. In general I've provided one or two sample variations on the phrases, and you can use those ideas to help you write your own.

Show your sentences to a native-Spanish-speaking friend or instructor, and they'll be able to give you pointers on where you need more work. This is one of the best ways to diagnose how you're doing and continue improving, actively working on your weaknesses.

You'll notice that about 20 of these phrases are highlighted in magenta or cyan. These are phrases that you can now say entirely in Spanish, and we require our coaching students to memorize these specific sentences.

Conjunctions

It's a house where a woman is living.	*Es una casa donde una mujer está* living.
It's a story where a man is worried.	*Es una* story *donde un hombre está* worried.
It's a boy who has a dog.	*Es un* boy *quien tiene un* dog.
It's about a woman who goes home.	It's about *una mujer quien va a casa.*

Prepositions

| From morning to night. | *Desde la mañana hasta la noche.* |
| We went from this house to that place. | *Fuimos desde esta casa hasta ese lugar.* |

There's a strange idiom that involves the preposition *desde:* The phrase *desde ya* most properly means something like "in advance". For example, "thanks in advance" might be *desde ya, ¡muchas gracias!* However, it's actually used in a very wide variety of ways. It is often used to mean something like "of course" or "by all means". Obviously, none of these meanings translates well into English.

| Sure, of course, I think the same. | *Claro, desde ya, yo* think *lo mismo.* |
| Sure, of course, he did the same. | *Claro, desde ya, él* did *lo mismo.* |

Countryside: Subjects and Articles

| You all do very strange things. | *Ustedes* do *cosas muy* strange. |
| They have very nice things. | *Ellos tienen cosas muy buenas.* |

| At the house of some friends. | *En la casa de unos amigos.* |
| First I need to have some things. | *Antes tengo que tener unas cosas.* |

The words *ellos*, *ellas*, and *ustedes*, just like *él* and *ella*, are used both as subject pronouns (sheep pastures) and as prepositional pronouns (where Joel sits in the tree dreaming in Lesson 5). So they can be used after prepositions, like *para*, *de*, and *sin*.

That is the hardest thing for me.	*Eso es lo más* difficult *para mí.*
That is the hardest thing for them.	*Eso es lo más* difficult *para ellos.*
This is the easiest thing for you all.	*Esto es lo más* easy *para ustedes.*
This is easiest thing for her.	*Esto es lo más* easy *para ella.*

Countryside: Objects

Let's start at the direct object scene. If you know how to use *lo*, *la*, *me*, and *te*, then you also know how to use *los* and *las* as direct objects.

I saw them many times.	*Las* I saw *muchas veces.*
I'm reading them again and again.	*Los* I'm reading *una y otra vez.*

(Oh by the way, if the word *veces* in that first example looks weird to you, just be aware that it's the plural of *vez*, "time". For some reason the Z turns into C in the plural version of the word.)

A strange thing often happens when Joel uses *le*. Consider this sentence:

He asked her if she had something.	*Le* he asked *si tenía algo.*

The person being asked is "her", represented by the word *le* (literally "to her"). But what if we wanted to clarify who that person is? For example, "He asked his mother if she had something"? In that case, "his mother" is the indirect object.

We might be tempted to phrase the sentence like this:

He asked *a su madre si tenía algo.*

But Spanish speakers don't do that. They do something a bit stranger. The sentence would look more like this:

Le he asked *a su madre si tenía algo.*

Wait a minute! What's the point of that *le* at the beginning? It looks like "<u>To her</u> he asked <u>to his mother</u> if she had something."

Yes, it's redundant. But unfortunately this is one of the awkward rules in Spanish: If an indirect object is involved, we almost ALWAYS put the indirect pronoun at the beginning, <u>even if the object is also named afterwards</u>.

Personally, I endearingly call this "the ridiculous redundant indirect object" (RRIO).

I told my father that I was here.	*Le* I told *a mi padre que estaba aquí.*
I told my friends that they are very nice.	*Les* I told *a mis amigos que son muy buenos.*
He asked his friend if he had something.	*Le* he asked *a su amigo si tenía algo.*

Say "Lo", Say "La"

Buckle up; it's time to learn about one of Joel's most bizarre and complicated habits. And we can't learn it without taking another trip through the bumpy countryside.

Something very strange happens when Joel uses more than one object pronoun.

When is that ever an issue? Let's use an English example:

"I gave it to you."

So there's a direct object, "it", which I'm giving to a recipient, "you". There's actually another way to say that sentence in English, though it's not quite as common:

"I gave you it."

Study that sentence. It's extremely valuable to us, because it provides a glimpse into Joel's mind.

As you can see, the recipient, "you", comes before the object, "it". In fact, if we replace the word "you" with other recipients, the structure stays the same:

"I gave them it."

"I gave her it."

In each of these cases, there are only two words other than "I gave". And the recipient always comes before the direct object.

For Joel, this is extremely important. When he uses words from more than one object scene (for example, an indirect object and a direct object), he always goes backward, moving back from the crossroads toward the scene with the hill and the tree.

So going back to our sentence, "I gave you it", here's how Joel would say it:

"*Te lo* I gave."

The word *te* is an indirect object, from the crossroads scene, and *lo* is from the direct object scene. He went backwards on his path, moving toward the hill instead of toward his home.

Here are some more sentences that use the same structure:

*"**Me lo** they gave."*

*"**Nos la** you gave."*

Are you ready for it to get worse?

Let's imagine that Joel wants to say, "I gave her it." By default, this should look like this: *"**Le lo** I gave."* ("To her it I gave.")

However, Joel really doesn't like the sound of that sentence. The words *"le lo"* together sound like singing, because of the "L" sound used more than once. Joel hates the sound of someone saying "La la la! Le lo! Le la!"

So any time Joel would say *"le lo"* or *"le la"* or anything like that, Joel stubbornly mispronounces it on purpose. He changes the word *le* to *se*.

For example, "I gave him it" is *"**Se lo** I gave."*

Don't be too confused: In this case, the word that looks like *se* is actually the word *le*. It just looks and sounds like se because of Joel's strange pronunciation habits.

It might help to think about it this way: The sheep that "lay" down, *le*, is also sometimes called *se*. But that only happens when Joel is moving backwards.

A few sentence examples will probably help you sort this out in your head. In each case, imagine yourself moving backwards from the crossroads scene to the direct object scene, but every time the term *le lo* or *le la* comes up, change it to *se lo* or *se la*.

As soon as that happens, I'll tell him it.	*Ni bien eso* happens, *se lo* I'll tell.
As soon as that happens, they'll give it to him.	*Ni bien eso* happens, *se lo* they'll give.
As soon as that happens, they'll give it to me.	*Ni bien eso* happens, *me lo* they'll give.
As soon as that happens, we'll tell it to her.	*Ni bien eso* happens, *se lo* we'll tell.
As soon as that happens, we'll tell it to you.	*Ni bien eso* happens, *te lo* we'll tell.

Countryside: Lake and Woods

While we're in the country, let's review the "lake" pronouns really quickly.

We've previously learned *esta*, *esto*, and *este* to mean "this", and we've learned *esa*, *eso*, and *ese* to mean "that".

For the nerds, these lake pronouns are called demonstrative pronouns, because they involve virtually pointing your finger, "demonstrating" what you're talking about ("this!" "that!"). (As a mnemonic for "demonstrative", with the stress on the syllable "monstr", think of the Loch Ness Monster, which might be living in this lake.)

These words have plural versions as well. "This" can turn into "these" when you put an S on the end of the words: *estas* means "these" feminine, and *estos* means "these" masculine or neuter. (For some reason *estes* isn't a thing; it's always *estos*.)

It's the same with turning "that" into "those": You turn esa into esas and you turn *eso* or *ese* into *esos*.

All those things at once?	*¿Todas esas cosas a la vez?*
All these years at home?	*¿Todos estos años en casa?*

Remember that Joel really likes to emphasize his own things. Very often, when he says "mine" (*mío* or *mía*), he puts the word "the" ahead of it: *el mío* or *la mía*. That also applies to the word *tuyo*, as well as *suyo*, which is the equivalent version of *su*.

Yours did very nice things.	*El tuyo* did *cosas muy buenas.*
Theirs did very strange things.	*La suya* did *cosas muy* strange.
Mine did very mean things to his friend.	*El mío le* did *cosas muy* mean *a su amigo.*

Plaza: Statue (Yes or No?)

For "boolean" adverbs (the ones on the statue), practice switching out *no*, *sí*, and *quizás* (remembering to use subjunctive verb forms along with *quizás*).

It's not very late.	*No es muy tarde.*
Maybe it be very late.	*Quizá sea muy tarde.*
Indeed he is there.	*Sí está ahí.*
Maybe he be there.	*Quizás esté ahí.*

Plaza: Steak (How Much?)

He's more tall than I.	*Es más* tall *que yo.*
He's less tall than I.	*Es menos* tall *que yo.*
He's as big as she.	*Es tan grande como ella.*

Plaza: Bread (When?)

The words *después* and *luego* are essentially synonyms, and since they're on the front of the baker's stand, they're used exactly like *antes*, normally followed by *de*.

Better before 2 in the afternoon.	*Mejor antes de las dos de la tarde.*
Better after 4 in the afternoon.	*Mejor después de las cuatro de la tarde.*
Better after 3 in the morning.	*Mejor luego de las tres de la mañana.*

But when these words are used without *de* after them, they mean something more distinct: *después* means "afterwards" (which sounds pretty specific), whereas *luego* means "later" (which is more vague).

Beforehand I left.	*Antes me fui.*
Afterwards he left.	*Después se fue.*
Later they left.	*Luego se fueron.*

Other "time" adverbs can be used the same way. You can stick them at either the beginning or the end of a sentence.

I'll meet you here tomorrow.	*Te* I'll meet *aquí mañana.*
I'll meet you here very late.	*Te* I'll meet *aquí muy tarde.*
I meet her here still.	*La* I meet *aquí aún.*
I've met them here always.	*Los* I've met *aquí siempre.*

Plaza: Fruit (Where?)

Over there there are many.	*Allí hay muchos.*
Over there he has a house.	*Allí tiene una casa.*
Over there she'll be fine.	*Allí estará bien.*

Plaza: Veggies (How?)

Here's a simple that uses *mal* to mean "badly" or "unwell".

She was doing very badly for a while.	*Ella estuvo muy mal por un tiempo.*
I was doing very badly for two days.	*Yo estuve muy mal por dos días.*
He was doing very badly that year.	*Él estuvo muy mal ese año.*

The word *mal* literally means "badly", just as *bien* means "well". These two words are opposites.

At the same time, these words sometimes have a broader, more moral meaning. In Joel's mind, if you do something "well" (*bien*), you're doing it "correctly" or "right". But if you do something "badly" (*mal*), you're doing it "incorrectly" or "wrong". So bear in mind that *bien* can mean "right" and *mal* can mean "wrong".

After many years I understood that it had been wrong.	*Después de muchos años* I understood *que había estado mal.*
After many years he understood that it had been right.	*Después de muchos años* he understood *que había estado bien.*

I want you to go with me.	I want *que vayas conmigo.*
They want her to be with you.	They want *que ella esté contigo.*

Comparative Adjectives

We have two idioms involving *menos*. First, to say "at least", Joel says *al menos* (literally "to the less/least").

At least, that's what I have.	*Al menos eso es lo que tengo.*
At least, that's what I think.	*Al menos eso es lo que* I think.
At least, that's what they hope.	*Al menos eso es lo que* they hope.

Second, the idiom *a menos que* means "unless". In other words, instead of "unless", Joel says "to less that". This is typically followed by a subjunctive verb.

Unless we are going later.	*A menos que vayamos luego.*
Unless you(formal) are leaving now.	*A menos que usted se vaya ahora.*

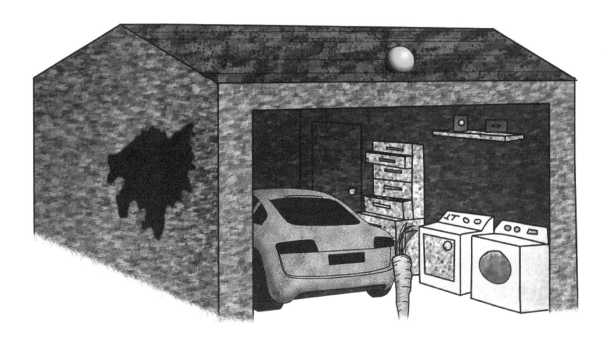

Indefinite Adjectives

To practice these words, I recommend first using various words from the scene in this sentence:

I'm going to many houses.	*Voy a muchas casas.*
I'm going to some house.	*Voy a alguna casa.*
I'm going to each house.	*Voy a cada casa.*
I'm going to every house.	*Voy a toda casa.*
I'm going to such a house.	*Voy a tal casa.*
I'm going to another house.	*Voy a otra casa.*
I'm going to so many houses.	*Voy a tantas casas.*

In English, we have an idiom to say that something is constantly increasing or decreasing: "More and more", "less and less", and so on. This is not the same in Spanish. Instead, it's common to say "each time more…" or "each time less…". So the equivalent to "more and more" is **cada vez más**, and "less and less" equates to **cada vez menos**.

He had more and more.	*Cada vez más tenía.*
She has less and less.	*Cada vez menos tiene.*

We've learned that **tal** means "such", as in "such a man": **tal hombre**. But the reason that **tal** is so common is because of frequently used idioms. For example, when you say "for such a reason", **"por tal razón"**, it simply means "for this reason". It's kind of like **por eso**, but slightly more formal and a bit more emphatic.

For such a reason there's a man in the house.	*Por tal razón hay un hombre en la casa.*
For some reason, there's a man in the house.	*Por alguna razón, hay un hombre en la casa.*

The word **tal** is actually used in many idioms that have no translation. For example, **tal vez** means "perhaps". It's used exactly the same way as our word for "maybe" (*quizá/quizás*), with a subjunctive in the following phrase.

Perhaps he has a place.	*Tal vez tenga un lugar.*
Perhaps they have a house.	*Tal vez tengan una casa.*

The idiom **como tal** means what it literally means in English: "as such".

And, as such, he almost went crazy.	*Y, como tal, he almost went crazy.*
And, as such, he also got well.	*Y, como tal, también estuvo bien.*

One more idiom involving **tal**. The phrase **¿qué tal?** literally means "What such?" By default, it's followed by a noun, and the meaning is "How is this thing?" or "What do you think of this thing?" For example, "How was the movie" would be "**¿Qué tal** the movie?"

Hi! How was your day?	*¡Hola! ¿Qué tal tu día?*
Hi! How was the party?	*¡Hola! ¿Qué tal la party?*

"Which" Adjectives

I left for a new house.	*Me fui a una nueva casa.*
I'll have the same job.	*Tendré el mismo trabajo.*

To say "at the same time", Joel says *al mismo tiempo*.

My friends were there at the same time.	*Mis amigas estaban ahí al mismo tiempo.*
The parents are reading at the same time.	*Los padres están* reading *al mismo tiempo.*

In English we often use the words "myself", "himself", etc. for emphasis; for example, "I'm doing it myself".

This "myself" is NOT an example of reflexive pronouns. Instead, it's an idiomatic way that English speakers re-state the subject: "I myself", "she herself", and so on, for emphasis on the subject. (There is no reflexive object in "I'm doing it myself"; that would end up meaning something like "I'm doing it to myself", which is obviously not the meaning.)

This is something new to learn, and it's an interesting situation where the word *mismo* comes in. To say "I'm doing it myself", with a strong emphasis on "myself", I would say "I'm doing it *yo mismo*."

So our word *mismo* doesn't just mean "same". It's also a word that's used for emphasis on "oneself" at the end of a phrase.

He had to be king himself.	*Tuvo que ser* king *él mismo.*
We have it ourselves.	*Lo tenemos nosotros mismos.*

And now for something completely different: You're about to see the word *sí* used in a way you would never expect. This word actually has a second meaning, entirely different from "yes"; it can also mean "himself" or "herself", as a reflexive prepositional pronoun. Technically, that means that *sí* belongs in the scene where Joel is dreaming in a tree.

More practically, it's usually used in phrases where someone is referring to himself or herself. For example, to say that someone is "sure of herself", that's *segura de sí misma*.

She's very sure of herself.	*Es muy segura de sí misma.*
I'm very sure of myself.	*Soy muy segura de mí mismo.*

Another idiom involving *mismo* is *ya mismo*, which is an informal phrase meaning "right now". (As you can see, the word *mismo* is very broadly used to provide emphasis.)

| Yes! If you tell me it right now. | *¡Sí! Si me lo you tell ya mismo.* |
| No! Unless you do it right now. | *¡No! A menos que lo you do ya mismo.* |

Something that English speakers have trouble getting used to is the use of *lo* to mean "the" when there's no noun. But this is pretty common with the adjective *mismo*. In English, when we say "I did <u>the same</u>", what noun is being used? "The same thing" would be *la misma cosa* (feminine), and "the same <u>type of thing</u>" would be *el mismo tipo de cosa* (masculine). But when we just say "the same", without a clear noun, the phrase is *lo mismo*.

| I'm thinking the same. | *Yo* think *lo mismo.* |
| They are doing the same. | *Ellos* are doing *lo mismo.* |

"Estar-ish" Adjectives

If you are female and talking about yourself, remember to use feminine adjectives.

| I'm not sure. | *No estoy segura.* |
| Are you sure? | *¿Estás seguro?* |

| It's clear. | *Está claro.* |
| It's clear that they aren't here. | *Está claro que no están.* |

"Ser-ish" Adjectives

| And is it safe? | *¿Y es seguro?* |
| And is it very big? | *¿Y es muy grande?* |

To say that someone is "confident", Joel often says that someone is "sure of himself", or "*seguro de* himself".

| He's very confident. | *Es muy seguro de sí mismo.* |
| I was very confident. | *Yo fui muy segura de mí misma.* |

People Nouns (Living Room)

I'll do you that favor, since we're friends.	*Te* I'll do *ese favor, ya que somos amigos.*
I'll help you with that, since you're my children.	*Los* I'll help *con eso, ya que son mis hijos.*

Bad people took everything and she had to leave.	*Gente* bad took *todo y tuvo que* leave.

I want to play with the serious-faced woman.	*Yo* want to play *con la mujer de* serious face.

Joel's word for "woman", *mujer*, can also mean "wife".

The man and his wife too!	*¡El hombre y su mujer también!*

Kitchen Nouns

Concurred!	*¡De acuerdo!*
They don't agree.	*No están de acuerdo.*

And does she have good work?	*¿Y tiene buen trabajo?*
And did he like his work?	*¿Y le* was pleasing *su trabajo?*

I had a problem.	*Tuve un problema.*
I had an idea.	*Tuve una idea.*
She had a reason.	*Tuvo una razón.*

Now we come to an idiom involving the word *razón*. Joel almost never admits that someone else is right about something unless he can see their logic. If he's forced to admit that someone else is right, the way that he says this is to say that they have *razón*, or "reason". For example, "You're right" is *tienes razón*.

You're right, this book is the best!	*Tienes razón, ¡este* book *es lo más!*

Time Nouns (Ballroom)

When Joel asks what time it is, he's thinking in terms of the colored lights; it's an easy question to answer simply based on what "aura" is currently shining.

In other words, to talk about the clock time, Joel doesn't use the versions of "time" found in the middle of the room. Instead, he always asks what "hour" it is.

What time is it?	*¿Qué hora es?*
What time was it?	*¿Qué hora era?*

To ask "at what hour" something happened, he uses the preposition *a*. So literally, instead of asking "at what hour", he asks "to what hour" something happened.

They'll be here at that time.	*Estarán aquí a esa hora.*
Will you be here at that time?	*¿Estarás a esa hora?*

At home there's never anyone during the mornings.	*En casa nunca hay nadie por las mañanas.*
At home there's always someone during the afternoons.	*En casa siempre hay alguien por las tardes.*

Dad and mom are arriving at any moment.	*Papá y mamá* arrive *en* any *momento.*
My friends are arriving at that moment.	*Mis amigos* arrive *en ese momento.*

Remember that references to time usually involve the preposition *a* ("to") rather than *en* ("at"). To say "sometimes", Joel always says "at times", or *a veces*.

Sometimes I think that I'm going to be able to enter.	*A veces* I think *que voy a* be able to enter.

Joel is a quirky bee, and all of his greetings are congruent with his quirkiness. Joel rarely says "good morning" or "good evening"; instead, he says "good days" or "good evenings".

Good morning!	*¡Buenos días!*
Good afternoon!	*¡Buenas tardes!*
Good evening!	*¡Buenas noches!*

To say that "it's time to do something", Joel actually words it as "it's moment of doing something", or "*es momento de* doing something".

It's time to go.	*Es momento de ir.*
It's time to have something else.	*Es momento de tener algo más.*

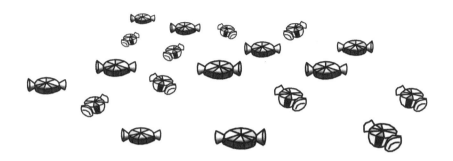

Place Nouns (Library)

The word *parte* means "place", but it's often used along with indefinite adjectives, the ones on the driveway. Practice switching out the word "otra" in this sentence with various other indefinite adjectives.

He sought her through every place.	*La* he sought *por todas partes.*
He sought her through another place.	*La* he sought *por otra parte.*
He sought her through many places.	*La* he sought *por muchas partes.*
He sought her through each place.	*La* he sought *por cada parte.*
He sought her through several places.	*La* he sought *por algunas partes.*

In another world.	*En otro mundo.*
In another place.	*En otra parte.*
In another place.	*En otro lugar.*

An idiom involving *mundo*: To say "everyone", Joel often says *todos*. But sometimes, to exaggerate how many people he's talking about, he says "all the world", or *todo el mundo*.

Everyone in the place was very sure.	*Todo el mundo en el lugar estaba muy seguro.*
Everyone in the house goes to that place.	*Todo el mundo en la casa va a ese lugar.*

Part Nouns (Bedroom)

We're going to do each part.	*Vamos a* do *cada parte.*
Aren't we going to do another part?	*¿No vamos a* do *otra parte?*

I'll give you the name of the place.	*Te* I'll give *el nombre del lugar.*
I'll give him the name of the thing.	*Le* I'll give *el nombre de la cosa.*
I'll tell them the type of the place.	*Les* I'll tell *el tipo del lugar.*

With a little bit of time.	*Con un poco de tiempo.*
With a part of the money.	*Con una parte del dinero.*
With many of the things.	*Con muchas de las cosas.*

Writing Assignment

Remember the theory portion of this lesson? We need to connect your thoughts to the Spanish language.

You want to be able not only to translate Spanish sentences, such as the phrase examples we just looked at. That's not enough.

You want to be able to THINK Spanish sentences.

The easiest way to start is by learning to *think* the sentences we just looked at. Practice saying them out loud while *thinking* the meaning.

But there's more: You should be able to modify these sentences by writing variations of them (kind of like the variations we provided). Then *think* those variations as well.

So in addition to "narrating your thoughts", as we discussed at the beginning of this lesson, you should also write several sentences down, in Spanish, every day, based on the native-written Spanish examples we've provided. Make it a routine. I recommend doing it in the morning, or whatever part of the day your mind is clearest. Carve out the time daily, because this is extremely important.

I also recommend showing your writings to a native speaker. That way you know you're practicing correctly. If you're an Accelerated Spanish member, you can send your sentences to our team of native-speaking Spanish coaches. We'll always provide you with detailed feedback on how you're doing and what you should be improving.

Dialogue Assignment

Let's apply our vocabulary to a couple of stories.

Over last several pages, some quotes (some of them slightly modified) have been highlighted in two different colors. In Volume 2, we're studying two separate dialogues: "Games with Sofía and Laura", and "Stories with Nicolás and Lucía".

Throughout this book, the highlight colors represent which dialogue they come from. Samples from our first dialogue (Sofía/Laura) are highlighted in magenta, and samples from our second dialogue (Nicolás/Lucía) are in .

You'll be expected to learn both of these stories in their entirety by the time you're finished with Volume 2. But we'll break it down throughout the book.

For now, I recommend focusing on just one dialogue: The one about two little girls, Sofía and Laura.

You'll find this story in its entirety at the end of this book. For now, we'll present just one part of the story, where Sofía and Laura are playing with two toys in a cardboard box, which they're pretending is a restaurant or a bar.

According to the story, "Man 1", Sofía's doll, is holding a box full of his brother's toys from when they were kids; he's hoping that this will remind his brother of the good times they had when they were young. Laura's doll, "Man 2", is trying to help Man 1 find his brother.

After you've worked with this conversation a bit, feel free to find the audio that goes with it at Spanishin1Month.com.

Searching for my Friend

Man 2: How nice to see you after so many years!

Man 1: I came to search for my friend, I have to tell him that I'm sorry.

Man 2: And that? What is it?

Man 1: It's my friend's… I mean, my brother's. We've know each other since childhood, it's as if we were brothers, but I did terrible things. After many years I understood that it had been wrong. Recently I realized that he was in problems. So I called him, but he told me that he didn't want to see me again. One way or another, I came to look for him. I told him: "No matter what, I'll help you. I'm going to be there.". I don't know why I called him; I guess it was in order that he would know that I was coming. It would be strange if he saw me around here all of a sudden. I have this with things from when we were kids, in order that he should not forget everything that we lived.

Man 2: And does he still live here?

Man 1: Yes, a month ago I spoke with Ignacio, a friend of both of us. He was with him until that day, and I know that his wife is here, so he's going to be here as well. I have to go to his house, but I don't know which one it is.

Man 2: Don't worry, you're going to find him.

Man 1: The most difficult thing for me is not to worry.

Hombre 2- *¡Qué bueno* to see you *después de tantos años!*

Hombre 1- I came to search for *mi amigo, le tengo que* tell que I'm sorry.

Hombre 2- *¿Y eso? ¿Qué es?*

Hombre 1- *Es de mi amigo… o sea, de mi* brother. We've known each other *desde* childhood, *es como si fuéramos* brothers, *pero yo* did *cosas muy* bad. *Después de muchos años* I understood *que había estado mal.* A little while ago I knew *que estaba en problemas. Entonces lo* I called, *pero él me* told *que no me* he wanted to see again. One way or another, *lo* I came to seek. *Le* I told: *"sea lo que sea, te* I'll help. *Voy a estar ahí." No* I know *por qué lo* I called. I guess que *para que* he would know *que* I came, *sería* strange *si me* he saw *por aquí* suddenly. *Tengo esto con cosas de cuando éramos* kids, *para que no* he forget *todo lo que* we lived.

Hombre 2- *¿Y* still he lives here?

Hombre 1- *Sí,* ago *un* month I spoke *con* Ignacio, *un amigo de los dos. Estaba con él hasta ese día, y* I know *que su* wife *está* here, *así que él va a estar aquí también. Tengo que ir a su casa, pero no* I know *dónde es.*

Hombre 2- Don't worry, *lo vas a* find.

Hombre 1- *Lo más* difficult *para mí es no* to worry.

Man 2: I'll help you with that, since we're friends Your friend, what's he like?

Man 1: He's tall, more tall than I. Many say that we look like each other, although I think not so much. He's very sure of himself, but I'm not. Whatever… I am what I am.

Man 2: Does your friend have a very large car?

Man 1: Could be! He always wanted to have a big car, maybe he finally did it after all.

Man 2: Now I know who he is! He works with a friend of mine. Someone, he or she, is around now. I'll give you the name of the place.

Man 1: Thanks so much, you have been of much help.

Hombre 2- It's nothing. All right, and when you see him tell him that I helped you.

Man 1: Haha. As soon as that happens, I'll tell him it. Perhaps it's too late; I hope not.

Hombre 2- *Te* I'll help *con eso, ya que somos amigos. Tu amigo, ¿cómo es?*

Hombre 1- *Es* tall, *más* tall *que yo. Muchos* say *que* we look alike, *aunque yo* think *que no tanto. Es muy seguro de sí mismo, pero yo no lo soy. Qué va a ser, soy lo que soy.*

Hombre 2- *¿Tu amigo tiene un* car *muy grande?*

Hombre 1- ¡It could *ser! Siempre* he wanted *tener un* car *grande, quizás lo* he did *de una vez por todas.*

Hombre 2- *¡Ya* I know *quién es!* He works *con una amiga mía. Alguien, él o ella, está por ahí ahora. Te* I'll give *el nombre del lugar.*

Hombre 1 - *Muchas gracias, has sido de mucha* help.

Hombre 2 - *No es nada. Bueno, y cuando lo* you see *le* you tell *que yo te* helped.

Hombre 1 - *Jaja. Ni bien eso* happens *se lo* I'll tell. *Quizá sea muy tarde,* I hope *que no.*

LESSON 8

Build Your Own Sentences

Until now, you've been speaking Spanish phrases that you've been taught. If you spoke your own meaning into it, it was simply by changing some of the words in the stock sentence.

That's all about to change.

Let's learn how to form entire sentences from scratch, combining Spanish phrases and clauses so that you can express yourself freely.

Lesson 8 Theory:

Build Your Own Sentences

"Whatever good things we build end up building us."
- Jim Rohn

"The face is a picture of the mind with the eyes as its interpreter."
- Cicero

IMAGINE YOU'RE in your "Spanish Zone", as described in the previous chapter.

Right now, this zone might feel small and uncomfortable. How are you supposed to say and think everything in Spanish… when your own Spanish sentences are so limited?

There are two ways to supplement your ability to think in Spanish:

(1) Expand your vocabulary.

(2) Expand <u>what you can do</u> with your vocabulay.

Right now, the 2nd option is our top priority.

We're about to study Spanish sentence structure in more detail than we ever have.

So far, you've been learning sentences by example. Instead of creating your own sentences word by word, you've been doing what native speakers do: Using existing sentences and slightly modifying them to adhere to your own meaning.

That's the most reliable way to form sentences in Spanish correctly.

But what if you want to say more? What if you want to add phrases, change the order of the words, or join multiple sentences together? Native speakers do that easily, so why can't you?

That's what this lesson is about.

Bookmark these pages. You'll probably be referring back to them pretty often as you begin to construct sentences in Spanish from scratch.

Let's dig into the theory of how Spanish sentences work.

Conjugated Verbs

Since all language learning is by imitation, we have to begin with the way that we know native speakers talk. So we'll start with stock sentences that you're already comfortable with.

Here are several sentences that you know, all structured in many different ways:

Yo no lo soy.

Quizá sea muy tarde.

Me fui a una nueva casa.

Es muy seguro de sí mismo.

Although these sentences are very different from each other, there's one thing that each of these complete sentences has in common… in fact, one thing that ALL Spanish sentences have in common:

A conjugated verb.

No more or less than ONE per sentence.

Yo no lo <u>soy</u>.

Quizá <u>sea</u> muy tarde.

Me <u>fui</u> a una nueva casa.

Es muy seguro de sí mismo.

Remember in Lesson 2 that we compared Spanish sentences to potato head toys, where you can switch out the different parts but maintain the same structure. Well, of course, there are all kinds of sentence structures, just like there are all kinds of potato head combinations. But they'll all have one thing in common.

Check out the various potato heads that you see on the next couple of pages. What's the common ground between all of them?

That's right: A pair of eyes. No more or less than one per potato.

It makes sense; potatoes always need eyes. Otherwise they wouldn't really be potato <u>heads</u>; they'd just be boring old potatoes. You can add or remove anything else, but the eyes have to be there for it to seem like a face.

Spanish sentences are the same way. You can add or remove subjects, objects, adverbs, and prepositional phrases, but every complete sentence has a single conjugated verb.

As a quick reminder, conjugated verb forms are the ones that we find <u>on the ground</u> of any verb shop, whether inside or outside.

However, unconjugated verb forms are found above the ground, such as the infinitive (e.g. *ser*), the participle (*sido*), or the gerund (*siendo*).

A sentence can have multiple <u>unconjugated</u> verbs. But it will still have just one <u>conjugated</u> verb.

For example, check out this sentence:

Todo va a haber estado bien.

Literally, "Everything is going to have been fine."

There is only one conjugated verb: *va* (from the present tense of Ir). But there are two unconjugated verbs: *haber*, an infinitive, and *estado*, the participle of Estar.

This little trick is really fun to play around with. You can create pretty long, wordy sentences, even with just one conjugated verb.

Let's start playing with this by learning about the several ways to embellish a potato's eyes.

Objects

Of course, the most direct way to modify a potato's eyes is simply to give it eyebrows.

When you think of eyebrows, think of <u>object pronouns</u>.

Just as eyebrows are always attached to the eyes, object pronouns are ALWAYS directly attached to the verb in a Spanish sentence.

Here are some examples:

Lo soy.

La tienen.

¿Los tenemos?

Each of these sentences is simply made of a verb (eyes) and an object pronoun (eyebrows). We can always change the verb out for a different one, and we can pretty easily change the object pronoun out, just as it's easy to change the eyes and eyebrows on the potato head. But you can't change the order. The eyebrows are always attached to the eyes, right "before" them (above them).

In fact, the core of Spanish sentence structure is described as *[obj][verb]*. Make that the heart of every sentence you speak in Spanish. The *[obj]* and *[verb]* are married to each other, as inseparable as the eyebrows and the eyes on our potato head.

Once you grasp this, you can do anything you want with the rest of the potato head. Everything else in a Spanish sentence is flexible and can pretty much do whatever it wants. But the conjugated verb is always the core of the sentence, and the object pronouns always belong right before the verb. This is a sacred connection that can never be violated.

Subjects

Check out the potato head we created on the previous page. Eyes and eyebrows are pretty cool. And they're all that's necessary for a Spanish sentence.

But wait a minute. Doesn't every sentence have a subject? If a verb indicates an action, shouldn't there be a person or item doing that action?

Well, in Spanish, the subject is often implied. Just because you don't see it, that doesn't mean it isn't there. Think about a lizard's ears: You can't see them, but they're there anyway.

In the same way, we can add ears to the potato head if we want. But even if we don't, the ear holes are still there. These represent the **subject** of the sentence: It's there, whether it's actually visible or not.

Consider again this sentence: *La tienen.* We could change this to *Ellos la tienen*, stating very clearly "<u>They</u> have it", though the *ellos* is

already implied in the original sentence.

Let's represent the subject of the sentence using sheep ears, since the creatures from the sheep pasture scene represent subject pronouns for us (*él, ella, yo, tú*, etc.).

So you might say that there are two ways to treat subjects in Spanish: Add sheep ears, or simply let the potato get along with earholes, which is also just fine.

As an interesting point, it's actually OK to put the subject either before or after the *[obj][verb]* structure, and as you can see in the picture, the ears are depicted "before" and "after" the eyes. Here are some examples that

follow this structure, with an *[obj][verb]* as well as a clearly stated subject:

<u>*Ella*</u> *lo es.*

<u>*Yo*</u> *lo soy.*

¿Los tenemos <u>nosotros</u>?

¿<u>Nosotros</u> los tenemos?

<u>Las mujeres</u> se fueron.

Se fueron <u>las mujeres</u>.

As you can see, in some cases we've used subject pronouns, such as *nosotros* and *ella*, and in others we've used entire nouns, such as *las mujeres*. These function the same way as the subject of a sentence, whether before or after the essential *[obj][verb]* "eyebrow-eye" structure.

Adverbs and Prepositional Phrases

Using just a verb, an object pronoun, and a subject, you can create a Spanish sentence that's about four or five words long.

But here comes the part where we start decorating: Adverbs (from the plaza) and prepositions (from the amusement park rides) add color and detail.

For example, let's imagine that adverbs are carrots (from the monkey's vegetable stand in the plaza). They can be stuck almost anywhere in the sentence, and they add interesting information.

Yo <u>siempre</u> lo soy.

¿Nosotros los tenemos <u>hoy</u>?

Se fueron las mujeres <u>así</u>.

You can stick a carrot (adverb) in the potato wherever you want. Except,

of course, between the eyebrows and the eyes.

Prepositions are similar, though they have a rule: You have to follow a preposition with a noun. Here are some common prepositions, with an example of a noun that might go after them:

* *en la casa*

* *en verdad*

* *de ese lugar*

* *por eso*

* *por muchos años*

These types of phrases are extremely flexible, just like adverbs. They can go almost anywhere in a sentence, and they add interesting information.

En verdad, yo siempre lo soy.

¿Nosotros los tenemos en la casa hoy?

Se fueron las mujeres así de ese lugar.

As you can see, it's possible to remove these prepositional phrases from the sentences. They

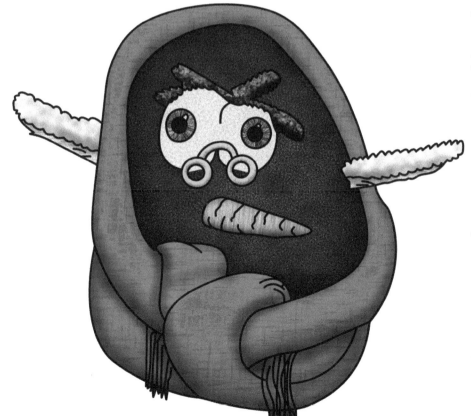

still function as complete sentences, even if you strip them down to the *[obj][verb]* structure:

Lo soy.

¿Los tenemos?

Se fueron.

But the subjects, adverbs, and prepositional phrases give extra information, detail, and color to these basic sentences.

I like to think of prepositional phrases as clothing that can be added to the potato head. Imagine a colorful scarf. You can dress the potato head up in a scarf, doing it in any way you like, as long as you don't cover up its eyes.

Conjunctions

Earlier I said that all Spanish sentences have one conjugated verb, no more or less than <u>one</u> per sentence.

However, the word "sentence" is a bit misleading, because it's actually possible to combine multiple "sentences" together into one larger sentence.

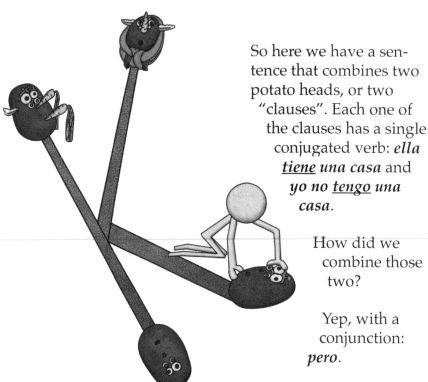

Take this example:

She has a house but I don't have a house.

Ella <u>tiene</u> una casa pero yo no <u>tengo</u> una casa.

It looks like we have two sets of eyes going on! How did we just put two potato heads together?

Well, in reality, a potato head does not equal a sentence; instead, a potato head equals a "clause". (If you want help remembering this term, imagine that all the potato heads are huge fans of Santa Claus and name themselves after him.)

So here we have a sentence that combines two potato heads, or two "clauses". Each one of the clauses has a single conjugated verb: *ella <u>tiene</u> una casa* and *yo no <u>tengo</u> una casa.*

How did we combine those two?

Yep, with a conjunction: *pero*.

Conjunctions are magic. You can use them to combine clauses all day long. Let's use them to combine some of those tiny sentences we reviewed at the beginning of this chapter:

Es muy seguro de sí mismo, <u>pero</u> yo no lo soy.

Quizá sea muy tarde, <u>aunque</u> me fui a una nueva casa.

Es muy seguro de sí mismo, <u>y</u> me fui a una nueva casa.

Yo no lo soy, <u>porque</u> quizá sea muy tarde.

The possibilities are endless!

Como

Check out this sentence:

Yo lo tengo como él lo tiene.

It means "I have it as he has it" (in the sense of "I have it <u>like</u> he has it" or "I have it <u>the way</u> he has it").

As you can see, there are two clauses there: **yo lo <u>tengo</u>** and **él lo <u>tiene</u>**. The word **como** is joining them together.

It turns out that the word **como** is a black hole in the universe of Spanish grammar. It's considered an "adverb", but it sort of works like a preposition or a conjunction; it always needs something after it.

In the sentence we just looked at, it's working like a conjunction. But in this sentence it's working like a preposition:

Yo lo tengo <u>como</u> él.

Here the **como** is simply followed by a noun.

This is one of the most hairy words in the Spanish language, but you can get used to it. Just imagine that whenever a potato head uses a comb, it tends to snag on things: Either a scarf (when **como** works like a preposition) or another potato head (when **como** works like a conjunction).

How To Practice

In Lesson 7, we talked about the importance of turning your English thoughts into Spanish sentences. This was a voice-changing exercise, training yourself to form thoughts in Spanish.

Now you should try doing the same thing, but think of it as a grammar exercise. Instead of forming Spanish thoughts, actually write down your English sentences and see if you can structure them in Spanish, using the potato head rules that you've learned.

Take this English thought as an example: "I wish the traffic weren't so bad."

We have two conjugated verbs: "I wish" and "weren't". So in Spanish, this would be two separate sentences connected by a conjunction: "I wish *que* the traffic weren't so bad."

Now that we know the basic structure, let's try to use Spanish wording.

Currently you don't have the Spanish word for "I wish", so let's re-word it to "I would be happier". Then our conjunction *que* can be replaced by the conjunction *si*: "I would be more happy <u>if</u> the traffic weren't so bad."

<u>**Estaría más** happy **si** the traffic **no fuera tan** bad.</u>

This is a perfectly structured Spanish sentence!

As you can see, creating your own Spanish sentences is not far from your reach. But it does take practice. You should work on writing several sentences a day, challenging yourself to reach new levels of comfort.

Also, make sure to run your sentences past a native Spanish speaker (such as a friend, or maybe the coaches from the Accelerated Spanish course), because you want to make sure that you're not training yourself in any errors.

Porks and Recreation

(Hacer, Poder, and Querer)

WHAT'S THE difference between "doing" something and "making" something?

In most languages, they're the exact same thing. There is no difference.

Most English speakers find this very bizarre. We seem to think that "making" and "doing" are two entirely different categories. In general, we "make" physical objects, such as meals ("they made breakfast"). We "do" actions, such as exercise ("I did my exercise").

But if you think about it, there's a lot of crossover. For example, a "mistake" is an action. So it should be "do", shouldn't it? But no, we always say "I made a mistake", not "I did a mistake."

As another example, if you come home to find that everything has been spilled off of your kitchen shelves, you would probably be angry that there's a mess. There are two questions you might ask: "Who made this mess?" or "Who did this?"

For Spanish speakers, "to make" and "to do" are the exact same thing. "Making a mess" is the same thing as "doing a mess"; "making dinner" is the same thing as "doing dinner".

One of our unfriendly neighborhood characters, Sarah, will come back to teach us this lesson.

Hacer: Do Your Own Dinner

Sarah spends most of her time at her apple shop, Ser, where she only concerns herself with being: "Are you a tall person?"

But when she feels more interested in doing or making something, she goes down the street to her restaurant, Hacer.

The infinitive *hacer* means "to do" or "to make". The stressed syllable sounds like "ser", although of course it has a completely different meaning. (Remember also that the H at the beginning is silent: "ah-SER".)

Hacer is a make-your-own meal restaurant that Ser manages. It may be strange that you would go to a restaurant and then make your own meal, but that's how Ser likes to run things. Actually, the main reason is for selfish purposes: She wants other people to make food for her. So unlike at the apple shop, at Hacer she isn't very picky about who comes in, as long as the guests are willing to make meals and give some of the food back to Ser herself. (Think "to Ser" or "a Ser", and you'll remember the pronunciation of *hacer*).

Joel and his friends come to Ser's restaurant because they want to make dinner for themselves. As soon as they come in, Ser tells them that they have to go ahead and prepare a "hog" right away. They're expected to prepare pigs for dinner, but Sarah always calls these pigs "hogs".

So she hands out a hog to each of her customers: one for Joel, one for the lizard, and one for the pandas to share. Each of them is expected to rub seasonings on the hog and then shove it into a hog-preparing machine that will do the cooking.

Since Joel is selfish and hungry, he insists on being the first to prepare his hog. He says, "I'll go do my hog first." The word he uses is *hago*, which sounds kind of like "I'll go" (remember that the H is silent, as always). This means "I do" or "I make".

But then something strange happens: Joel hears a grunting noise, coming from the direction of the lizard's pig. It seems that the lizard's hog is trying to say something.

"What did the lizard's hog say?" asks Joel. Then the same sound begins to come from the pandas' hog. "What are the hogs saying?" This is very unsettling: The hogs seem to be talking. In Joel's confused rush, he pronounces the word "hog" wrong, leaving out the H and the G, so it sounds like "AH-say" and "AH-saying".

The words *hace* and *hacen* are used for the lizard and the pandas. *Hace* means "it does" or "it makes" (and can also be applied to "he" or "she", such as "she does" or "he makes"). *Hacen* means "they do" or "they make".

Of course, the word *haces* is used for "you do" or "you make", so it's what Joel says to Sarah: "You gave us live hogs to cook? What are you doing??" To say "what are you doing", Joel says *"¿Qué haces?"*

But it's too late; the hogs are already locked behind oven-like doors. Staring at the hogs through the glass, Joel and the pandas all simultaneously say, "oh no…" and at the exact same time, they see the hogs saying the same thing:

"Oh no."

"Did you see that?" shouts Joel. "The hogs all said the same thing that we did! What are we doing? What we are doing isn't good." When he says "we are doing", he uses the word *hacemos*, which has the stressed syllable "same" (based on the fact that they all said the "same" thing at once).

The hogs disappear into the workings of Hacer's giant hog-preparing machines. As they meet a strange fate, let's quickly review the variety of words in this scene: *hago* for Joel, *hace* for the lizard, *hacen* for the pandas, *haces* for Ser, and *hacemos* (with the stressed syllable "same") for "we do" or "we make".

Hacía

Joel is disturbed by the notion that he and his friends have sent hogs into a meal-preparing machine while they were still alive.

By examining the chutes that the hogs were sent through, he can tell that they must have been directed to a large machine behind the counter.

When Ser isn't looking, Joel sneaks behind the counter to get closer to this machine. It has very tiny windows, like peep holes, and Joel hopes he can spy into the machine to see what's going on with the hogs: "I want to see what I can see."

The stressed syllable "see" goes with the word *hacía*, which is the imperfect past tense for Hacer. *Hacía* applies to both Joel and the lizard, so it can mean "I was doing", "I was making", "he was doing", "she was making", and so on.

Meanwhile, other words can be derived from this word: *hacían*, *hacías*, and *hacíamos*, all of which use the same stressed syllable, "see".

If you're paying close attention, you might already realize that the verb Hacer is an action verb. In other words, it's like Ir: You usually do it one time, not for a long period of time. The imperfect past tense isn't nearly as common as the preterite past tense (which we'll learn soon).

However, this version behind the counter, hacía, is occasionally used when something has happened multiple times in the past. To demonstrate, let's see what happens when Ser catches Joel spying through the peep holes.

"What are you doing back here?" she demands to know. "You aren't authorized to come behind the counter. This area is for experienced chefs only."

Joel makes an excuse: "But I AM an experienced chef! I used to make dinner all the time when I was a young bee growing up, because my mother was too lazy to do it herself."

To say "I used to make dinner all the time", Joel says "*Hacía* dinner all the time." This is used for a recurring event in the past, something that someone "used to do", rather than a single event.

More often, of course, Hacer is regarded as a one-time action, so the preterite tense is more common than the *hacía* tense. We'll learn the preterite forms as Joel and his friends find the prepared hogs coming out the other end of the machine.

hacía

76

Red

Recall that inside every store, we always have a present tense, a general (imperfect) past tense, and a "red" (preterite) past tense.

For example, in Estar the preterite "red" tense was between the shelves, where the lizard and Joel found the beef stew cauldron. In Ir, we used the doctor's closet for the preterite tense.

In Hacer, the "red tense" takes place at the table area of the restaurant, to the left of the entrance. This is where the guests are expected to finish preparing the hogs and then eat them.

Joel hears some thumping noises and looks at the tables. The hogs have fallen out of chutes and onto the

tables, now fully cooked and almost ready to eat, with an apple in each hog's mouth.

Following the directions, Joel picks up some sauce and garnish, and he spends about five minutes carefully decorating the hog, hoping that it will look nice. When he's finished with this, dinner is ready to eat!

"Wow," says Joel, "I did that myself? That wasn't hard at all! Making dinner was very easy."

Joel's word for "I did" (or "I made") is *hice*.

But then Joel looks over at the lizard. He's amazed to see that although the lizard spends only a few seconds throwing the garnish and sauce onto

the hog, the lizard's hog somehow looks even better than Joel's.

"HE'S SO good at that!" says Joel. "He made his dinner even faster than I did."

The word for "he made" (or "she made", or "he did", etc.) is *hizo* (pronounced "EEH so").

Meanwhile, Ser enters the scene and shouts "Remember to give me some of the food!" But as she comes in, she slips on some sauce on the floor, spilling the food that she's holding all over this part of the restaurant.

Joel is angry. "Cease and desist!" he shouts, in his mischievous, formal voice. "Look what you did! While we were making very nice meals, you just made a big mess!"

The word for "you did" is *hiciste*, with the stressed syllable "cease".

What about the pandas?

This is a bit disturbing. When the pandas' hog emerges from the chute, the pandas freeze with their mouths hanging open. One of them finally utters, "Our hog… it's breathing!"

Joel looks at the pandas' hog. It seems to be lying motionless, but the apple in front of its mouth is the giveaway: The hog's breath can be seen on the apple, with condensation rhythmically appearing and fading on the apple's surface as the hog inhales and exhales.

"Look, Ser!" says Joel. "You can <u>see air on</u> the apple in front of the pandas' hog's mouth! Something's very wrong here."

The word *hicieron*, pronounced "eeh-see-AIR-on", means "they made" or "they did". Associate "see air on" with the pandas, and you'll remember *hicieron*.

Joel looks around at the rest of the hogs. It seems that air is blowing on all of the apples! "What have we done?" says Joel.

The lizard feels the hogs' necks to see if there's a pulse. He shakes his head "no": The hogs are indeed dead.

Joel is a bit relieved. "I guess the air just makes it seem like all the hogs are alive," he says. "They aren't really breathing."

The word *hicimos*, with the stressed syllable "seem", means "we made" or "we did". Associate the syllable "seem" with the entire group.

Practice the Preterite

Let's quickly practice using our five new "red" preterite words.

"I did it": *Lo hice.*

"He/she did it": *Lo hizo.*

"You did it": *Lo hiciste.*

"They did it": *Lo hicieron.*

"We did it": *Lo hicimos.*

You might recognize something familiar about *hiciste*, *hicieron*, and *hicimos*. They're very similar to the equivalent words in Ir's closet.

"You went there": *Fuiste ahí.*

"They went there": *Fueron ahí.*

"We went there": *Fuimos ahí.*

Hiciste rhymes with *fuiste*, *hicieron* rhymes with *fueron*, and *hicimos* rhymes with *fuimos*. (Meanwhile the words *fui* and *fue* from Ir are extremely irregular, so they don't match the *hice*/*hizo* pattern.)

In conversations, you'll want to be able to think of these words quickly. Make sure you have the "-iste" strongly associated with "you", "-eron" strongly associated with "they", and "-imos" strongly associated with "we".

Here's one exercise you can do right now: Pretend you're watching the pandas going various places and doing different things. As they do these things in your imagination, narrate their story in the past tense, using *fueron* ("they went") and *hicieron* ("they did"). Use the voice of a spy who's reporting on each thing they do, but in very general terms.

For example, *"Fueron a algún lugar… hicieron algo… fueron a otro lugar… hicieron algo más… ya fueron a casa."* Make sure to imagine the pandas the whole time and associate these words with them.

Next, switch to the first person plural. Imagine yourself doing those same things, along with Joel. Narrate each thing using *fuimos* ("we went") and *hicimos* ("we did"). *"Fuimos a algún lugar… hicimos algo… fuimos a otro lugar… hicimos algo más… ya fuimos a casa."*

Practice that story three more times, first using *fuiste* and *hiciste*, then *fue* and *hizo*, and finally *fui* and *hice* (picturing yourself doing these things alone).

If you're now somewhat comfortable with all the preterite tenses of Hacer, feel free to move on with the lesson. Or, if you like, you can continue this exercise to keep practicing, perhaps using present tense verbs such as *hacemos* and *van*.

Hurray! It's the Future!

Joel and his friends are horrified by what happened in the restaurant. They refuse to eat the hogs and decide to go home and make their own dinners.

As they leave through the front door, Joel tells the pandas, "I'll make dinner for all of us at home." As he says this, he actually gets kind of excited about it because he's so hungry: "Hooray! I'll make dinner at home." His word for "I'll make" or "I'll do" is *haré*.

Meanwhile, the lizard says "Rah!" His word is *hará*.

Based on these words, we also have *haremos* ("we'll do" or "we'll make"), *harán* ("they'll do" or "they'll make"), and *harás* ("you'll do" or "you'll make"). If you want an extra mnemonic for *harás*, imagine that Ser comes out and tries to harass them into staying and making more food here. Joel says, "You'll do that. We'll go home."

But instead of going straight home, Joel and his friends go to the side of the store and check out the wood pile that fuels the machines inside. They observe that this wood pile is sitting next to an air conditioning unit, which keeps the building cool when the wood burns too hot. (For the nerds, the air conditioning unit will help you remember that the "would" forms of a verb are officially known as the <u>conditional</u> forms.)

The word for "I would do", "he would do", or "she would do" is *haría*. In case you haven't figured it out yet, "Ría" is ALWAYS the stressed syllable for the "would" versions of any verb, and Hacer is no exception.

However, you may have noticed that these words are shorter than normal. Most conditional words put -ría at the end of the infinitive, which would make a word like "<u>hacería</u>", just like future tense words usually put -ré at the end, as in "<u>haceré</u>". But Hacer is used so often that Joel likes to shorten all of these forms of the verb.

Practice using them all. Here are a few examples:

> *Haré algo.* ("I'll do something.")
>
> *Harían algo.* ("They would do something.")
>
> *Harás algo.* ("You'll do something.")
>
> *Haríamos algo.* ("We would do something.")

Once you're comfortable with these, it's time to visit the muddy back yard.

Hog Sty

Sarah's hogs are kept in a sty in the back yard. This makes the subjunctive versions of Hacer very easy: *haga*, *hagas*, and *hagan* all have the stressed syllable "hog" (with a silent H). The longer word, *hagamos*, has a stress on the middle syllable (like any word with "mos" at the end"), so it may take some more practice.

I recommend trying these words out in this sentence structure: "I hope *que haga algo*." Practice exchanging *haga* for the other subjunctive forms of Hacer.

Beside the building, on the side where we normally have a moving sidewalk,

Joel discovers how Ser powers the restaurant when she's not burning wood.

An ox has been enslaved by Ser, walking on the moving sidewalk as a treadmill. The ox is working very hard, and its movement creates enough energy to power the machines in Hacer.

If the ox ever gets tired or tries to stop, Ser gets angry. She says, "Do the work!" Her word for "do", as an imperative, is *haz*, which sounds like a cross between "ass" and "ox". This is how you order someone to do something; "do the work" is *"haz el trabajo."*

81

H is for Helicopter

On the roof is a giant landing pad for helicopters, which deliver hogs to the restaurant. The giant "H" on the roof represents the word *hecho*, which is the participle. For example, "I have done it" is *lo he hecho*, and "they have done the work" is *han hecho el trabajo.*

Hanging from the chimney is a bell, which looks exactly like the bell from Ser's apple store. Normally, people are expected to ring this bell at "the end" of a pleasant visit. At Ser, the word was *siendo*; here, the word is *haciendo*, based on *hacer*. In both cases, the stress is on "end": "see-END-o" and "ah-see-END-o".

For example, to say "I am doing it", you say *lo estoy haciendo.*

We'll see more examples involving hecho and haciendo soon. For now, Joel and his friends are going to leave Hacer and eat dinner at home. While they do, make sure you can remember all the forms of Hacer that we've learned.

hecho

haciendo

Poder: Dare To Get in Shape

After dinner, Joel and his friends decide to try to burn off some calories at the local gym.

The verb that we're about to learn is almost always used <u>along with other verbs</u>. It roughly means "to be able", but for practical purposes, it replaces the English words "can" and "could".

As some quick examples, check out these sentences:

- You <u>can</u> have it now.

- He <u>couldn't</u> be there yesterday.

As you can see, "can" and "could" are used before other verbs to indicate someone's ability to do something. But in Spanish, the words "can" and "could" don't exist.

Instead, you'd use some form of "to be able". In these cases, you'd say:

- "You <u>are able</u> to have it now."

- "He <u>not was able</u> to be there yesterday."

The verb for "being able" is Poder.

Poder represents all kinds of ability. The owner of the store, Darrel, goes by the nickname "Dare", and he's physically very gifted. He expects no less from his patrons, and his gym has one clear motto: "Dare to get in shape!"

Dare's shop includes lots of different workout equipment, but it's mainly known for being really hard to get around in. He has designed it so that it's impossible to enter without getting a workout. The shop itself is almost an obstacle course.

When Joel and his friends first arrive in Poder, they are discouraged by the obstructions. Right inside the door is a giant pool of water that they have to wade through. It's not deep enough to swim in, but it's a lot of work to wade through it.

The stressed syllable here is "wade", and it helps us remember the words *puedo*, *puede*, *puedes*, and *pueden*. As you might have guessed, *puedo* means

"I am able", *pueden* means "they are able", and so on. In every case, the stressed syllable is "wade".

For example, "he can wade through the pool" is "*puede* wade through the pool."

Meanwhile, the sunlight streaming through the window makes the water warm, and Joel and his friends feel hot. "This takes all day!" says Joel. The word for "we are able" is *podemos*, with the stress on "day".

You might not need the mnemonic to remember *podemos*. It's actually based on the infinitive, *poder*, but the R is replaced with "mos". This is the case with almost every verb:

estar: estamos

tener: tenemos

hacer: hacemos

poder: podemos

As we learn more and more verbs, we'll rely on these patterns more and more often. Nevertheless, you should make sure that you can remember all five of the present tense forms of Poder here in the entrance where they belong.

Día

Dare loves the daylight. He thinks it's great for fitness, and for getting vitamin D.

Behind the counter where Dare himself hangs out, he has pictures of sunshine and paintings of the letter D, just like the ones we saw on the wall in Joel's ballroom. Normally the letter D represents the word *día*, which means "day". Here, it helps us remember the words *podía*, *podías*, *podían*, and *podíamos*, all of which have the stress on "*día*".

Of course, these are the normal past tense versions of Poder. For example, while "I am able to do this" is *puedo hacer esto*, "I was able to do this" is *podía hacer esto*.

Pudo

Joel and the lizard want a break after all that wading. They try to find the place that they're least likely to have to work hard: The aisles of merchandise.

Dare has red shelves of merchandise, but in reality, he doesn't sell much. He's always more interested in training people, so although Joel and the lizard don't know it, these shelves are actually a trap.

As they round a corner, suddenly Dare jumps on the lizard from behind a shelf. He tackles the reptile and ties it up with its own tail.

"Ha!" says Dare. "You've been Pudo'd!"

Apparently, "pudo" is Dare's favorite martial art. He named it after judo, but it's not related at all; instead of throwing your opponent, you're expected to tie them up with one of their own bodily features.

Dare is about to pounce on Joel, probably to tie him up with his wings, but he hesitates. "I'll let you be," he says. "Your yellow color reminds me of the daylight. I like you!"

Joel is relieved that he was able to avoid such a humiliating situation. "I was able to avoid this!" he brags as he helps the lizard untie his tail.

The word *pudo* means "he was able" or "she was able" in the preterite tense. Meanwhile, the word *pude* sounds very similar, though it ends with "day", and it means "I was able". For example, "I was able to avoid this" is "*Pude* to avoid this."

You might notice that this pattern is similar to the one we learned in Tener and Estar:

pude / tuve / estuve

pudo / tuvo / estuvo

Obstacle Course

If you thought the inside of Poder looked like an obstacle course, wait till you see the back yard.

This is a real obstacle course, with ropes, ladders, and swinging objects. If you fall off the equipment, you land in some very thick mud.

Joel and his friends decide not to use the equipment; instead, they try wading through the mud. This was a really bad idea. The mud proves to be much harder to wade through than the water inside the store.

Most of the subjunctive forms of Poder have the stressed syllable "wade": *pueda*, *puedas*, and *puedan*.

Joel says, "That was really dumb of us! We should have just climbed over the mud. I hope that we can avoid being so dumb in the future." The subjunctive of "we can" is *podamos*, with a stressed syllable that sounds like "dumb".

Beneath the ground, under all the mud, is the storm shelter that Yol standards require. This storm shelter, however, serves a double purpose: Dare uses this underground chamber to make bricks. He doesn't want the

mud to go to waste, so he lets some of the mud sit in heaps for a long time, and when a heap of mud has sat still for 12 months, it turns into a heavy brick that he can use to lift as weights.

The word *pudiera*, with the stressed syllable "year", means "were able" as a past tense subjunctive. We'll learn how this is used soon. For now, just remember to stress "year" to represent how long these bricks have to sit underground before they can be lifted.

Every Deed

After Joel and his friends have gone through the obstacle course, they stagger away, covered with mud. Dare is very proud of them, because they have been able to face his gym's challenges successfully.

"You all have been able to perform every deed!" he says in praise.

The word for "been able" is *podido*, with the stress on "deed".

Querer: Rare Jewels

Our last verb in this lesson is Querer.

Querer is a jewelry shop that stands across the road from Hacer. It's run by a koala named Kay Rare, but her last name, Rare, is what she prefers to be called, because she likes to emphasize the fact that she sells very rare jewels.

The verb Querer means "to want", or in some cases, "to love". Joel associates this word with wealth. Whenever he wants something, he thinks of rare jewels.

When Joel first arrives in Querer, his eye is caught by the shiniest item in the store: A diamond necklace with the form of an arrow. "I want it!" he exclaims. His word for "I want" is *quiero* (pronounced "kee-AIR-ow", stressing "arrow").

Meanwhile, most of the other words here also have the stress on "air": *quiere*, *quieres*, and *quieren*.

The word for "we want" is *queremos*, with a stress on "ray". This is because of

Querer's security system: Rare insists on shining a "ray" of light on each customer in her store, like a spotlight, to keep track of them and make sure they aren't stealing.

Review the words in this scene, and practice using them before a noun, such as "a house":

Quiero una casa.

Quiere una casa.

Quieres una casa.

Quieren una casa.

Queremos una casa.

Joel doesn't like the rays of light shining on him, so he goes behind the counter to see if he can rip Rare off.

Quería

What Joel finds behind the counter are some extremely precious emeralds. Gems like these are very hard to find in Yol.

"Where did they come from?" asks Joel.

Rare proudly responds, "Oh, I wanted emeralds for a long time, but they can only be found deep under the mountain of Ría." She points to a picture of the mountain that she keeps behind the counter.

The normal past tense forms of Querer have a stress on "Ría":

quería: I wanted

quería: he/she/it wanted

querías: you wanted

querían: they wanted

queríamos: we wanted

You might think this is strange, since the syllable "Ría" is normally used to indicate the conditional "would" forms of words, not the past tense. But it's because Querer is a strange verb, with an R in the middle. Compare *quería* with *hacía* or *tenía*, and you'll see that it's not very different from the past tenses of those other verbs.

Keys

The merchandise area in Querer's store is where rubies, diamonds, and many other types of jewels are stored. They're all locked behind doors.

Joel asks if he can hold one of the rubies, but Rare has to thumb through several dozen keys. She keeps putting the wrong key in the lock, and says, "Oops! That's not what I meant to do."

The most common preterite forms of Querer have the stress on the syllable "key": *quise* and *quiso*. These literally mean "I wanted" and "he/she/it wanted", but they're also used instead of "I meant". So "That's not what I meant to do" is *"Eso no es lo que quise hacer."*

The other preterite forms of Querer are created like the preterite forms of Hacer that we learned earlier:

hice/hizo: quise/quizo

hiciste: quisiste

hicieron: quisieron

hicimos: quisimos

As you can see, the two verbs are closely related, which is why they're right across the street from each other. For now, though, focus on remembering the stress on "key" for *quise* and *quiso*.

Junk Jewels

Joel doesn't want to pay for jewelry, so Rare invites him to go into the back yard and dig through the rejected jewelry to find something free.

Querer's back yard has a huge heap of ugly, dirty jewels that are either inauthentic or simply too ugly to be of any worth in Yol. Some of these are not only fake, but they're hollow; they look like large jewels, but they're inflatable toys made of plastic filled with air.

With the stressed syllable "air" we get most of the subjunctive forms of Querer: *quiera*, *quieras*, and *quieran*.

Meanwhile, Querer's storm shelter underground is where she secretly sources many of her gems. It seems to defy logic, but somehow there's a mountain range underground that looks like the Sierra Nevada. These miniature mountains supply diamonds for Querer.

The past tense subjunctive of Querer is *quisiera*, with the stress on "Sierra". (You may also notice that it sounds a lot like other past tense subjunctives we've learned: *fuera* and *pudiera*. In each case, the stress is on the syllable that sounds like "air".)

quiera

quered

Rid

Joel and his friends never find the underground diamonds, but they do make off with a bunch of fake, plastic jewels from Querer's back yard.

Rare stands on the roof and watches them leave. "Oh good!" she privately says to herself. "I've been able to get rid of all those fake jewels that I didn't like or want."

The participle is *querido*, with the stress on "rid". For example, "I have wanted it" is *lo he querido*.

Make sure to review all the forms of today's three verbs. We're about to put some intense work into using them.

Lesson 8 Application:
Verb Contractions

WE'VE LEARNED THREE new essential verbs this week, but there's one more thing that you can do with verbs that we haven't talked about yet: <u>contractions</u>, or combining two words into one word.

This is most common with Hacer, but you can actually do it with basically any verb.

To begin, you've been taught that object pronouns happen before the verb. "I do it" would be *lo hago*, and "they did it" would be *lo hicieron*.

However, we pointed out in Lesson 6, when we learned Ir, that the imperative actually has an object at the end. The word *vete*, which you use when you're ordering someone to leave, literally means "go yourself". The imperative of "go" is *ve*, but "go yourself" is *vete*. And it's considered one single word.

Similarly, "let's leave" is *vamonos*, which literally means "let's go ourselves". The object is at the end, but only because it's actually part of the same word. (Fun nerdy fact: *vamonos* should be "vamosnos", but in the evolution of the language the extra S in the middle got dropped.)

Now let's take that idea and go to Hacer. The imperative is where the ox is walking on the moving sidewalk like a treadmill. "Do the work" is "*Haz* the work." However, if we want to say "do it", the word is *hazlo*. Again, that's just one word; this is simply the way that imperatives work.

This doesn't work with normal conjugated forms of a verb, which always get the object before them (e.g. *lo hago*). However, with the infinitive and the imperative, it's actually quite common to put the object at the end. It's most common with the infinitive. Recall that infinitives, such as *hacer*, are basically treated as nouns. So "I like to do my work" would be "I like <u>*hacer* my work</u>". It's like saying "I like <u>your house</u>". You're treating the idea of "to do" as a noun, so you use the word *hacer* and treat it as a noun.

But what if you wanted to talk about the idea of "doing it"? We can use a single word for that, too, and the word is *hacerlo*. So "I like *hacerlo*".

It's important to emphasize that you CAN'T do this with most forms of a verb; as we've drilled into your head before, object pronouns go before verbs. But you can append objects to the end with the imperative (like *hazlo*) and with the infinitive (like *hacerlo*).

Let's go ahead and study plenty of sentence examples with our new verbs. As before, some of the sentences are highlighted in either magenta or turquoise. If the information in this chapter is overwhelming to you, focus for now on memorizing the highlighted sentences, and you'll find it easier to expand your comfort with these verbs from there.

Infinitives

Let's look at some examples of just the infinitive being used of Hacer, Poder, and Querer. Practice getting very comfortable with these before moving on to the conjugated forms of these verbs.

As you work with these sentences, practice using infinitive contractions, such as *hacerlo*.

One of the easiest ways to use an infinitive is in the "Ir + *a* + infinitive" construction:

We aren't going to be able.	*No vamos a poder.*
I'm not going to do it.	*No voy a hacerlo.*
He won't be able to do it.	*No va a poder hacerlo.*
You won't want it.	*No vas a quererlo.*
They won't want to do it.	*No van a querer hacerlo.*

Aren't we going to do that part?	*¿No vamos a hacer esa parte?*
Won't you be able to have the money?	*¿No vas a poder tener el dinero?*
Isn't he going to want to do everything?	*¿No va a querer hacer todo?*
I'm not going to be able to love her.	*No voy a poder quererla.*

Remember that infinitives sometimes function like nouns.

In the next example, *hacer* is being treated as a noun. It's being used after a preposition, *sin*, to say "without doing anything" (grammatically equivalent to "without food" or "without a house"). Practice switching out this preposition with other prepositions.

Without doing anything?	*¿Sin hacer nada?*
Without wanting anything?	*¿Sin querer nada?*
In order to do everything?	*¿Para hacer todo?*
Because of being able to do that?	*¿Por poder hacer eso?*
Upon doing it?	*¿Al hacerlo?*

You may have noticed that the previous list of five examples did NOT include a complete sentence. How do we know that? Because none of these examples has any <u>conjugated verb</u> (potato eyes).

The example *¿Sin hacer nada?* is only a prepositional phrase. However, the next example uses such a phrase at the beginning of a true complete sentence:

Without doing anything, she went to her house.	*Sin hacer nada, fue a su casa.*
Without wanting, she went to her house.	*Sin querer, fue a su casa.*
Without doing it, she went to my house.	*Sin hacerlo, fue a mi casa.*
In order to have it, she went to your house.	*Para tenerla, fue a tu casa.*
Upon doing it, she went to her house.	*Al hacerlo, fue a su casa.*

This next one also uses *hacer* after a preposition, this time at the end of the sentence. To talk about the amount of time or resources available for doing something, you commonly use *para*, as in *para hacerlo* ("to do it" or "in order to do it").

He only has three hours to do it.	*Sólo tiene tres horas para hacerlo.*
We only have a moment to do it.	*Sólo tenemos un momento para hacerlo.*
You'll only have four days to do it.	*Sólo tendrás cuatro días para hacerlo.*

Conjugating Hacer

Let's practice our conjugations of Hacer. First, practice all your present-tense conjugations with variations on this sentence:

And what are YOU doing here?	*¿Y tú qué haces aquí?*
And what are YOU ALL doing there?	*¿Y ustedes qué hacen ahí?*
And what are YOU[formal] doing here?	*¿Y usted qué hace aquí?*
And what are WE doing here?	*¿Y nosotros qué hacemos aquí?*

In the next sentence, **hace** is used to indicate a passing of time. This is a very common sentence structure in Spanish, phrased as "It makes three years that you are here". The "you are here" may sound strange; in English, we'd be more likely to put that phrase in a past participle ("It makes three years that you <u>have been</u> here"), but Spanish speakers always use the present tense if the activity is still ongoing.

It makes three years that you are here!	*¡Hace tres años que estás aquí!*
It makes four days that I don't have it!	*¡Hace cuatro días que no lo tengo!*
It makes two hours that you haven't been here!	*¡Hace dos horas que no estás!*

Now let's practice the preterite conjugations of Hacer:

He did what he had always wanted.	*Él hizo lo que siempre había querido.*
I did what I had always wanted.	*Yo hice lo que siempre había querido.*
They did what they had always wanted.	*Hicieron lo que siempre habían querido.*
You did what you had always wanted.	*Tú hiciste lo que siempre habías querido.*
We did what we had always wanted.	*Nosotros hicimos lo que siempre habíamos querido.*

The next example is a reflexive use of Hacer. Instead of meaning that something "does itself", it means that something "is done". For example, "how is this done?" can be said as *¿Cómo se hace esto?*; that's literally "How does this do itself?", though that's not how it's translated.

Nothing is done.	*No se hace nada.*
How is this done?	*¿Cómo se hace esto?*
This is always done that way.	*Esto siempre se hace así.*

Doing something to oneself can also mean that you're "making yourself something", or "turning yourself into something". For example, you can make yourself a friend. For this one, practice using different tenses of Hacer: The participle, the present, the past, etc.

She had made herself a good friend.	*Ella se había hecho muy amiga.*
They had made themselves good friends.	*Ellas se habían hecho muy amigas.*
He's making himself a good friend.	*Él se hace muy amigo.*
We made ourselves good friends.	*Nosotros nos hicimos muy amigos.*

Let's review Hacer's subjunctive uses:

I want you to do it like this.	*Quiero que lo hagas así.*
I want them to do it like this.	*Quiero que lo hagan así.*
I want it to be done like this.	*Quiero que se haga así.*
I want us to do it like this.	*Quiero que lo hagamos así.*

Let's talk about another use of the subjunctive.

You may remember this sentence example from earlier lessons: "How nice that it's you!" as "How nice that you be you!": *¡Qué bueno que seas tú!*

The beginning of the exclamation signifies a feeling, "how nice", and the second part (after the *que*) expresses what the feeling is about. That second part is always subjunctive.

Let's modify this sentence: Instead of "how nice", let's say "I don't like it". This would be "I don't like it *que seas tú.*"

This is a pretty common sentence structure. In the next examples, we're going to use it to indicate, "I don't like you to do that", or literally, "I don't like that you do that."

I don't like you to do that.	*No* I like *que hagas eso.*
He doesn't like you to do the work.	*No* he likes *que tú hagas el trabajo.*
I don't like when they do me favors.	*No* I like *que me hagan favores.*

In that last case, note that the plural word *hagan*, meaning "they do", might simply refer to a general "they", as in "I don't like it when any people do me favors".

Now for some imperatives:

Fine, do the work.	*Bueno, haz el trabajo.*
Fine, do it.	*Bueno, hazlo.*
Fine, let's do the work.	*Bueno, hagamos el trabajo.*
Fine, let's do it.	*Bueno, hagámoslo.*

Conjugating Poder

Use this example to practice the present tense of Poder, followed by an infinitive:

And can I go?	*¿Y yo puedo ir?*
And can we go?	*¿Y nosotros podemos ir?*
And can you all go?	*¿Y ustedes pueden ir?*
And can he have it?	*¿Y él puede tenerlo?*
And can you do it?	*¿Y tú puedes hacerlo?*

Now use this one to practice various tenses:

Another day we can go.	*Otro día podemos ir.*
Another year she was able to go.	*Otro año pudo ir.*
Another day they were able to go?	*¿Otro día podían ir?*
Another time I managed to go.	*Otra vez pude ir.*

This next example uses two phrases: The first with *cuando* followed by a subjunctive, and the second with a normal sentence.

When I'm able to go there, I'll do it.	*Cuando pueda ir ahí, lo haré.*
When they're able to go there, they'll do it.	*Cuando puedan ir ahí, lo harán.*
When we're able to go there, we'll do it.	*Cuando podamos ir ahí, lo haremos.*

We're going to learn a new idiom: The <u>reflexive</u> version of Poder.

Remember that Hacer, when reflexive, means that something "is done". *Se hace* literally means "it does itself", but it's used to mean "it is done".

Poder has a similar transformation when it's reflexive. *Se puede* has no literal translation (it would mean "it is able itself", which is nonsense), but it basically means that something is possible to do. For example, *se puede hacer* means "it can be done", and *se puede tener* means "it can be had". But *se puede*, by itself, means "it's possible", implying that it's possible to do something.

If it's possible…	*Si se puede…*
If it's possible to do…	*Si se puede hacer…*
If it's possible to have that…	*Si se puede tener eso…*

The verb Poder has a secondary meaning. Normally it means that someone "can" do something or is "able" to do something. But occasionally, the word simply means "might". To say that something "might" be true, it's common to say *puede ser* ("it might be").

That might be.	*Eso puede ser.*
That might be a problem.	*Eso puede ser un problema.*
Afterwards it might be a problem.	*Después puede ser un problema.*

More broadly, *puede* can be used before any verb to indicate that it <u>might</u> be the case.

He might be here.	*Puede estar aquí.*
There might be problems.	*Puede haber problemas.*
They might be friends.	*Pueden ser amigas.*

When Poder is used to mean "might", one idiomatic use is simply to put *puede que* at the beginning of a sentence. It doesn't translate literally, but it means that something might be true. This phrase is typically followed by a subjunctive verb.

It might be that it's not safe.	*Puede que no sea seguro.*
It might be that they're there.	*Puede que estén ahí.*
It might be that she wants something else.	*Puede que quiera algo más.*

In our previous examples, we've used the imperfect (*podía*) and preterite (*pude/pudo*) somewhat interchangeably. But how do you know when you should use one or the other?

Normally, when you use the general imperfect tense, it means that something "was possible" in the past. That's pretty straightforward.

But when Poder is used in a preterite sense, this indicates that someone actually made an attempt to do something, at a specific moment.

Let's compare two situations. Consider the English sentence, "I couldn't get out of the house".

This could mean two different things. If you said "*no podía* to get out of the house", this is just a general inability; you wouldn't have been able to get out of the house if you had tried.

However, if you instead phrase it as "*no pude* to get out of the house", this implies that you actually tried to leave the house and couldn't, at a particular moment. (Maybe you tried to open the door and it was stuck.)

So words like *podía* indicate the general past, but *pude* and *pudo* imply that some action was taken.

But I couldn't because they weren't there.	*Pero no pude, porque no estaban ahí.*
But he couldn't, because he didn't have it.	*Pero no pudo, porque no lo tenía.*
But she couldn't, because she wasn't there.	*Pero no pudo, porque no estaba.*

When the conditional *podría* version of Poder is used, this is sometimes used as a "softer" version of being able to do something. For example, imagine you want to request something, there are multiple options, even in English. "Can you give me food?" is a little demanding, but "Would you be able to give me food?" is a little softer. That's what *podrías* often indicates.

But could you do the work?	*¿Pero podrías hacer el trabajo?*
But you might be nicer!	*¡Pero podrías ser más bueno!*
But could they be nicer?	*¿Pero podrían ser mas buenas?*
But he would be able to be here beforehand!	*¡Pero podría estar aquí antes!*

Conjugating Querer

Querer can be used before a noun, as in *quiero una casa*.

I want more money in my life.	*Quiero más dinero en mi vida.*
We want a new house.	*Queremos una nueva casa.*
Do you want something else?	*¿Quieres algo más?*
They wanted another job.	*Querían otro trabajo.*

But very often, Querer is used exactly like Poder, right before a verb, as in *quiere hacerlo*.

After a while, I wanted to do it.	*Luego de un tiempo yo quería hacerlo.*
After a while, he's going to want to do it.	*Luego de un tiempo él va a querer hacerlo.*
After a while, they always want to leave.	*Luego de un tiempo siempre quieren irse.*
After a while, one wants to leave.	*Luego de un tiempo uno quiere irse.*

Don't get too weirded out by the *hacerle* contraction in the next example. It simply means "do to him/her" (or perhaps "do for him/her").

I want to do something nice to him.	*Quiero hacerle algo bueno.*
They want to do something nice for me.	*Quieren hacerme algo bueno.*
He wanted to do something nice to him.	*Quería hacerle algo bueno.*
They wanted to do something nice for her.	*Querían hacerle algo bueno.*

Remember that Querer can mean both "want" (for a thing) and "love" (for a person).

She loved him a lot.	*Lo quería mucho.*
They loved her so much.	*La querían tanto.*
He wanted it just a little.	*Lo quería muy poco.*

Something strange happens when you put the person after Querer. Check out this example:

He loves his wife.	*Quiere a su mujer.*

What is that extra *a* doing right before *su mujer*? Well, for some reason, Spanish speakers like to put an extra *a* before direct objects when the direct object is a person. It's their way of respecting people more than items.

Here are some more examples in the same sentence structure. Practice alternating objects after *quiere* in this sentence, sometimes using an inhuman object, sometimes using *a* and then a person.

They love their parents.	*Quieren a sus padres.*
They want their things.	*Quieren sus cosas.*
They love their friend.	*Quieren a su amigo.*
They want more money.	*Quieren más dinero.*
They love the man.	*Quieren al hombre.*

When followed by *que*, Querer indicates an intention that something should happen; for example, "I want that this should happen". Of course, since this is an intention, the verb within the *que* phrase is going to be subjunctive.

I want that we go to the house!	*¡Quiero que vayamos a la casa!*
They want that I go to the house!	*¡Quieren que yo vaya a la casa!*
We want that they go to the house!	*¡Queremos que vayan a la casa!*

Very often, when a preterite of Querer is used (*quiso*, *quise*, etc.) instead of imperfect (*quería*, *querían*, etc.), it means that someone didn't just "want" to do something, they actually tried to do it, as an action. It's kind of like the difference between "I <u>wanted</u> to do it" and "I <u>meant</u> to do it". Since preterite implies an action, *quiso* and *quise* imply the action of "meaning", maybe even "trying", to do something.

When I meant to go there, I went somewhere else.	*Cuando quise ir ahí, fui a otra parte.*
When I meant to say "please", I did something else.	*Cuando quise* to say "please", *hice algo más.*
When he meant to say that, he messed up.	*Cuando quiso* to say *eso,* he messed up.

One more idiom: Remember *lo que sea* to mean "whatever it be"? Well, in general, when *lo que* is followed by a subjunctive, it means "whatever" in some unique way. A good example is *lo que quiera*, which generally means "whatever [someone] wants".

I can do whatever I want.	*Puedo hacer lo que quiera.*
We can do whatever we want.	*Podemos hacer lo que queramos.*
You can do whatever you want.	*Puedes hacer lo que quieras.*
They can do whatever they want.	*Pueden hacer lo que quieran.*

Hacer: Advanced Use

Let's revisit the meaning of Hacer.

Remember that it means both "to do" and "to make". In English, sometimes we use the verb "make" to mean "to force", as in "to make him do this".

Hacer has that meaning as well: You can make someone else do something. This is generally an *hacer que* structure, followed by a subjunctive. For example, "He makes her do it" is literally "he makes <u>that she do it</u>", or *él hace <u>que ella lo haga</u>*.

Our final example for this lesson uses this construction, and you'll notice that it conveniently uses all three of our verbs: Poder, Hacer, and Querer.

They're able to make it so that nobody wants to do it.	*Pueden hacer que nadie quiera hacerlo.*
He was able to make it so that nobody wanted to do it.	*Él podía hacer que nadie quisiera hacerlo.*
I'm able to make it so that you don't want to do it.	*Puedo hacer que no quieras hacerlo.*
She managed to make it so that I didn't want to do it.	*Pudo hacer que yo no quisiera hacerlo.*

Hagámoslo Cada Día

After Lesson 8, you should be very close to basic fluency.

Now that you have Hacer, you can use this verb to express an enormous variety of things about yourself, your thoughts, what you've done, and what you'd like to do.

Not only that, but thanks to the guidance from the beginning of Lesson 8, you can now form sentences freely in Spanish, not limited by strict sentence structures.

In other words, the sky is the limit. You now have the ability write an infinite variety of things in Spanish.

From now on, you should plan to **write two full paragraphs in Spanish every day**, at least five days a week.

We're working on fluidity in producing your own Spanish sentences. This type of fluidity and confidence comes through <u>writing first, not speaking first</u>.

Plan to do this while in your "Spanish Zone". See how closely you can get your Spanish sentences to match your English thoughts, while maintaining good Spanish syntax and grammar.

Be focused and deliberate. Concentrate on your work, and piece together Spanish sentences that meet the following criteria:

(1) They follow the Spanish sentence patterns that you've learned, but they reinforce them in new ways.

(2) They practice Spanish phrases and vocabulary that are difficult to you.

(3) They are personal to you, based on your own experiences, interests, and hopes.

And every day, you should show these sentences to a native Spanish speaker. Since they're written out, your friend or coach will be able to offer very specific, tangible critique (which is sometimes harder in a conversation since that's not written out).

Dialogue Assignment

On the next few pages, you should study how your vocabulary is being used in the context of another game that Sofía and Laura are playing.

Laura makes up a story about a little girl who is friends with a big, scary monster. Sofía plays the "monster", which is just a large teddy bear. Laura uses her doll to play the part of a little girl who was sleeping in bed. She starts by asking the monster how it managed to get into the house today.

La Cosa

Laura's Doll: How did you get here?

"Thing": I came in through the back door.

Laura's Doll: How strange! Dad is the one that always makes sure that that shouldn't happen.

"Thing": Doesn't matter. I'm able to pass through any kind of place.

Laura's Doll: And why did you come?

"Thing": I was always going to see another girl, but she left from her house to another one very far away, and I was very lonely all this time.

Laura's Doll: But you might be more nice! You shouldn't enter like that because it's scary.

Laura- *¿Cómo* did you arrive *aquí?*

La cosa- I entered *por la* back door.

Laura- *¡Qué strange! Papá es el que siempre* makes sure *que eso no* happens.

La cosa- *No* it matters. *Yo puedo* pass *por* any *lugar.*

Laura- *¿Y por qué* did you come?

La cosa- *Siempre iba a* see otra girl, *pero se fue de la casa a otra* muy far away *y estuve muy solo todo este tiempo.*

Laura- *¡Pero podrías ser más bueno! No* you should come in *así porque* it's scary.

"Thing": I'm sorry, I really like being here. And obviously you wouldn't have let me enter.

La cosa- I'm sorry, I like *mucho estar aquí. Y claro que no me* you would have let come in.

Laura's Doll: It's not that way at all. If you were to have done it nicely, I would have done it.

Laura- *No es así para nada. Si lo* you were to have *hecho* nicely, *lo* I would have *hecho.*

"Thing": But I'm very large and strange.

La cosa- *Pero soy muy grande y* strange.

Laura's Doll: Well, whatever, you're nice one way or another. If you had wanted to do something bad you already would have done it.

Laura- *Bueno, sea lo que sea, eres bueno sí o sí.* Si you were to have *querido hacer algo* bad *ya lo* you would have *hecho.*

"Thing": All right. And what's up with you? Why do you have that face?

La cosa- *Bueno, ¿y qué te* is going on? *¿Por qué tienes esa* face?

Laura's Doll: My brother did something that he shouldn't have done. Our father doesn't know it yet, and for that reason my brother is so worried.

Laura- *Mi* brother *hizo algo que no podía hacer. Nuestro padre no lo* knows *aún, y por eso mi* brother *está tan* worried.

"Thing": Well, I'm sure that everything is going to be fine.

La cosa- *Bueno, estoy seguro de que todo va a estar bien.*

Laura's Doll: Thanks… Where do you live?

Laura- *¡Gracias!… ¿tú dónde* live?

"Thing": In another world! Do you want to meet my house?

La cosa- *¡En otro mundo! ¿Quieres* to see *mi casa?*

Laura's Doll: Of course! What's it like?

Laura- *¡Claro! ¿Cómo es?*

"Thing": I'm not able to say it with words; you have to go, but you can only go at night and now it's almost day.

La cosa- *No lo puedo* to say *con* words, *hay que ir, pero sólo se puede ir de noche y ya casi es de día.*

Laura's Doll: All right, let's go before to-night. I'll find you here tomorrow before it becomes night, all right? I'll be with José at home until you're here.

"Thing": Who is José?

Laura's Doll: My dog! He's my best friend, he always understands us. Before, we had a little girl dog; her name was Luna. She was very lonely and Jose came along. But Luna died, and now José is as lonely as she was. Now get out of here 'cause dad and mom are coming at any moment.

Laura- *Bueno, vamos antes de esta noche, te* I'll meet *aquí mañana antes de que se haga de noche, ¿sí? Estaré con José en casa hasta que estés aquí.*

La cosa- *¿Quién es José?*

Laura- *¡Mi* dog! *Es mi mejor amigo, siempre nos* he understands. *Antes teníamos una* little girl dog, she was called Luna, *estaba muy sola y* arrived *José, pero Luna* died *y ahora José está tan solo como ella. Ahora vete de aquí que papá y mamá* arrive *en* any *momento.*

LESSON 9

Leverage Essential Vocabulary

Now that you're thinking in Spanish and building your own sentences from scratch, it's time to expand your vocabulary so that you can begin to express your thoughts more accurately.

But be warned: Some words are much more important than others.

Let's learn why native speakers strongly prefer certain words. Then we can continue to follow in their footsteps.

The **elefante** can **corre** away! And **gatos** like to drink **leche**!

Her Spanish is getting so advanced!

Lesson 9 Theory:
Active Ignorance

"We first make our habits, and then our habits make us."
- John Dryden

"One who is faithful in a very little is also faithful in much."
- Jesus

YOU NOW know about 300 words. But how well can you use them?

Not long ago, I received an email from a student whom we'll call "Nate". Nate was dissatisfied with his small vocabulary.

He had recently tried to converse with a 5-year-old who was a native Spanish speaker. This kid was talking about what he'd had for breakfast that morning, and Nate couldn't understand the items that the kid described.

Nate wrote to me:

"I can't express very much without more nouns, adjectives, and adverbs… I would like you to introduce common words of basic conversation."

I get this kind of complaint a lot. Students like Nate don't really like relying on pronouns such as *esto* and *eso*, or on vague verbs like *hacer*. They'd rather have more colorful words like "oatmeal" and "slurping".

The reasoning is simple: "If I had just had the vocabulary from that conversation, I would have understood everything!"

Well, yes. Maybe.

If you train for one specific conversation, sure, you might be able to understand that <u>one</u> specific conversation. But where does that lead you?

Conversation Training Is a Dead End

Which of the following sentences do you think you'll find yourself saying more often?

(A) "The eggs and milk are in the kitchen, with the apples and carrots."

(B) "I want you to do it as soon as you can."

Each of these sentences requires approximately

the same amount of vocabulary. But the second one will obviously be useful in many, many more situations.

And yet many second-year Spanish students can easily say the first sentence, but they have no idea how to assemble the second one in Spanish.

Why do most people make this mistake?

It's a simple temptation: The first example is visual and physical, while the second one is abstract. But that's exactly why the second one is SO much more valuable.

Let's think about Nate again for a second. If Nate had just happened to study the exact words that the 5-year-old kid was going to use in the short conversation about breakfast, he could have understood him. That vocabulary list would probably include about 20 obscure words like "blueberries", "stuffed", and "sloppily". And this specific knowledge would have prepared Nate for a grand total of one conversation.

However, there are BILLIONS of potential conversations you might have. You can't specifically prepare for each one. As soon as the other person goes off script, you'll be lost.

Instead, if you want to talk about anything and everything, you need to begin with the vocabulary that will allow you to talk about anything and everything.

This means learning the words that are used all the time every day in Spanish, the top 600 words by frequency.

It means perfecting those words until they're second nature, until you can say them without thinking about them, and until you can perfectly understand them in a conversation with a native speaker.

It means learning to stretch each word that you know to its maximum potential until you know every function that you can get out of it.

And although it's counterintuitive, it means temporarily avoiding

learning words outside that essential realm, until you've perfected this critical core of your Spanish knowledge. These incredibly foundational skills must come first, with exclusive priority.

Syntax: Essential Skills

One of the fundamental rules of accelerated language learning is very simple:

Until a certain point in your language journey, restrict your knowledge to a very small amount of vocabulary.

Instead of entertaining ourselves with shiny objects like foods and animal names, we need to focus on clear, perfect communication. And this actually requires us to ignore certain information for a while.

One day, after a certain point in your language learning journey, you'll be ready to expand your horizons. Then you can confidently absorb every single thing that you find important… And it will work! But ONLY because of the foundations you've laid first.

We've learned almost all the essential syntax of the Spanish language, and in this lesson we're going to be learning a lot more labels (especially descriptive labels).

It's easy to learn new labels. You've been doing it your whole life. Learning labels in Spanish is no different than learning labels in English; learning to call the bathroom the *baño* or the *aseo* is just like learning to call it the "loo" or the "water closet". It's a simple, entertaining way to learn new names for things.

And when you focus on entertaining yourself, you'll find that you can move very fast without getting anywhere.

Let's imagine you want to improve your baseball game. You're terrible at hitting, you can't pitch, and you're really bad at throwing and catching the ball.

But your favorite part of the game is running between bases.

So every afternoon, your 1-hour practice schedule looks like this:

- 4:00: Practice running from home to 1st base.

- 4:15: Practice running from 1st to 2nd.

- 4:30: Practice running from 2nd to 3rd.

- 4:45: Practice running from 3rd to home.

Does that look like productive practice? Of course not. When you practice running from one base to another, you aren't practicing baseball at all. You're just practicing running, which is a basic skill common to most sports, not baseball specifically.

Labels are just as unproductive to learning Spanish. If you're practicing animal names or memorizing lists of action verbs, you're not practicing Spanish. You're just learning lists of labels, which is a skill common to all languages.

What's a better baseball practice schedule?

- 4:00: Practice hitting the ball in a batting cage.

- 4:15: Practice throwing the ball at a vertical line, learning from errors to perfect your aim.

- 4:30: Play catch with a friend, standing at a distance just at the edge of your comfort zone.

- 4:45: Practice with a friend who is slightly better than you, focusing on hitting and pitching.

If you practice like this, you'll actually improve in your baseball skills. That's because you're actually focusing on the essential skills inherent to the game, which are the most difficult skills.

Strangely enough, you don't get better at baseball simply by playing the whole game. You get better by restricting yourself to a small set of essential skills and focusing on those.

It's true of other sports as well. Professional basketball players don't spend most of their time playing. They focus on very specific skills: Shots and ball handling. Sure, practicing basketball is more fun when you're playing a game. But if you're a professional player, you know to spend most of your time focused on the essential skills inherent to the game.

Every basketball player looks forward to passing the ball across the court in a real game.

Every baseball player is excited to make an epic, game-winning home run.

Every language learner is excited to use hundreds of nouns and verbs in a passionate conversation on a personal topic.

But in all of these cases, the fastest way outward is inward. The more focus you put inside the realm of essential skills, the faster you'll be able to explode outward from there.

In a language, the "essential skills inherent to the game" are syntax: Mastering the top few hundred words that hold the entire language together.

So When Do We Get Labels?

The good news is that if you focus on this most essential vocabulary, you can learn the language much more quickly. Instead of spending time and attention on learning

new vocabulary but not knowing exactly how to use it, you'll direct that effort toward using your core vocabulary as effectively as possible, like a native speaker.

One day, after a certain point in your language learning journey, you'll be ready to expand your horizons. After you've truly mastered everything in this book, you can confidently absorb every single thing that you find important… And it will work! But ONLY because of the foundations you've laid first.

Remember what I said about the word "exculpate" in Lesson 1? An English speaker has an easy time integrating new, obscure vocabulary, even in complex sentence structures, because of a strong existing foundation.

So when, exactly, will you be ready for more colorful vocabulary?

After you're basically fluent.

Until then, you should outright refuse to learn

any words other than the minimum amount to make you fluent.

This is extremely important. If you set yourself the goal of only mastering the top 600 words of Spanish, in all of their possible uses, you can make tangible progress. With each lesson in this book, you'll know that you're closer to your goal.

But if your goal is to learn "everything", you'll end up going in circles… which is sadly what most people do. They think that just learning more words, like "strawberries" and "yummy", will make them fluent. But they would serve themselves much better by focusing on the core essence of the language and not moving beyond there until it's mastered.

The more comfortable you make your essential vocabulary, the more easily you'll be able to learn thousands more words and express yourself fluently in Spanish.

Don't Get Distracted

I have to emphasize this warning: It's essential that we stick with this core vocabulary for a while, even when it hurts.

The temptation is strong. Sometimes it's a lot easier to learn a new word instead of finding a way to describe something with your current vocabulary. But in order to master the language, it's critical that we fully conquer all the most frequent vocabulary.

You should especially plan to practice sticking to these essentials while in your "Spanish zone".

Recall Lesson 7, where we started training ourselves to think exclusively in Spanish, for example by using words like *esta cosa* instead of more specific nouns.

You can also use *hacer* instead of most verbs, and *así* instead of most adjectives or adverbs.

Instead of saying "I don't really plan to play many sports", you can say *yo no voy a hacer esas cosas mucho.* It conveys the same meaning, though in a more abstract way.

Here's what all of this means: If you've made it through the first eight lessons of this course, you've come a long way. In fact, a whole year of classroom Spanish would normally teach very little of what has been taught so far, and you've learned more grammar than some fourth-year Spanish students. Ultimately, you should congratulate yourself for a strong knowledge of how the language works.

Now it's time to move forward with our vocabulary, learning more words in this lesson than we've ever learned before. But even so, don't get distracted with outside vocabulary! There will be time to explore later, but for now, we'll continue focusing on the most frequent words.

Lesson 9 Vocabulary:

Adverbs and Adjectives

(and some other words)

WE'RE ABOUT TO learn an immense number of new words.

Since we have so many to learn, we won't get to practice using every single one individually. There simply isn't enough time. We'll just quickly learn each word and where it belongs in the memory palace.

But the good news is that you already know how to use these words! If you have correctly learned all the words through Lesson 7, you'll also know how to learn the new vocabulary in Lesson 9: The same way as the other words around them in the same scenes.

We're about to explore almost every place in Yol. Buckle up for the quickest, craziest feast of vocabulary you've ever seen.

Walls (Our Last Conjunctions)

Even though Joel loves the amusement park's rides, sometimes he can't even make his mind up. Today is one of those days. Joel is so indecisive that he wastes tons of time and money at the binoculars feature in the park. In fact, he pays the binoculars so many times that he ends up with no money left in his pockets.

The pandas are getting impatient, and they tell him that they want to go and ride something. Joel now feels nervous because he doesn't want to admit that he's wasted all the money, so he says hesitantly, "Well, if we're out of money, then we can't ride anything." But he's thinking of the word "waste", and so he ends up saying, "Well, if we're out of money, *pues* we can't ride anything."

Joel points at a wastebasket, which is hanging on the side of the binoculars, to strengthen his point.

The word *pues* is used in logical statements like this, particularly after "if" (*si*). It means something roughly equivalent to "then" or "since".

Now look closely at the path. Something has changed since the last time we were here: Walls have been built around some of the paths, separating them more distinctly. These walls represent the word *cual*, which means "which". This word can be used in place of *que* in certain situations.

The line for the water slide is very long and moves slowly, since only one person can ride at a time. Many of the people in line have fallen asleep. Since Joel is out of money, he decides to steal the Yen that's sticking out of their pockets. He tells the pandas, "I'm stealing Yen from them while they're asleep waiting in line."

His word for "while" is *mientras*, with the stressed syllable "Yen". As you can see, *mientras* (with the snoozing people) is stored right next to *cuando*.

Suddenly an earthquake shakes the amusement park. A giant crack in the ground opens up next to Joel's magic wand and his newly stolen Yen. At first Joel is afraid for his possessions, but then he sees that they're fine. "I still have a magic wand and a bunch of money, <u>even though</u> there was an earthquake."

The word *aunque*, pronounced "aUN-kay", sounds a little bit like "earthquake", and it means <u>even though</u>.

Now let's take a look at the things hanging between rides. We have the shoes, that represent *y* ("and"), the tire, representing *o* ("or"), and the knee pads, representing *ni* ("neither" / "nor").

Sometimes Joel changes these words based on what comes after them. The word *y* changes to *e* if it's followed by an "eeh" sound, and the word *o* changes to *u* if it's followed by an "oh" sound. This is because Joel wants to be clear instead of repeating the same vowel sound twice.

For example, "Sofia and Isabella" is *Sofia e Isabella*, and "some day or another" is *algún día u otro*. As you can see, *y* turned into *e* and *o* turned into *u*. This is fairly easy to remember, since it's always a very closely-related vowel sound.

Now stop for a second and look at this entire scene. This is all the conjunctions we're going to learn. We have no more stories or mnemonics between the rides here, because we're done. If you have all of these words down, you're done learning conjunctions. (Breathe deeply and let that sink in for a second.)

Still, we have a few more words at the rides themselves. So let's move on to our last prepositions.

Durante (Our Last Prepositions)

Joel glances at the carousel and is shocked: The con man is on the carousel!

But instead of riding on a horse, the con man is walking around, bumping into all the horses.

"What are you doing there?" asks Joel.

"I'm walking against the horses!" says the con man. "Every time the ride starts (oof!), I walk in a contrary direction. That way (ouch!), I'm not

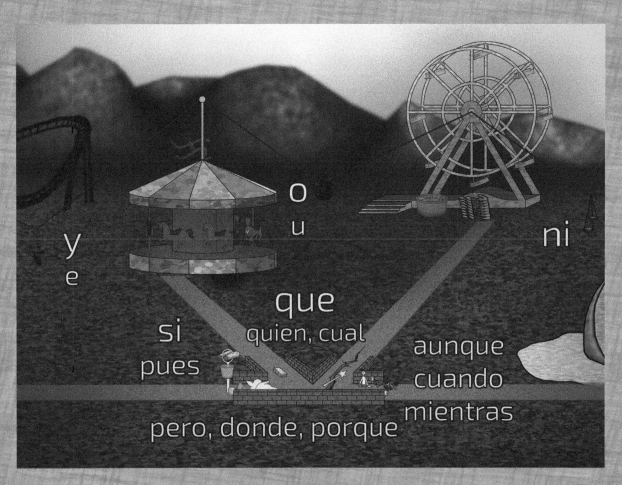

actually moving at all (oof!), and so I get to be on the ride without having to pay for it, since I'm (ouch!) technically not riding it."

Joel begins to see how clever this is: The con man is on an amusement ride without paying! And what he's doing is moving against the flow of the horses, defying the conventional way of riding a carousel. The word for "against" is *contra*.

"How can I join you without paying?" asks Joel.

"Join me!" says the con man. "It's not hard to get on (ouch!). Just enter <u>between</u> the horses after the ride starts."

Joel tries to "enter" the ride by going between the horses, but it's difficult because the horses are moving. Still, he sees that a snake is succeeding in getting on by slithering <u>between</u> and <u>among</u> the horses. The word for "between" or "among" is *entre*.

Meanwhile, a backhoe is slowly digging underneath the carousel. The word for "underneath" is *bajo*.

Before we learn our next word, let's review what Joel did in Lesson 7 when he crawled from the carousel to the ferris wheel. He crawled *desde* the carousel *hasta* the ferris wheel.

This time, Joel does the same crawl again, but this time he gets lost in the weeds because nobody mowed the park. By the time he finds the ferris wheel several days later, he arrives on the wrong side.

The ferris wheel operator looks at Joel and sees the trail of trampled weeds that he left behind. "Did you make that trail?" he asks.

"Yes," says Joel. "I've been crawling ever since I left the carousel on Saturday."

"How long ago was that?" asks the carousel manager.

"A whole week ago," says Joel. "*Hace* a whole week."

The word *hace* here could be translated as "it makes", as in "It makes a week." But Joel also uses the word hace to mean "ago", and it's used before nouns. So "a day ago" is *hace un día*, and "three years ago" is *hace tres años*. It's like saying "it makes three years", but *hace* is not being used as a verb here. Instead,

desde hasta hace

hace is a special kind of preposition, categorized much like *desde* and *hasta* at the ferris wheel.

We have two last prepositions to learn. Joel continues crawling through the weeds, this time in the direction of the water slide because he's extremely thirsty from all this work.

Joel can't look up because he's so tired, but he knows what direction to go because he hears music playing: It's a recording of Jimmy Durante singing "Make Someone Happy". The music stops when nobody's riding the water slide, but the music always plays during the ride. The word for "during" is *durante*, represented by the gramophone record player floating down the slide.

He almost reaches the water slide before he runs completely out of energy, dehydrated and unable to continue. At this point, he finally cries for help: "Where are the pandas when you need them? Won't they help me get to the water slide?"

The pandas hear Joel and call back: "Where are you?"

"I'm in the weeds, crawling toward the water slide."

"Did you get to the water slide?"

"No, I didn't get TO it, but I've been going TOWARDS it," he yells back with the last of his strength.

Previously we learned the word *a* to mean "to". This is the word Joel would use if he was able to reach the water slide. But the word *hacia*, with the stress on the first syllable, means "toward". Joel thinks of *hacia* as a more dehydrated, frustrated word.

Before we go on, see if you can remember all the prepositions that we have learned at each ride. Try to use each one with a noun (e.g. *de la casa, en la casa, sobre la casa, bajo la casa, hacia la casa*).

Next, let's wrap up our pronouns with a quick, final visit to the countryside.

hacia   durante

Swamp Walls

Joel rushes through the countryside but stops at the swamp because of something strange.

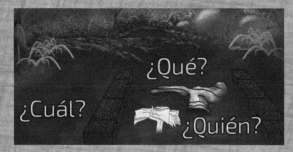

In the water, surrounding the dead hand (*"quién?"*) and the robe (*"qué?"*), are two walls. Joel wonders if he can walk across the swamp using a wall as a pathway, but he isn't sure <u>which</u> path to follow.

The word *cuál?* means "which?" As you can see, it's like the word that we learned in the amusement park, but in this case it's used as a question.

Holes and "O"s

Remember that one time when Joel came to the marketplace, he ran into the fountain and got his head stuck in the large hole. Here he said *hola!* as a greeting.

But he doesn't usually like saying "hello" to this hole; often, he just says "goodbye" to it. To remind himself that he doesn't want to get his head stuck here, Joel paints some circles on the stone, as a warning not to get stuck in these odd "O"s. (His head is shaped like the letter O, so he's susceptible to getting it stuck in an O-shaped hole.)

The term <u>odd "O"s</u> represents the word *adiós*, which means "goodbye". So the hole itself represents *hola* ("hello"), but the circles painted around it represent *adiós* ("goodbye").

We store other exclamations here at the fountain as well. Previously, Joel said *"oh"*. This so-called word is extremely simple, and it's used pretty much exactly the same way in Spanish as it is in English.

A few other simple exclamations, which we'll store in the water fountain, are *"hey"*, *"okay"*, and *"ay!"* That last one is Joel's favorite thing to say when he's gotten hurt.

Below the hole, we've seen that the word *bueno* is depicted as another exclamation. This particular exclamation is used as a filler word, generally used while Joel is thinking, kind of like how we say "All right…" in English.

Another filler word is *pues*. This is used at the beginnings of phrases, just like *bueno*, but it's a little less positive; it's more equivalent to the English word "well…"

To represent this, Joel paints a waste basket (remember the stressed syllable "waste") around the word *bueno*. Both *bueno* and *pues* are often used as meaningless filler words at the beginning of a sentence.

Dolly

We have several more exclamations to learn here at the fountain.

Remember that the patch of grass represents the word *gracias*, which means "thanks!" or "thank you!" This is where we keep some exclamatory words that Joel often uses all by themselves, in place of complete sentences.

Today, a living doll is standing on the left side of the grass. The doll looks like it wants to walk across the grass, but it's hesitant; maybe it feels guilty about the idea of trampling down the grass. Joel tells the doll, "Go ahead! It's fine." To say this, Joel says *dale*, which basically means "sure!" or "go ahead!"

But the doll responds to Joel: "There's a giant claw in the grass. I don't want to hurt my feet on it."

Joel looks and sees the sharp "claw" sticking out of the grass. Joel says, "Oh, of course! Got it."

The word *claro* is used as a positive exclamation to mean "of course" or "got it".

On the right side of the grass, opposite the dolly, is a stop sign made of pasta. The sign says, *"basta!"*

The word *basta* means "stop!" or "that's enough!" It's normally used out of anger, and in some ways it's the opposite of *dale*.

Meanwhile, standing on a ledge above the grass, there's another doll. This one looks like a man, and he's bowing slightly and holding his hat out, saying "Pardon me, madame!" The hat that he's holding is painted the colors of the sunrise (or the "dawn").

The exclamation *perdón*, with a stress on the syllable "dawn", means "sorry" or "pardon me".

Quickly review all of these words: *dale*, *gracias*, *claro*, *basta*, and *perdón*. Remember where they are and what they mean, and you'll be able to use them easily in a conversation since they are simply used by themselves. *"Claro!" "Perdón!"*

125

Boo! More Booleans

The statue, whom Joel calls "Tom" (and he imagines that it says "boo!"), has several new boolean words for us today.

realmente

exactamente

siquiera

casi

tampoco

ni siquiera

Remember that on the statue's face, we store words exchangeable with *sí* ("yes" / "indeed"), whereas on the ground behind the statue we have words exchangeable with *no* ("not").

Let's start with Tom's head. Since nobody takes care of the statue very frequently, stuff grows on it. In the statue's hair grows a proliferation of mint leaves. These mint leaves store two useful words: *realmente* and *exactamente*.

As you might have guessed, *realmente* means "really" and *exactamente* means "exactly". They're very similar to English words, but in each case, the stress is on the syllable that sounds kind of like "mint".

On the statue's face, we've learned the words *hasta*, *también*, and *sólo*, which can be used before a true sentence (just like *sí* and *exactamente*) but can also be used before a noun ("even the house", "also the house", "only the house"). We have one more word to learn on the statue's face, and it belongs in the statue's mouth.

Remember that Joel found money in Tom's ears. Now Joel peers into the stone mouth, but he's disappointed to find it completely empty. In fact, it's so empty that it doesn't even have any air in it!

Joel says, "I thought that I would see something in the statue's mouth, at least some air!" The word for "at least" is *siquiera*, pronounced "see-key-AIR-ah". "At least the house" is *siquiera la casa*.

Further down Tom's body, we have words that don't quite mean "yes" and don't quite mean "no". On the neck of the statue hangs a price tag. Yep, the statue is for sale! In fact, Joel almost bought it at one point, but the cost was just a bit too high for him. The word for "almost" is *casi* (stress sounds like "cost").

Let's keep moving down. We've seen previously that the word *quizá* (or *quizás*), in the statue's leg, represents

126

"maybe". Further down, on the ground, we have the word *no* to mean "no" or "not".

We actually have a couple of other words that are negative. One is the word *tampoco*, which is essentially a synonym for *no*. This word has the stress on "poke", because there are nail heads poking out of the bottom of the statue. Joel Imagines that Tom tries to poke people with these nail heads.

Tampoco is often used to mean "not" at the beginning of a sentence. Other times, it's used to mean "neither", as in "me neither" (*yo tampoco*). In both cases, it's used like the word *no*.

Another term for "not" is *ni siquiera*. Of course, we already learned *siquiera* in Tom's mouth to represent "at least", but in reality, this word is more often used in a negative way. Some people would even almost consider *ni siquiera* to be its own word (even though it's two words) because that's how *siquiera* is most idiomatically used.

igual

The term *ni siquiera* means "not even". At the bottom of the statue, between the nails, is a small hole. Joel hopes to find something in this hole, but he finds nothing, not even air ("*ni siquiera* air").

The Wall in the Bucket

There's one more strange word to learn here at the statue.

As you may have noticed before, the statue is holding a bucket that pours water into the fountain. This bucket is divided, pouring water in two streams. Joel calls the division in the bucket a "wall" that separates the water. This is a very simple device to store the word *igual* (pronounced "ig-WALL").

Igual is a strange word. It can be used like the boolean words that we learned on the statue. But it's generally used at the very beginning of a sentence, kind of like the exclamations that we learned in the fountain below the statue.

The word means "but at the same time" as a filler. In English, for example, you might hear someone say, "But at the same time, I think I'll stay home," or "But still, I think I'll stay home." That's how the word *igual* is used: "*Igual*, I think I'll stay home."

For now, just add *igual* to your arsenal of words that can be used at the beginning of a sentence. It's time to go get some meat.

Steak and Spice

When Joel arrives at the steak stand today, he finds a few new options on the surface of the stand.

Remember that the words *muy*, *más*, *menos*, and *tan* can be used to affect a description. For example, if you want to call yourself "very lonely", you can say *estoy muy solo* (or *estoy muy sola* if you're female). To say "I'm less lonely", you can say *estoy menos solo*. All of these words work the same way.

On the negative end of the stand, to the left of the *menos* steak, is a bone. This bone has absolutely no meat on it, and it swings back and forth in the wind, making a back and forth motion, or "nodding", as Joel likes to say. This represents the word *nada*. We previously learned this word to mean "nothing" (in the swamp), but here in the plaza it can be used as an adverb to mean "not at all". For example, *nada solo* means "not at all lonely".

Above this, hanging off the very edge of the stand, is a strange foot. We'll learn more about this foot later, but for now, notice that it doesn't seem to belong to anyone, and it has very large, strange toes. Joel wonders, "Whose toes are those?"

The word *justo*, which sounds like "whose toe", can be used to mean "just", "barely", or "just barely". For example, "Just before the house" would be *justo antes de la casa*.

On the positive end, to the right of the *más* steak, is another steak that has an extremely large bush of "moss" on it. There's so much green growth that Joel thinks the steak looks like his own "messy yard". This represents the word *demasiado* ("de-mossy-YAD-o"), which resembles the sound of the phrase "messy yard". This word means "extremely" or "too" (*demasiado solo* can mean either "extremely lonely" or "too lonely").

In an awkward place near the middle of the stand, a wishbone from a chicken is perched, slightly leaning against a piece of steak. Joel remarks, "That's quite strange. How does it stand there like that?" The word *bastante* (stress sounds like "stand") means "quite" (*bastante solo* means "quite lonely"). Just remember that it's somewhat positive, toward the positive end of the stand.

In the middle is a simple steak that looks partly cooked. Joel asks, "How well is this steak cooked?" and the butcher responds, "Medium." The butcher has also tried to chop the steak in half, though he only got halfway through. The word *medio*, stored in the middle of the stand, means "kind of" (*medio solo* means "kind of lonely").

Run through those words again. These all indicate degree in some way, and they can all be used before adjectives such as *solo*.

But there's another type of degree adverb that's used in a different way, generally to affect entire phrases. These are hanging from the top of the stand.

Most importantly, there's a hook hanging in the middle of the stand, and it says "WANT" in big letters. This puzzles Joel until the butcher explains this new feature: When you buy a steak, you're allowed to put spices on it for free. You can use as much spicing as you want. But it still has to be measured on the scale, just so the butcher knows how much you took.

The word *cuánto* is used in questions to mean "how much?" (The stress of *cuánto* sounds like "want".)

Meanwhile, some answers to this question are hanging to the left and to the right. On the left is a tiny salt shaker that's extremely small, with such a tiny top that it looks like it would feel weird to poke someone with it. This represents the word *poco* as an adverb.

On the right end is a spice shaker that looks like a horned toad with a wide-open mouth. This represents *mucho*, which means "much".

Between the two is a shaker with some very red, zesty spices in it. This represents the word *tanto*, which means "so much". (The stress is on "tan", the color of both the red spices and the butcher's skin.)

All of these words can be used to show the degree to which something is done. That sounds very abstract, but try it out in the following sentence: "I do it a lot." In Spanish, that would be *"Lo hago mucho."* To say "I do it so much…" you would say *"Lo hago tanto…"* and to say "I do it only a little, you say *"Lo hago poco."*

We'll explore the usage of these words later. For now, make sure you've learned where all of them are located.

Ticking Bread Wand

Joel comes to the bread stand and sees something new: A magic wand is swinging back and forth above the stand, making a ticking noise.

This represents the word *cuándo?*, which means "when?" Remember that at other stands, we have stored the interrogative (question) adverbs as hanging from the stand; for example, at the steak stand it's *cuánto?* (how much?), at the fruit stand it's *dónde?* (where?), and at the vegetable stand it's *cómo?* (how?). At the baker's stand, the word is *cuándo?* (when?).

Of course, the answer for the baker is usually "never". To represent this word, the baker has a piece of bread that he hides behind the stand, and it looks like a clock that has struck noon for *nunca*.

Today, the baker has wrapped this *nunca* clock with his fuzzy blue pajamas. This represents another word for "never", which is *jamás* (stress on "moss", though it looks like part of the word "pajamas").

The words *nunca* and *jamás* are stored behind the stand, because they represent a time that never happens. However, we have several words for times that do happen, including *ahora* ("now"), *siempre* ("forever"), and *ya* ("anymore").

One of these words is *aún*, which means "still". It's represented by the V-shaped piece of bread that the baker owns. There's another word for this piece of bread: *todavía*. That's because the bread looks kind of like a toad, but in a V shape (toad-ah-VEE-ah).

Both *aún* and *todavía* mean "still", though *todavía* is often used to replace the English word "yet". (If you think about it, "yet" and "still" are pretty much synonyms in English, even though we idiomatically use them in different situations.) Just remember that both words are stored on this V-shaped loaf of bread that stretches into the past, the present, and the future.

Let's learn a new word that happens in the future. We've already learned *tarde*, which means "late" and is located on the right side of the stand. Closer to the center, there's a small prawn (a type of sea creature) that is starting to eat from the right side of the *hoy* loaf of bread. Another prawn is nibbling at the *mañana* loaf.

The word *pronto* means "soon". It represents something that's going to happen in the near future, maybe some time between today and tomorrow, as you can see by where we've placed the prawns.

As Joel looks at the prawns, a strange movement catches his eye. Joel never noticed this before, but under the glass covering of the bread stand, some Yen bills are sliding by, underneath all the bread on the surface. These old paper

bills are a bit greasy and covered with crumbs, but Joel can't help wishing that he could break the glass and access the money.

The word **mientras**, with the stress on "yen", represents the word "meanwhile". (We already learned this in the amusement park to mean "while", but it has this other meaning as an adverb as well.) As you can see, everything that's happening on top of the stand (*entonces, hoy, pronto*, etc.) is unaffected by the yen that are moving below the surface in the mean time.

Make sure you can remember where **cuándo, jamás, todavía, pronto**, and **mientras** are located. We have one more word to learn here.

On the front of the stand, you've seen that the baker has painted "aunties" and "uncles" to represent the words **antes** ("beforehand") and **después** ("afterwards"), as well as **luego** ("later").

These words all have to do with the order that something happens in. The word **antes** means "first" or "beforehand". All of these aunties are in line before the uncles.

But the aunt in the very front is a horse. She's a mare, in fact (a female horse). The word for "very first" or "first of all" is **primero** (with the stress on "mare").

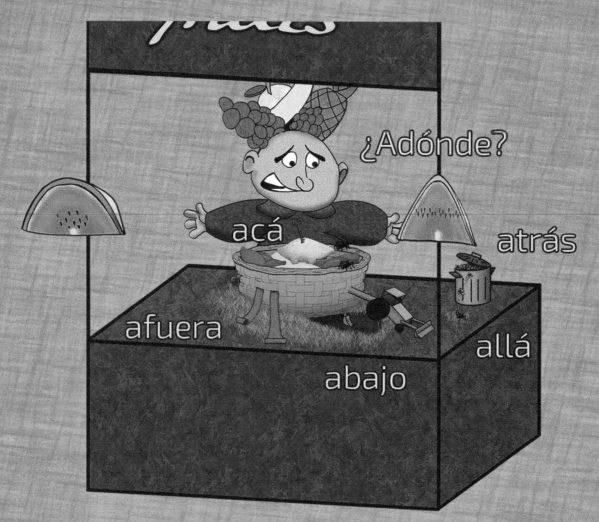

Basket Case

The crazy fruit vendor has not been getting much business lately, mostly because the spiders drive customers away. So he's been trying to implement some interesting new marketing strategies.

At the fruit stand, Joel notices that the two melons hanging on the stand look different from each other.

We've learned the word *dónde?* to mean "where?", and it's represented by these "dawn-day" melons. But one of them looks like it's been squeezed into the shape of the letter A. This represents a new word, *adónde*, which means "to where?" (It's equivalent to the antiquated English word "whither?")

In the fruit vendor's basket, we've already learned the word *aquí*, illustrated by a key. It turns out that *aquí* has a synonym, *acá*. This word sounds almost like "a car", and as you can see, the key is stuck into a lemon that's shaped like a car. Both *aquí* and *acá* mean "here".

Today there's a third spider in addition to *ahí* ("there", near you) and *allí* ("there", somewhere else). The word *allá*, with a stress on "ya", is represented by a spider that's even further away than the *allí* spider. The *allá* spider is sitting on a patch of grass on the stand, far removed from the basket. *Allá* is used to mean "way over there" or "yonder", and it's used in some idioms that we'll learn soon.

Joel is fascinated by the grass growing on the stand. "It's like you're growing a lawn here," he tells the fruit vendor.

"Oh yes!" says the vendor. "I'm cultivating my fruit stand, and I hope to grow fruit right here on the stand so I don't have to import it all."

Joel notices that a backhoe (a large machine) is digging in the stand, underneath the basket. It causes the basket to keep moving further and further down into the stand. This represents the word *abajo*, which means "downward".

There's another movement taking place as the basket is lowered: Some cloth is pouring out from the cracks in the basket, spreading out in all directions. The fruit merchant tells Joel, "Hey, get a T-shirt! I want people to get excited about my fruit. Put that on!"

Joel looks at the cloth seeping out of the basket. "How am I supposed to wear this?" he asks. The fabric keeps flowing out, without ever ending; it's not divided into smaller pieces. He

starts to wrap it around himself like a toga, but he stops because he finds it too strange.

The word *afuera* (stress on "wear") means "out" or "outward". This is the motion that the cloth is making, coming out from the basket.

One more word on top of the fruit stand. In the corner of the stand, near the back, the *allá* spider is eating a small piece of fruit, and it keeps throwing tiny pieces of the peel over its own shoulder, into the tiny trash can. The word *atrás* means "back" or "backward", as illustrated by the spider throwing the trash backward.

"Day" Peel

Have you ever wondered what kind of special fruit is locked inside the fruit vendor's drawers?

We're about to explore some more adverbs related to location, but these are used differently from the ones on top of the stand. Words like *aquí*, *ahí*, and *afuera* are used all by themselves. But the words that we're about to learn are often followed by the preposition *de*.

In the drawer, there actually isn't much fruit, just a piece of a peel of an expensive fruit that has been eaten. Apparently the fruit vendor got hungry and ate his best fruit, so there's just part of the peel left. It's colored yellow, like the the sunshine or the "day" as Joel calls it.

At the center of this peel is a sharp dent. This represents the word *dentro*, with means "inside". For example, to say "inside the house", you would say *dentro de la casa*.

Surrounding the peel are some cloth strips, representing the stressed syllable "wear" as we learned it on top of the stand. The word *fuera* means "outside", though it doesn't indicate outward motion as the word *afuera* did (it's missing the "ah" syllable that indicates movement). So to say "outside the house", you would say *fuera de la casa*.

Just around this cloth, a yellowish circle is drawn to outline this merchandise. The circle represents the word *cerca*, which means "near". For example, "near the house" is *cerca de la casa*.

Further away from the peel, against an edge of the drawer, lies a green hose.

This hose is as far away from the peel as possible, and represents the word *lejos*. (This word is pronounced "LAY-hose", except that the S makes a "ss" sound, not a "zz" sound.) *Lejos* means "far away".

The strangest thing about this yellow peel is that it has a yellow hand and a very long arm. This arm is stretched all the way from the peel's main body to the front of the drawer. It's surprising how long this arm is, and the word *adelante* (stress sounds kind of like "long") means "forward" or "in front".

The fruit merchant is very serious about the security in this drawer. In addition to locking it with the *aquí* key, he has installed some bone "ribs" across the top of the drawer to prevent people with big hands from grabbing what is left of his expensive fruit. The ribs are located above the peel, so the word *arriba* means "above", "on top", or "up".

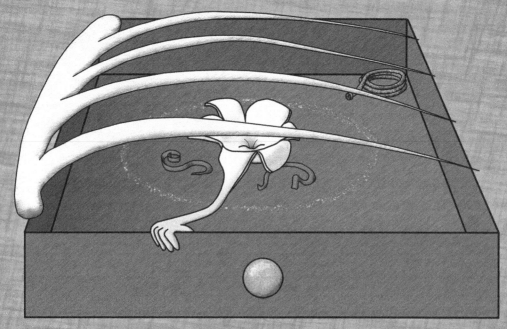

There are several idiomatic ways to use some of these words, but for now, practice with the following phrases:

dentro de la casa

fuera de la casa

cerca de la casa

lejos de la casa

adelante de la casa

arriba de la casa

If you've stored all these words, we're ready to go over to the vegetable stand.

Loudly and Softly

On the top of the stand, we've already learned *mal* on the left, *bien* on the right, and *como* and *así* in between them.

But today, the farming monkey has stacked two cans of vegetables on top of each other. He asks Joel, "would you like me to talk loudly or softly?"

When he says this, he is speaking through the top can. This one looks like a stop sign with a picture of music notes, and as the monkey speaks, the can changes his voice, auto-tuning it and amplifying it so it sounds like he's singing in a very high, loud voice.

"HALT!" shouts Joel, very annoyed at the shrill notes. "I hate the sound of that."

The word *alto*, which sounds kind of like "halt" (or like something you'd call a female singer), means "high" or "loudly" when applied to sound.

So the monkey moves his face down to the lower can. "How do you like this?" he asks. Suddenly, the monkey's voice sounds very quiet, like the low grumbling of a machine. In fact, this vegetable can has a picture of a backhoe on it.

"That's much better," says Joel.

The word *bajo* means "low" or "quietly" when it refers to sound. As you can see, it's possible to use all these words to refer to the way that someone talks: You can talk *bien*, you can talk *mal*, you can talk *bajo*, or you can talk *alto*.

Suddenly, the monkey starts to talk about these cans, the vegetables inside them, and where they come from. But he keeps repeating himself. This is very boring to Joel.

"What are you talking about?" asks Joel. "You just seem to be talking around in circles."

"I am!" says the farmer, apparently proud of himself. "I'm talking circles around the cans."

Looking closely, Joel realizes that the monkey is reading a script. There are words written on the stand in tiny yellow letters, displayed around the cans in a circular fashion. "Oh," he says, "You really ARE talking in circles about the cans."

The word *acerca* means "about", in the sense that you can talk "about" something. But it's used in a very particular way, always with the preposition *de* after it. So to talk "about the house", you would talk *acerca de la casa*.

On the right side of the stand, beside the money can, is a unique type of water fountain. This device sprays a stream of water on the lettuce to keep it fresh, but it sprays it so hard and so fast that sometimes the leaves of lettuce go flying off into the distance. This water represents the word *rápido*, which means "quickly".

Between the fountain and the cans is a blue wall. Joel asks, "What does that wall do?" and the monkey says, "Whatever I want it to do." To demonstrate, he shouts, "I'm an igloo!" at the wall. Three seconds later,

136

the wall itself repeats, "I'm an igloo!", exactly the same as the monkey said it.

The word *igual* can mean "the same way". Whereas the vegetable cans modify the monkey's voice, this wall says things the exact same way that the monkey does.

Practice switching out these adverbs, imagining that you're describing the ways that people talk. They can talk *alto*, *bajo*, *acerca de la casa*, *rápido*, or *igual*.

Of course, you can use any of our other words from this location as well: People can talk *bien*, *así*, *contigo*, and so on.

The Whole Plaza

We've been looking at tiny, individual spots in the plaza throughout this lesson, one adverb category at a time.

But now it's time for you to review the entire plaza, as a whole, in your imagination.

Walk between the statue and each of the stands. Are you able to picture all of the words in each location, including the vocabulary that we learned in previous lessons?

If you can, you're ready to go back to Joel's yard for some new adjectives.

My Oar

At Joel's car, we've learned the comparative words *más* ("more"), *menos* ("less"), and *mejor* ("better").

Recently Joel decided to prepare for travel, in case he ever goes to the wonderful *lugares* that he wants to visit some day. He has put a tiny kayak on top of the car in case he encounters water. But instead of a paddle for the kayak, Joel has an enormous oar that's even bigger than the boat itself. "My oar is bigger than my boat!" he declares. The word for "bigger" is *mayor* ("my OAR").

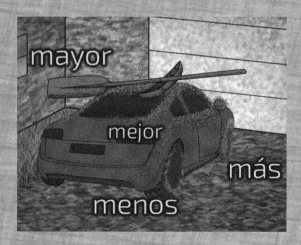

Ents and Wall Air

On the wall of Joel's garage, Joel now has some kneepads suspended next to the mud splotch. But strangely enough, when anyone asks Joel about these kneepads, he insists that they don't belong to anyone, and that they weren't put here by anyone: "No person put them here, and they don't belong to any goon in the world."

Recall that the mud splotch represents *algunos*, which means "some" or "several", as in *algunos hombres* ("some men" or "several men"). Now we have a new word: *ningún*. This means "no" as an adjective, and it's used the exact same way as *algún* but means the opposite. For example, *ningún hombre* means "no man".

Next to the toad in the grass that represents *mucho* ("much") and *todo* ("every"), Joel has planted a tree. But this tree now looks like it has a face, which makes Joel think it could be not a tree, but an <u>ent</u> (the talking tree-like creatures from The Lord of the Rings), and maybe it's here to take care of the things in Joel's yard! This "ent" represents the word *suficiente*, which means "enough" or "sufficient".

Leaning against the tree is a very similar word: The wishbone from the butcher's stand. This represents the word *bastante* (stress on "stand"), but here instead of "quite", it means "quite a bit of" or "enough". So while *mucho dinero* means "much money", *bastante dinero* means "quite a bit of money" or "enough money".

However, if we move too far to the right, we get "too much". As you can see, this tiny part of Joel's yard has become very crowded and messy, and to add to the mess is a framed picture of this mess! The word *demasiado*, which resembles the sound "messy yard", means "too much" or "an enormous amount". *Demasiado dinero* means "a ton of money" or "too much money".

Inside the garage, the set of drawers beside Joel's *otro* car is completely empty. Joes keeps air in the more special drawers, but the rest of the drawers are devoid even of air. He likes to say that some of the drawers, or "certain drawers", have air in them. The word *ciertos* (which sounds like "certain" but stresses air) means "certain" or "some of". For example, "certain men" would be *ciertos hombres*.

A muffled chirping voice is the loudest noise in this scene, coming from above the washing machine. A bird seems to have its head stuck in the wall.

"Help!" shouts the bird. "I don't have any air in here!"

Joel isn't convinced. "How are you talking if you don't have any air?"

"Well, I want good air," responds the bird. "This wall air isn't good enough for me. I can't sing properly with just ANY old air."

The word *cualquier* may sound complicated, but it stresses the sounds "wall" and "air". What it means is "any", or "any old"; for example *cualquier hombre* means "just any man".

On the corner between the garage and the "messy yard" by the driveway, another item from the butcher's stand has made an appearance: The hook that represents the word *cuanto* (as in "as much as you want"). Here, the word does not have an accent mark, and it means something like "as much as"; this word is complicated, and we'll learn how to use it idiomatically later.

For now, review all the words in this scene and make sure you can list each one individually by walking mentally around the garage area.

Which Horse?

Joel's neighbors in the apartments to the west have a custom of putting weathervanes on top of their chimneys. There are many apartment buildings, but Joel finds the first four most interesting.

The weathervane on top of the first building looks like a pink, female horse, and Joel calls it a "mare". The word for "first" is *primero* (stress on "mare").

The weathervane on the second apartment building is of a horse that looks like it's choking on the smoke produced by this apartment's ongoing fire. Joel calls this horse a "goon", and his word for "second" is *segundo*. (stress on "goon").

The third weathervane depicts a horse with an apple-shaped head and a stern expression. This horse reminds Joel of Ser, who owns this particular apartment building. His word for "third" is *tercero* (stress on "Ser").

The horse on the fourth weathervane has giant green bumps that Joel thinks of as warts. His word for "fourth" is *cuarto*.

Nobody lives in Ser's apartment building, because she's so mean, and very few people live in the smoky apartment building (for understandable reasons). But plenty of people live in the first "mare" apartment building, and quite a few live in the fourth "wart" building.

We've already been introduced to the new waving neighbor (*nuevo*) and the girl who stares in the mirror (*mismo*).

These both live in the mare apartment building, on the first two floors.

On the top floor lives the strangest human being Joel has ever seen. This boy has a horn growing from his forehead, like a unicorn, and he's the only person in Yol who has this condition. Since he's so unique, Joel calls him *único* (stress on "oon" and pronounced almost like "unicorn"). This word means "only" or "unique".

With him is a group of kids playing a game they call "ultimate frisbee". But this isn't normal ultimate frisbee. Their version of "ultimate" is more like hot potato: The last person holding the frisbee loses. So they pass it to each other very quickly, hoping not to be the last. The word for "last" is *último*.

All of these words in the first apartment, *nuevo, mismo, único,* and *último*, are generally used before a noun (*nuevo hombre, último hombre,* etc.). But the words we're about to learn in the fourth apartment tend to be used after a noun.

Here, Joel likes to critique the neighbors' choice of furniture.

One neighbor has very old, sad-looking furniture.

Another has furniture that's too plain, boring, and common (too many people have furniture like that), and it's all on black wheels and rolls around the apartment.

But one neighbor has very comfortable-looking new furniture. Joel thinks that this neighbor made the correct decision.

Joel's adjective for the old, sad furniture is *pasado* (stress on "sad"), which means "previous" or "from the past".

The simple, plain, common furniture that rolls around is called *general* (hen-eh-RAL), which means "general". Remember to stress the syllable "ral", which may remind you that this furniture "rolls" around.

But the "right" or "correct" furniture is called *correcto*.

Practice using these three words after nouns. "The last year" is *el año pasado*, "the general people" is *la gente general*, and "the correct house" is *la casa correcta*.

ALL the Numbers

You should remember *uno*, *dos*, *tres*, and *cuatro* from previous lessons.

We're about to learn all about that legendary night when Joel got scared by animals in his back yard. But first, I'm going to give you a summary of the entire story:

(1) It was dark, and Joel got scared and damaged his own things while trying to run away from the animals.

(2) The sun came up, and he realized there really wasn't much to be afraid of. He went inside and slept.

(3) In his troubled sleep that morning, Joel had a bad dream that he was on trial for breaking his own things.

This storyline is important, because it separates our small numbers from our big numbers. We're going to use a few landmarks to show how this works.

The most important landmark is the sunrise. When the sun came up that morning, Joel shouted, "Yes! It's finally daytime!" If you look at the sun coming up over the horizon, it looks like a sideways 10, which is of course a pivotal number. This word is *diez* (with the stress on "yes").

ciento

mil

"yawn"

After this, Joel went inside and counted his money, just to put himself in a better mood (money always makes him feel better). The word "Yen" is the stressed syllable for our word for 100, *ciento*.

Then he ate an extremely late "dinner", or "breakfast"; it's hard to define this meal, since he had been up all night. One way or another, it was a meal, and the word *mil* means "a thousand".

Finally, Joel went to sleep. By the time he got to bed, he was yawning constantly. Since this is the last part of the story, this represents the biggest number we'll learn, *millón* (pronounced "me-YAWN"), which means "a million".

Make sure to get these in proper order: *uno* (1), *diez* (10), *ciento* (100), *mil* (1000), and *millón* (1,000,000). Remember the storyline as you go over these numbers.

Now for the details of the story.

Joel (*uno*) went into his back yard one night, and he encountered two does (*dos*) lying in the grass. This frightened him, so he traced his wings on the ground to try to create a decoy (*tres*). But while doing this, he wore himself out so that he became too tired to fly, which added to the problem. And the flagpole that he climbed up has four low-wattage light bulbs in the shape of the number four (*cuatro*).

Next, Joel found that he was trapped by the stream of water that flows through his back yard. He was able to see that there was a boat floating down this stream, but this boat was very strangely shaped like the number 5, which has a very unstable look to it. Joel climbed across the stream on the boat, but as he did, it almost sank into the stream. The Spanish word for "five" is *cinco*.

Uno, dos, tres, cuatro, cinco.

Once Joel was on the other side of the stream, he came up with another plan. He decided to create a new decoy, but instead of being a picture of himself, it would be a recording of himself speaking. He pulled out a microphone that he had handy, and he spoke into the microphone the first thing he could think of: "What should I say!" Then he set the microphone down, upside down, on the ground, and it kept echoing the last part of his sentence: "I say! I say! I say!" The number 6, which looks like a twisted, upside-down microphone, is pronounced *seis*.

Next, Joel ran into something that looked in the dark like a giant mouth with sharp teeth. He literally ran into it, as if the mouth had eaten him. In reality, this "mouth" was just a sideways tent that Joel had left in his yard and forgotten about, but it terrified Joel: "Help! This giant mouth just ate me!" The word for 7, a number that looks kind of like an open mouth, is *siete* (stress on "ate").

Joel scrambled away from the tent but got caught in a chain that was holding it to the ground. His head went through one link in the chain, and his posterior went through the next link. "Ouch!" shouted Joel. (You would too, if you were bent into this position.) The word for 8, which looks like two links in a chain, is *ocho*.

Finally, Joel used his free arms to grab the first thing he could find, a tent peg, and wave it around wildly. The tent peg ripped the tent as he waved it around. The number 9, which might look sort of like a tent peg, is *nueve* (stress on "wave").

This is the part where the sun came up and Joel realized that he wasn't actually in any danger. "Yes!" said Joel. "It's daytime." (*Diez.*)

Joel extricated himself from the tent chain and was about to go inside when he heard a voice: "You silly bee, you've caused a lot of damage here!"

The man who yelled this was a strange human dressed as a king and sitting in the 5-shaped boat. "What did the king say?" Joel said to himself. The word for 15 is *quince* (sounds like "KING say").

"I said, you've caused a lot of damage! Just look at your yard," said the king.

Joel looked at the flagpole. The flag was now torn to shreds, probably from when he was climbing on it to turn on the lights. The word for 14 is *catorce* (stress on "tore").

Notice that the words *quince* and *catorce* both have "say" at the end. These are similar to the words for 11, 12, and 13, which are all based on the numbers for 1, 2, and 3. Compare each of these numbers with its counterpart:

uno (1): *once* (11, pronounced "ON-say")

dos (2): *doce* (12, "DOES-say")

tres (3): *trece* (13, "TRES-say")

Fortunately, these are all the new numbers we have to learn in the yard. If you can remember these numbers in order, you'll be ready to move on.

- From Joel's arrival to the stream: *uno*, *dos*, *tres*, *cuatro*, *cinco*.

- From the microphone to the tent to the sunrise: *seis*, *siete*, *ocho*, *nueve*, *diez*.

- Revisiting 1-5 with "say" at the ends: *once*, *doce*, *trece*, *catorce* ("tore"), *quince* ("king").

All right, now remember everything he did when he left the yard: First, he counted his money (*ciento*), then ate a meal (*mil*), then yawned and went to bed (*millón*).

Next we're going to learn the words 20, 30, 40, and so on.

In Joel's troubled sleep that morning, he dreamed that he was on trial for everything in his yard that he broke. In his imagination, each of the items has been brought forward as evidence on a big, round plate. (The circular plate represents the zero at the ends of the numbers 20, 30, etc.)

First, the two does are presented as evidence. When the two does are on a platter, they appear with all of their blood vessels showing through their skin, which is a horrible sight. But Joel says, "They're not wounded or bleeding; that's just their <u>veins</u> showing through their skin." The word for 20 is *veinte*. (Make sure to connect this in your imagination to the does sitting on a platter.)

Next, when the tracing of Joel's wings is shown, Joel insists, "I didn't do that. That was caused by a train running through my yard." The word for 30 is *treinta*.

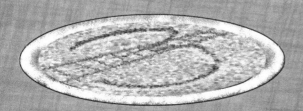

When the flag is presented, Joel declares that the damage was caused by a storm of rain. The word for 40 is *cuarenta* (stress on "rain").

When the *cinco* boat is brought forward on a platter, it doesn't have a king; it now has a miniature queen. The queen is sitting in the lower part of the boat, so Joel makes up a story: "The boat sinking isn't my fault; the king was trying to sink the queen! He's the evil one." The word for 50 is *cincuenta* (the stress is on "kwhen", which sounds kind of like "queen"; think "sink queen").

Next, the microphone is brought forward. Remember that in real life, Joel made it say "I say!" over and over. But here in Joel's dream, it's instead repeating "I saint!" Joel tells the jury, "See, even the microphone is testifying in my favor. I'm a saint." The word for 60 is *sesenta* (stress on "saint").

The tent that "ate" Joel is next. Now that it's right-side-up, it doesn't look like a mouth, it just looks like a tent. The word for 70 is *setenta*.

When the tent's chain is brought on a separate plate, Joel says, "Oh, it's a chain." The word for 80 is *ochenta*.

The last piece of evidence is the tent peg that Joel waved around. But something very strange has happened to this tent peg. It's standing up straight on the platter, and like the does, it seems to be covered in blood vessels or "veins". The word for 90 is *noventa*.

Before going on, make sure you can remember the words distinctly. In particular, review the differences between the numbers 2-9 and the numbers 20-90:

> *dos* ("does") vs. *veinte* ("vein")
>
> *tres* ("trace") vs. *treinta* ("train")
>
> *cuatro* ("watt") vs. *cuarenta* ("rain")
>
> *cinco* ("sink") vs. *cincuenta* ("quen")
>
> *seis* ("says") vs. *sesenta* ("saint")
>
> *siete* ("ate") vs. *setenta* ("tent")
>
> *ocho* ("ouch") vs. *ochenta* ("chain")
>
> *nueve* ("wave") vs. *noventa* ("vein")

Later we'll learn how to express all the numbers that we haven't specifically covered (complicated numbers like 17, 35, and 1832). For now, make sure you have all these important numbers stored where they belong.

"Estar" Adjectives

On the east side of Joel's house, we've already learned *está claro* ("it's clear") from the dining room window and *estoy seguro* ("I'm sure") and *estoy solo* ("I'm alone") from the "goo" below it.

This "goo" indicates how Joel feels a lot of the time, so let's put two more emotions here.

First of all, there's a sign that says the word "Lease" on it. But the "lease" has been crossed out, and a big smiley face has been drawn on the gooey sign. Joel is very happy that he now owns his house (it's no longer leased to him), and his word for "happy" is *feliz*.

Next, there's a piece of paper in the goo that lists all the things in Joel's cluttered yard. When he hides in the goo, he uses this list to review all of his belongings. Usually, he's not ready to get out of the goo until he's checked every item off the list. The word for "ready" is *listo*.

Speaking of the clutter in the yard, check out the items to the right of the dining room window, particularly the rope that goes up to one of Joel's ballroom windows. This rope is useful for storing adjectives related to location.

At the top of the rope is a large stop sign with the word "HALT" scribbled on it. Joel tries to warn people not to climb too high on the rope, and the word for "high" is *alto*.

At the bottom is a tiny robotic toy backhoe digging the rope into the ground. The word for "low" is *bajo*.

Tied into the middle of the rope are two hunters that look like conjoined twins. Sometimes they go up the rope, and sometimes they go down the rope (apparently by moving the knot around), but wherever they are, they're always together. The adjective for "together" is *juntos*.

viejo (with a stress on "yay" but ending in the sound "ho").

Next to the grave is a lantern, a lot like the "lantern of life" in Joel's bedroom. It's shaped like a V, and Joel's word for "alive" is *vivo*.

On top of the lantern is a very young man whose feet and arms look like garden hoes. Joel considers this kid to be very young, and he calls him *joven* (stressed syllable "hoe"). *Joven* is the opposite of *viejo*, just like *vivo* is the opposite of *muerto*.

Near the rope is a tombstone. Joel is superstitious and thinks that some creatures may be immortal, but whenever he sees a dead creature (such as a dead panda or a dead human), he writes that word down on the gravestone, as if to announce "that proves that pandas are mortal!" or "humans are mortal!" Joel's word for "dead" is *muerto* (which sounds kind of like "mortal").

Sitting on top of the grave is an old man who looks like Santa Claus. When Joel first saw this man, he exclaimed, "Yay! It's Santa! Have you brought me money?" But the old man responded, "Oh ho ho, I'm not Santa, I'm just an old man." Joel's word for "old" is

The last word in this scene is represented by a crazy cow that keeps coming into Joel's yard. It rolls around on its back near the goo, and it's obviously insane. Joel calls this the "low cow", and he's not too scared of it because it's so crazy that it doesn't even seem to be able to stand up. His word for "crazy" is *loco*.

Joel often uses any of these words near the rope to comment on other people: "You're crazy" is *estás loco*, and "she's dead" is *está muerta*.

Practice using all of the words in this scene after conjugations of Estar before moving on.

"Ser" Adjectives: Size

In Joel's enormous front yard, we store adjectives that tend to be used with Ser. For example, *es bueno* or *son grandes*.

Today let's start with the trees. We've learned *grande* for "large" or "big". Next to the large "grand" tree is a tiny tree that's shaped like a cane, which represents that the word for "small" is *pequeño* (stress on "cane").

Another tree is not very large, but it's extremely tall. This tree has a "HALT" sign at the top, just to remind people not to climb too high in the tree, and Joel's word for "tall" is *alto*. (This word was in both scenes, but as you can see, it refers to size when used with Ser, but it refers to location when used with Estar.)

"Ser" Adjectives: Facts

Let's go to the wall where we learned bueno. This word is used in many ways, but for now, let's talk about how it can be used in two-part sentences like this one:

Es bueno que estés aquí.

As you can see, there are two phrases here, separated by *que*. First we have

es bueno, and second we have *estés aquí*. The first sentence uses a normal Ser conjugation, and the second is subjunctive.

The word *bueno* in the first phrase comments on the fact described by the second phrase. Of course, *bueno* isn't the only way to comment on a sentence; "it's strange", "it's important", and "it's fair" are some other ways you might comment on a fact. So let's put other words like "strange" and "important" in this scene.

First of all, a toy train has crashed through the wall here. Joel thinks this is very strange, and he says, "It's strange that a train is in my wall!" The word for "strange" is *extraño*, with a stress on "tran".

Sitting in one of the cars of this train is a tiny human that taunts Joel: "We humans are better than you bees! Look at us! We invented trains and are good at driving them! We're much more important than you!"

This argument doesn't convince Joel, but he now associates the word "important" with this human's taunts. The word *importante* stresses the syllable "taunt".

Then the human points to the person in the car next to him: "This is my sibling, Taylor. Taylor isn't a human. I'm more important than Taylor."

Joel is baffled: How can this taunting guy be siblings with Taylor if Taylor isn't a human? And is Taylor his "sister" or his "brother"? He just called Taylor his "sibling". Joel wonders, "How is it possible that Taylor is your sibling?"

The word for "possible" is *posible*, with a stress on "sib".

Below the train, some feet are sticking out of the bottoms of the cars. Joel doesn't know whose feet they are, but

he decides to try to tickle their toes. When he does, they always yell "No fair!"

Joel doesn't know whose toes these are, but his word for "fair" (as in "it's not fair") is *justo* (sounds like "whose toe").

All of these words are connected to the protruding stage. But there's one related word that's in a different place: *cierto*.

Here's the thing. The window above Joel's stage is cracked, and it has been the cause of nasty drafts for a long time. The air has been blowing in and out of the house for a year, even though he's tried hiring lots of people to fix it. It is now certain to him that the window will be drafty for years to come, and to say "it's certain", he says *es cierto* (sounds like "certain", but the stress is on "air").

This word is in a slightly different place from the other words. This is because it works a little differently: Instead of being followed by a subjunctive phrase, it's followed by a simple phrase; for example, to say "it's certain that you're here", you would say *es cierto que estás aquí* (no subjunctive involved).

"Ser" Adjectives: Gossip

Among crusty bachelors like Joel, sometimes gossip is an activity reserved for rocking on the front porch ("front porch talk" and "gossip" are the same thing to Joel). Well Joel doesn't have a front porch, per se, but the path in front of his front door does the job. This is where Joel like to make descriptive statements about other people.

First of all, Joel has painted an apple to look like Ser's face. This apple is badly bruised because Joel has stepped on it many times (usually on purpose). Whenever he sees the apple, he says, "Why so serious?" His word for "serious" is *serio* (or of course *seria*).

Joel often describes people he doesn't like as "too serious". But a stronger, more negative word is *malo*, which means "bad" or "mean". To represent this, he has a toy monkey holding cymbals and trying to "maul" the apple with them.

Beside the path is a chicken wearing cowboy boots. Joel is a huge fan of American Westerns (imported to Yol from Earth); he thinks they're brilliant. The chicken likes to use the word "yall", which Joel thinks is an ingenious word. (If you think about it, "yall" is somewhat equivalent to ustedes in English, which Joel thinks is smart.) Joel often tells the chicken, "You American Westerners are amazing and brilliant." His word for "amazing" or "brilliant" is *genial* (stress on "yall", but starting with "hen").

Next to the hen is yet another magic lantern, but this one has feet. It runs quickly around, to the door and back. Joel says that this little fellow is very "energetic" and "lively". His word for "lively" is *vivo*.

Joel's door has been subjected to vandalism: Someone scratched a picture of Santa Claus at the top, and lower down, they made a picture of the young man whose arms and legs are made of hoes. We use these pictures to store the words *viejo* and *joven*.

All of the words in this scene are commonly used with Ser conjugations to talk about people. *Eres mala* means "you're mean", and *es viejo* means "he's old". Whenever you use a word from this scene with a Ser conjugation, you're describing someone's identity, or something about their character.

151

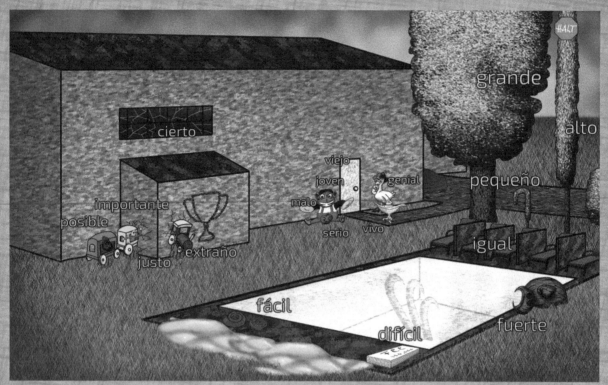

Of course, the words *viejo*, *joven*, and *vivo* are in both scenes, but they have different senses based on where they are. Here in the Ser scene, *vivo* is a comment about what type of person someone is: "He's a lively person." In the other scene, it's just how that person is doing: "He's alive." In Spanish, the words *viejo* and *joven* are also perceived to have different meanings based on whether you use Ser or Estar, though the change is somewhat subtle.

Easy, Hard, and Difficult

The words near Joel's door typically refer to people, but the words that we learn around the pool are more often used for non-human nouns.

We've already learned *claro*, which means "clear", "transparent", or even "light-colored". We also learned *seguro*, which means "secure".

On the near side of the pool is Joel's swimsuit, which, strangely, is made of wood. Joel says that he likes to wear something "strong" as he swims, just to help protect him from the claws at the bottom of the pool. He refers to this swimsuit as *fuerte* (stress on "wear"), which means "strong" or "hard" (physically).

On the closer side of the pool are some interesting formations in the cement. Joel has made a lot of money by selling fossils, which are very expensive in Yol. But for him, finding fossils is an extremely easy task, because an abundance of fossils can be found in the surface of the ground just next to his pool. He says that finding fossils is *fácil*, which means "easy".

But something that's not so easy for him is paying the legal fees involved in selling fossils. In Yol, there's a levy for every fossil that's sold, and sometimes Joel neglects to pay this money; the stack of fees piles up next to his pool because he finds it very difficult to part with his money for these fees. His word for "difficult" is *difícil* (stress on "fee").

On the right side of the pool are several pool chairs. The custom in Yol is to have some privacy while lying on a pool chair (so that nobody stares awkwardly at you), and so some walls have been built between them. All of these walls are made of equal height, and Joel's word for "equal" is *igual*.

...Difficult?

If you found today's vocabulary overwhelming, you're not alone. Most students struggle with this enormous lesson.

To clarify your goals, simply focus on one thing: Remembering <u>where</u> each word is located.

You'll have plenty of opportunity to review these words later. You're also very likely to use all of them quite a bit in real Spanish conversations, so although they may be unfamiliar now, they'll be your old friends before long.

For now, just make sure everything is where it belongs, and then you'll be ready to practice them in phrases.

Lesson 9 Application:
Descriptiveness

LET'S APPLY our new vocabulary to full sentences in Spanish, using our new conjunctions, prepositions, adverbs, and adjectives to create a richer variety of descriptions in our expression.

Conjunctions

There are many books, which are all very good.	*Hay muchos* books, *los cuales son todos muy buenos.*
It was my sister, which is very nice.	*Era mi hermana, la cual es muy buena.*
There's a man, which is my friend.	*Hay un hombre, el cual es mi amigo.*
He was here today, which was very strange.	*Estaba aquí hoy, lo cual era muy extraño.*

In the last case you may be confused by the *lo cual*, but that indicates just a general "which"; instead of a specific masculine or feminine noun, we're saying that the entire fact of him "being here yesterday" is what is strange. *Lo cual* is actually a pretty common way to say "which".

The knight had it and he was going to kill someone.	*La tenía el* knight *e iba a* kill *alguien.*
I was at home and I was going to do it.	*Yo estaba en casa e iba a hacerlo.*

Or another day we can go.	*U otro día podemos ir.*

All three of the conjunctions at the area of the path near *cuando*, including, *aunque* and *mientras*, tend to be followed by a subjunctive.

Though it be true…	*Aunque sea verdad…*
When it be difficult…	*Cuando sea difícil…*
While he be here…	*Mientras esté aquí…*

Prepositions

Between them there was nothing.	**Entre ellas no había nada.**
Against us there was nothing.	**Contra nosotros no había nada.**
Toward the north there was nothing.	**Hacia** the north **no había nada.**
During that year there was nothing.	**Durante ese año no había nada.**

A month ago I spoke with Ignacio.	**Hace un** month I spoke **con Ignacio.**
A few days ago I did it with my parents.	**Hace unos días lo hice con mis padres.**

Swamp Pronouns

In the swamp, we've learned *¿cuál?* to mean "which?" and *¿quién?* to mean "who?" We can easily make these words plural by adding -es to the end: *¿quiénes?* and *¿cuáles?*

Who are they?	**¿Quiénes son ellos?**
Who are your friends?	**¿Quiénes son tus amigos?**
Which are mine?	**¿Cuáles son las mías?**

Very often for some reason Joel likes to ask "which?" instead of "what?" This means that the word *cuál* (or *cuáles*) is more common than "which?" is in English. When in doubt, Joel shows favoritism toward *cuál* instead of *qué*.

For example, instead of saying "what problems?", Joel might prefer to say "which problems?"

Which problems?	**¿Cuáles problemas?**
Which friends?	**¿Cuáles amigos?**

Exclamations

Stop, let me read!	**Basta,** let me read!
Sorry, I have to read.	**Perdón, tengo que** read.
Sure, you can read.	**Dale, usted puede** read.
Of course, I can read.	**Claro, yo puedo** read.

Booleans and Igual

It's almost daytime.	*Casi es de día.*
Is it even daytime?	*¿Siquiera es de día?*
It's not daytime.	*Tampoco es de día.*
It's not even daytime.	*Ni siquiera es de día.*

Do you even know where she is?	*¿Siquiera you know dónde está?*
Do you really know where they are?	*¿Realmente you know dónde están?*
You don't even know where we're going?	*¿Ni siquiera you know adónde vamos?*
Do you almost know where you're going?	*¿Casi you know adónde vas?*

At the same time, I think that there might be problems.	*Igual, I think que puede haber problemas.*
Still, I think that there might be fewer friends.	*Igual, I think que puede haber menos amigos.*

Steak Adverbs

It's kind of hard to stay for so much time.	*Es medio difícil to stay tanto tiempo.*
It's too hard to stay for so much time.	*Es demasiado difícil to stay tanto tiempo.*
It isn't at all hard to stay for so much time.	*No es nada difícil to stay tanto tiempo.*
It's quite hard to stay for so much time.	*Es bastante difícil to stay tanto tiempo.*

He liked it so much…	*Le it was pleasing tanto…*
They liked it a lot.	*Les it was pleasing mucho.*
We only liked it a little.	*Nos it was pleasing muy poco.*

The adverb *justo* is almost exclusively used along with the time adverbs from the front of the baker's stand, as in *justo antes de* ("just before") or *justo después de* ("just after").

We did it right before that.	*Lo hicimos justo antes de eso.*
They did it right after this.	*Lo hicieron justo después de esto.*
Your house is right after mine.	*Su casa está justo después de la mía.*

Time Adverbs

Although the word *jamás* technically means the same thing as *nunca*, it's usually used for particular emphasis, almost like "never ever". (Sometimes you'll even hear Spanish speakers say "¡nunca jamás!")

No, never.	*No, jamás.*
Yes, tomorrow.	*Sí, mañana.*
Maybe, later.	*Quizás, luego.*

And does he still live here?	*¿Y todavía he lives acá?*
And will he soon be here?	*¿Y pronto estará acá?*
And meanwhile does he have something?	*¿Y mientras tiene algo?*

Location Adverbs

English speakers tend to have trouble with the location adverbs that we've learned at the fruit stand today. So for this exercise, practice only switching out one word: The adverb. Leave the other words in the sentence the same; just change the adverb out.

Here are all the adverbs that are inside the fruit drawer, adverbs that are followed by *de*:

He was inside the house.	*Estaba dentro de la casa.*
He was outside the house.	*Estaba fuera de la casa.*
He was near the house.	*Estaba cerca de la casa.*
He was in front of the house.	*Estaba adelante de la casa.*
He was on top of the house.	*Estaba arriba de la casa.*
He was far from the house.	*Estaba lejos de la casa.*

These same words are often used by themselves, without de after them, at the end of a sentence:

A man that was very far away.	*Un hombre que estaba muy lejos.*
A man that was very near.	*Un hombre que estaba muy cerca.*
A man that was on top.	*Un hombre que estaba arriba.*
A man that was inside.	*Un hombre que estaba dentro.*

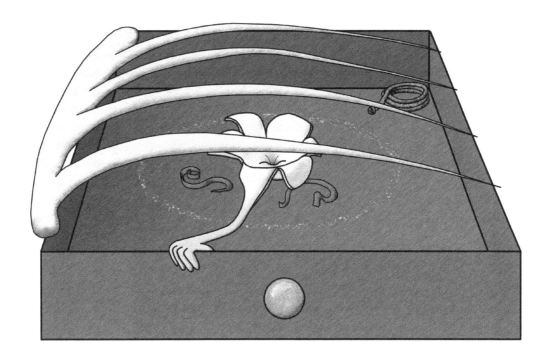

Next let's go over the adverbs on the top of the fruit stand. We're going to use a simple sentence example that uses *ir ahí* ("go there"), but then we'll modify the adverb *ahí* to use some of our new adverbs.

She was going to go there also.	*Ella iba a ir ahí también.*
She was going to go over there also.	*Ella iba a ir allá también.*
She was going to go outside also.	*Ella iba a ir afuera también.*
She was going to go backwards also.	*Ella iba a ir atrás también.*
She was going to go down also.	*Ella iba a ir abajo también.*

Veggie Adverbs

One moves the hand quickly.	*Uno* moves *la* hand *rápido.*
Move the hand the same way.	Move *la* hand *igual.*
Speak the word loudly.	Speak *la* word *alto.*
Talk more softly.	Talk *más bajo.*

Had you heard about this book?	*¿Habías* heard *acerca de este* book?
Had you talked about this house?	*¿Habías* talked *acerca de esta casa?*

Comparative Adjectives

The word *mejor* means both "better" and "best". In English, we have two separate words for those things, but they're the same in Spanish. In the same way, *mayor* can mean either "bigger" or "biggest".

In general, for the nerds, Joel's <u>comparative</u> adjectives can also be used as <u>superlative</u> adjectives.

I hope to go to the best place of all.	I hope *ir al mejor lugar de todos.*
I hope to have the biggest house of all.	I hope *tener la mayor casa de todas.*

Indefinite Adjectives

He stays in the story too much time.	He stays *en la* story *demasiado tiempo.*
He stays in the house enough time.	He stays *en la casa suficiente tiempo.*

Stop, I already gave you enough reasons.	*Basta, ya te* I gave *suficientes razones.*
Stop, I already gave you many reasons.	*Basta, ya te* I gave *muchas razones.*
Stop, you didn't give me any reason.	*Basta, no me* you gave *ninguna razón.*

Someone can stay at any moment?	*¿Uno puede* stay *en cualquier momento?*
Someone can stay at another moment?	*¿Uno puede* stay *en otro momento?*
Nobody can stay at any moment?	*¿Nadie puede* stay *en ningún momento?*

She had made herself a good friend of a certain man.	*Ella se había hecho muy amiga de cierto hombre.*
He had made himself a good friend of some woman.	*Él se había hecho muy amigo de alguna mujer.*

The word *cuanto* is used in certain idioms that relate to correspondence. For example, in English, we say "the more you search, the more you find", using a comma in the middle. Spanish uses very different wording: "*Cuanto más* you search, *más* you find."

This use of *cuanto* is impossible to translate literally. The best way to learn is simply by memorizing an example and then modifying that:

The more you search, the more you find.	*Cuanto más* you search, *más* you find.
The more they have, the more they want.	*Cuanto más tienen, más quieren.*
The more I want it, the more I do it.	*Cuanto más lo quiero, más lo hago.*

The next idiom, *en cuanto a*, makes absolutely no sense when translated literally. But it means "regarding". It's somewhat comparable to the English idiom "as far as...", for example, "as far as that goes..."

As far as that goes...	*En cuanto a eso...*
As far as our house goes...	*En cuanto a nuestra casa...*
As far as the general problem goes...	*En cuanto al problema general...*

Sometimes the adjective *cuanto* actually gets an accent over it: When Joel asks "how many"? In these cases, *cuántos* is used, which has both an accent and an S at the end; it looks a lot like *cuánto* from the butcher's stand, but it's technically being used as an adjective (because it expects to be answered by a number, not an adverb).

In particular, when Joel asks how old someone is, he prefers to think in terms of how many years they "have". So instead of "How old is the boy?", Joel would ask "How many years does the boy have?"

How old is the boy?	*¿Cuántos años tiene el boy?*
How many houses does the woman have?	*¿Cuántas casas tiene la mujer?*

"Which" Adjectives

In this example, switch out adjectives that tend to go after the noun (like *"problema general"*).

The general story is about a boy.	*La story general is about un boy.*
The past story is about a man.	*La story pasada is about un hombre.*
The correct story is about a woman.	*La story correcta is about una mujer.*

With the following examples, practice switching out adjectives that go before the noun.

In the first part…	*En la primera parte…*
In the new part…	*En la nueva parte…*
In the third part…	*En la tercera parte…*
In the last part…	*En la última parte…*
In the fourth part…	*En la cuarta parte…*
In the same part…	*En la misma parte…*
In the only part…	*En la única parte…*

The word *lugar* is used along with ordinal adjectives in idioms that are similar to English idioms. For example, Joel might list reasons for doing something and say "in the first place…"

In the first place…	*En primer lugar…*

Notice here that *primero* gets shortened to *primer* when it's used right before a masculine noun. We'll see soon that some other adjectives do this as well.

Numbers

When describing amounts, Joel sometimes informally uses *como* to mean "around" or "like". For example, "There are about a thousand people here" would be "*Hay como mil* people here" (literally "there are like a thousand people here").

It makes like a thousand hours that you've been here!	*¡Hace como mil horas que estás aquí!*
It makes like a million years that you haven't been home!	*¡Hace como millón años que no estás en casa!*

Now that we know all of our single-digit numbers (1, 2, 3, etc.) and also building blocks for larger numbers (20, 30, 100, 1000, etc.), let's talk about combining these parts for complex numbers, such as 35 or 1832.

Here are the rules:

- Teens: We've already learned 11-15 as *once, doce, trece, catorce,* and *quince.* For the rest of the teens, the idea is "ten and six", "ten and seven", etc, but said as a single word: *dieciséis, diecisiete, dieciocho,* and *diecinueve.*

- <u>Twenties</u>: The twenties are a lot like the teens. The basic idea is "twenty and one", "twenty and two", etc., but as a single word with altered spelling: *veintiuno*, *veintidós*, *veintitrés*, etc.

- <u>30-100</u>: When we get past thirty (*treinta*), we use separate words: *treinta y uno*, *treinta y dos*, etc. This applies all the way to 99 (*noventa y nueve*).

- <u>101-999</u>: The thing about three-digit numbers is that you list the parts, but you only put *y* near the end, right before the last digit.

- In terms of place value, think "<u>hundreds, tens, and ones</u>". That's exactly how you'll say it in Spanish. For example, 832 is "8 hundreds, 30, and 2", or *ochocientos treinta y dos*. 469 is "4 hundreds, 60, and 9", or *cuatrocientos sesenta y nueve*.

She's ten years old.	*Tiene diez años.*
She's sixteen years old.	*Tiene dieciseis años.*
She's twenty-eight years old.	*Tiene veintiocho años.*
She's thirty-five years old.	*Tiene treinta y cinco años.*
The house is 347 years old.	*La casa tiene trescientos cuarenta y siete años.*

Keep practicing with more examples on your own. There are a couple of rarely-encountered exceptions to these rules, such as the strange word for 500, *quinientos*. But you won't find it hard to learn these later; such exceptions will be easy to smooth out after you've become confident with numbers in general.

Here's one idiom to learn regarding numbers: In English, we say "the fifties" to refer to the years from 1950 to 1959. In Spanish, we would instead say "the years fifty", or *los años cincuenta*.

It's from the 60s.	*Es de los años sesenta.*
It's a house from the 40s.	*Es una casa de los años cuarenta.*

Adjectives Associated with Estar

He was a little crazy.	*Estaba un poco loco.*
She was very crazy.	*Estaba muy loca.*
They were pretty high.	*Estaban bastante altas.*
He was very young-looking.	*Estaba muy joven.*

Once the king is dead…	*Una vez que el* king *esté muerto…*
Once the man is ready…	*Una vez que el hombre esté listo…*
Once the woman is kind of happy…	*Una vez que la mujer esté medio feliz…*

Let's read this together.	Let's read *este juntos.*

Adjectives Associated with Ser: Size

Although grande and pequeño literally refer to size, these types of words can refer to age instead. For example, a when someone refers to a person as grande, they probably mean "old" or at least "grown up" rather than referring to the person's size.

He's not a very old/big kid.	*No es un* kid *muy grande.*
She's a very small/young kid.	*Es una* kid *muy pequeña.*
He's a pretty tall guy.	*Es un tipo medio alto.*

Something interesting happens with certain adjectives if they come right before a noun. The word *bueno* is shortened to *buen* when it happens right before a masculine noun; for example "a good man" is un *buen hombre*.

Similarly, the word *grande* is shortened to *gran* if it occurs just before any noun (not just masculine nouns).

He's a nice guy.	*Es un buen tipo.*
It's a big house.	*Es una gran casa.*

Adjectives Associated with Ser: Facts

Each of the following examples uses two phrases, separated by *que*. The phrase after *"que"* is subjunctive, unless *cierto* is used.

It's important that one do it.	*Es importante que uno lo haga.*
It's not fair that you be here.	*No es justo que estés aquí.*
It's possible that they do it.	*Es posible que lo hagan.*
It's strange that he loves her.	*Es extraño que la quiera.*
It's certain that we have it.	*Es cierto que lo tenemos.*

As if *cierto* wasn't a confusing enough word, it has an idiom: *por cierto* often precedes a sentence that's inserted awkwardly into a conversation. It can mean either "by the way" or "in fact", depending on context.

In fact, your mother is here now.	*Por cierto, tu madre está aquí ahora.*
By the way, your mother is here now.	*Por cierto, tu madre está aquí ahora.*

Adjectives Associated with Ser: Gossip

The king was young and the knight old.	*El* king *era joven y el* knight *viejo.*
The woman was serious and her friend mean.	*La mujer era seria y su amiga mala.*
The man was brilliant and his wife very lively.	*El hombre era genial y su mujer muy viva.*

Adjectives Associated with Ser: General

It wasn't so easy to do it.	*No era tan fácil hacerlo.*
It was very difficult to do it.	*Era muy difícil hacerlo.*

Dialogue Assignment

Today we'll look at the beginning of the story between Sofía and Laura.

They're both at Laura's house. Laura is kind of bossy and seems to have a way of losing her toys.

After some discussion, they decide to play with two woman dolls. "Woman 1" is Laura's doll, and "Woman 2" is Sofía's doll.

"Me tuve que ir de Argentina."

Sofía- I want to play with the woman with the serious face.

Sofía- *Yo quiero* to play *con la mujer de* face *seria.*

Laura- I don't have her. She was around, but I never saw her again.

Laura- *No la tengo. Estaba por ahí pero nunca la* I saw again.

Sofía- That always happens to you with everything you have.

Sofía- *Eso siempre te* happens *con todo lo que tienes.*

Laura- That's not true.

Laura- *Eso no es verdad.*

Sofía- Yes, last time you couldn't find the dog.

Sofía- *Sí, la última vez no pudiste* to find *el* dog.

Laura- Well, that was only one time.

Laura- *Bueno, eso sólo fue una vez.*

Sofía- And now the woman with the serious face!

Sofía- *¡Y ahora la mujer de* face *seria!*

Laura- Well, it doesn't matter, it's not here.

Laura- *Bueno, no* it matters, *no está.*

Sofía- I'd rather play in your mom's room.

Sofía- *Mejor* let's play *en el* room *de tu mamá.*

Laura- No, better after five in the after-

Laura- *No, mejor después de las cinco de*

166

noon. By that time she will have left and we can do whatever we want. Now let's play here, I'll play with this one and you play with this other one. Yeah? They were friends since they were girls; both of them are doctors and police officers and also they play on important teams.

Sofía- All those things at once?

Laura- Yes. So when mine calls yours by telephone, yours doesn't know who it is.

Sofía- But they were friends from childhood. How is she not going to know?

Laura- It's that she had left for many years. She had been in Argentina. But one day she ended up without anything; bad people took everything and she had to leave. When she arrives in the country she doesn't have money so she calls you in order that you might help her.

Sofía- They took everything?

Laura- Yes, everything, even the house.

Sofía- All right, let's go.

Mujer 1- Hi! How is your day?

Mujer 2- Who is this?

Mujer 1- It's me!

Mujer 2- María? How nice that it's you!

Mujer 1- How have you been?

Mujer 2- I've been better than ever!

la tarde. Para entonces se habrá ido y podemos hacer lo que queramos. Ahora let's play *acá, yo* play *con esta y tú* play *con esta otra. ¿Sí? Eran amigas desde* childhood, *las dos son* doctors *y* police officers *y también* they play *en* teams *importantes.*

Sofía- *¿Todas esas cosas a la vez?*

Laura- *Sí. Entonces cuando la mía* calls *por* telephone *a la tuya, la tuya no* knows *quién es.*

Sofía- *Pero eran amigas desde* childhood, *¿cómo no va a* know?

Laura- *Es que se había ido por muchos años. Había estado en Argentina. Pero un día* she ended up *sin nada, gente* bad took *todo y tuvo que irse. Cuando* she arrives *al* country *no tiene dinero entonces te* she calls *para que la* you help.

Sofía- *¿Todo* they took?

Laura- *Sí, todo, hasta la casa.*

Sofía- *Bueno, dale.*

Mujer 1- *¡Hola! ¿Qué tal tu día?*

Mujer 2- *¿Quién es usted?*

Mujer 1- *¡Soy yo!*

Mujer 2- *¿María? ¡Qué bueno que seas tú!*

Mujer 1- *¿Cómo has estado?*

Mujer 2- *¡Estuve mejor que nunca!*

Mujer 1- Great! And the kids?

Mujer 2- They're both very well. How are you? Where are you?

Mujer 1- I'm in the country. I had to leave Argentina. I had a problem; they took all my things and I had to come back. It's not so bad, it was time to be at home, but now I don't have a place to stay. Can I stay at your house?

Mujer 2- I left for a new house. It's small, but it has some of everything, even a bed for you. Of course you can stay. And I can give you money.

Mujer 1- What luck! Thanks so much! I don't really like people to do me favors, especially with this type of things, you know, money.

Mujer 2- Don't be that way. Fortunately I don't have to worry much about those things. All right, I'm going to work; I'm sorry, but at home there's never anyone in the mornings. I arrive at seven. You can come at that time.

Mujer 1- Perfect, I'll sit in some bar and wait. I'll be happy to be at home.

Mujer 2- Until tonight!

Mujer 1- *¡Qué bueno! ¿Y los* children?

Mujer 2- *Están los dos muy bien. ¿Cómo estás tú? ¿Dónde estás?*

Mujer 1- *Estoy en el* country. *Me tuve que ir de Argentina. Tuve un problema,* they took *todas mis cosas y tuve que* come back. *No es tan* bad, *era tiempo de estar en casa, pero ahora no tengo donde* to stay. *¿Puedo* to stay *en tu casa?*

Mujer 2- *Me fui a una nueva casa, es pequeña, pero tiene de todo, hasta una* bed *para ti, claro que puedes* stay. *Y te puedo* give *dinero.*

Mujer 1- *¡Qué luck! ¡Muchas gracias! No* I like *que me hagan favores, sobre todo con este tipo de cosas, tú* know, *de dinero.*

Mujer 2- *No seas así, por* luck *no tengo que* worry *mucho por esas cosas. Bueno, me voy a* work, I'm sorry, *pero en casa nunca hay nadie por las mañanas,* I arrive *a las siete, puedes* to come *a esa hora.*

Mujer 1- *Muy bien,* I'll sit *en algún bar y* wait. *Estaré feliz al estar en casa.*

Mujer 2- *¡Hasta esta noche!*

LESSON 10

Listen Well

We're approaching the brink of fluency. But this final push will be incredibly difficult.

At this point, you'll find that comprehension becomes a major obstacle in the way of comfortable conversation.

You learn most effectively when you're both challenged and affirmed, with both of those elements in balance. Let's turn listening from a weakness into a strength.

Lesson 10 Theory:

Immersion Is NOT the Answer

"Deep practice is built on a paradox: Struggling in certain, targeted ways — operating at the edges of your ability, where you make mistakes — makes you smarter."

- Daniel Coyle, "The Talent Code"

THERE'S A popular myth among language learners that simply "immersing yourself" is a good way to learn Spanish.

In my own experience with hundreds of students, I've seen that this attitude almost always leads to catastrophe. Especially for their listening skills.

If you go out on the street and talk to some random Spanish speaker, you might be overwhelmed and discouraged that you can't understand them and they can't understand you, creating a negative experience. Your strongest, most memorable association with Spanish would then be a vivid event of stress, failure, and discouragement.

Imagine you're being guided up a very challenging staircase. A good guide will always know which step you're on, and they'll be able to lead you gently but firmly to the next one.

Immersion, on the other hand, expects you to be at the top of the stairs right away. This encourages you to skip steps, which can be more disastrous than you might think.

I'm going to tell you the story of "Austin".

Now, Austin is not a real person; he's a composite character of several students I've had in the past.

Austin was convinced that immersion would be the savior in his language-learning story.

After a couple of months in the Accelerated Spanish coaching course, Austin wasn't making the progress he wanted to make.

Unfortunately, the fault was his own. The reports that I was receiving from his native-speaking Spanish coaches weren't good: Austin wanted to move forward too quickly, but he simply wasn't doing his assigned work.

I arranged a call with him to encourage him to get back on track, but Austin wasn't interested in slowing down:

"I've been watching some Spanish movies. I turn the subtitles off and try to see how much I can understand."

"Okay, how much is that?"

"Well, usually not much of anything, but I can pick out words here and there."

Even though he couldn't seem to make the time to study, he did have time to watch movies and listen to Spanish radio.

I strongly advised him against this practice.

"You really need to master the essentials first. The words you're picking out aren't going to help you become fluent. Have you been doing the assigned listening practice?"

"Some of it. It's been hard for me to make the time."

"Okay, we can slow things down if needed, but you really need to master these essentials."

"Well actually, I've made a decision that will make a big difference. I'm taking my work on the road and flying to Spain very soon."

"Oh. Really?"

"Yeah, I've already bought the plane ticket. I think it will force me to immerse myself and help me really learn everything quickly."

I sighed. Austin was in for some serious disappointment.

The Mythical "Tipping Point"

Austin was a victim of the classic mistake that many beginning language-learners make.

Instead of following his teachers' guidance and limiting himself to one specific goal at a time, he was throwing himself into the language like a rock into the ocean, hoping to absorb enough to find himself magically fluent one day. But that doesn't work.

The legendary "tipping point" to sudden fluency doesn't exist. I know many language learners and have worked with hundreds of coaching students, and nobody has experienced such a thing.

However, there are pivotal moments that ARE pretty common. Here are examples:

- "Today, I suddenly realized that I could fully understand this story I've been studying. I don't even have to think about the English anymore! It's incredible."

- "Today it occurred to me that I can express almost anything I want to say with my own vocabulary. It's a very freeing feeling!"

- "I can now understand about 90% of what people say in a conversation with me! My patience (and theirs) has really paid off in the last several months. I'm finally having entire conversations in Spanish on lots of subjects."

Note that these are three sequential moments, not one sudden "tipping point into fluency". The objective is to work toward each of these, one at a time. You want to have measurable goals that you're trying to meet.

Unfortunately, Austin was ignoring the milestones and simply trying to leap toward this nebulous concept of "fluency", hoping that some day he would suddenly be at the top of the stairs.

In Lesson 4 (Volume 1) of this course, I demonstrated that the best growth happens when you're practicing on the fringes of your comfort zone, pushing the boundaries of familiarity further and further out. If you stay within your comfort zone, that zone won't get any bigger. But it also won't get any bigger if you jump with both feet outside of it and completely lose track of everything you're familiar with.

As it was, Austin was practicing by listening to things he couldn't understand, such as Madrid radio. This not only did nothing to improve his listening skills, it actually reinforced the habit of not understanding what he heard. This meant that he was frustrating himself by constantly exposing himself to things he couldn't comprehend. Whereas he could understand everything he heard in <u>English</u>, 90% of the <u>Spanish</u> that he heard was beyond his comprehension, psychologically creating an association of futility with his intended second language.

Active Listening

Take a moment to listen to the sounds around you. What is the highest pitch you hear? If you listen closely, what is the lowest rumble that is audible to you right now?

Were you fully aware of these noises before you gave them your attention?

No. You're aware of them now, but only because you told your brain to

pay them specific attention.

Whether you are conscious of it or not, your brain is not registering all the sounds that you hear. Every single second, your mind filters the sounds it recognizes as meaningful from what it hears as simply meaningless noise.

For example, a few months ago in Tulsa, a construction team began tearing up a parking lot across the street from my downtown apartment. They currently spend about 10 hours per day making loud, violent noises as they work on raising a new five-story building in the Tulsa Arts District.

At first, I was alerted to the noises each time I heard them. They were new and interesting.

But soon, the loud crashes, beeps, and jackhammer noises became normal. My brain realized that this was simply a new type of background noise. Now I rarely notice the sounds. My subconscious mind finds these sounds meaningless and decides to ignore them.

Here's the scary question:

Do you want that to happen to you with Spanish?

What would happen to you if your mind decided to register Spanish as meaningless noise, something that should automatically be shut out when you hear it?

If you spend a lot of time listening to Spanish that you don't understand, your brain will subconsciously train itself to ignore Spanish. You'll get used to not understanding Spanish, and that will be the norm for you, as it was with Austin

Effective listening practice doesn't overwhelm you with information that you don't understand. A good Spanish teacher will always work at the fringes of your comfort zone (NOT miles outside the comfort zone) which is absolutely necessary for progress in your listening skills.

This is why I require my students to listen extensively to Spanish that is fully within their vocabulary. That means listening to a wide variety of uses

of the essential vocabulary that we talked about in the previous lesson. The dialogues from the course are extremely useful for this. Keep practicing with them until you understand them so perfectly that you comprehend the meaning of every sentence you hear effortlessly.

My best students stick to the top 600 words of the language, working with them until they know them so well that they can use them flawlessly and understand them in almost any context.

This means that while they listen extensively to dialogues using these 600 words, they avoid listening to Spanish radio or watching Spanish films until they've mastered them. They understand what they're listening to, and they're able to imitate it so that they can use those same phrases themselves.

Later, when it's time to practice listening with further media such as real Spanish videos and songs, they study the exact vocabulary that they need for what they're practicing with in order to understand it 100%. This is much more valuable than listening passively.

Let's say a student chooses a song that she's never heard before. Although she currently knows 600 words fluently, she may need about 20 new words to understand this particular song. That's very doable. Once she's learned the meanings of these 20 new words, she studies the text of the song and then practices listening to it with the written transcript in front of her (and maybe singing along) until she has perfect understanding of it.

This active form of listening practice is radically different from the common approach, which is simply to turn something on and hope that the sounds stick in your brain somehow.

If you're practicing with a good Spanish teacher (such as the excellent native-speaking coaches on my staff), they will also tailor their conversation to your current level of ability, even in spontaneous conversations.

If you don't perfectly understand something that your coach says, ask her to explain it to you. She'll be happy to repeat herself and to write the phrase out for you; then you can copy that sentence into your own personal flash cards and study them on your own.

A good teacher will work on expanding your personal comfort zone one step at a time, neither keeping you stuck inside it nor throwing you helplessly outside it.

Lesson 10 Vocabulary:

Verb Geography

("The Shops Around the Corner")

IT'S TIME TO DO an exercise that involves a strong, active imagination. You're going to have to imagine yourself walking out of Joel's house and down the street.

The goal here is to learn the entire layout of the verb neighborhood near Joel's house.

We've been introduced to some of the verb shops nearest to Joel, including Ser and Ir (the two closest), Haber, Hacer, Querer, and Poder (a stone's throw down the road, at the fork), and Estar and Tener (to the right).

Before we start walking around in our imagination, let's talk about why these shops are where they are.

As you've learned, all of these verbs are pretty complicated. Each one seems to follow its own rules. In particular, the preterite past tense of each verb seems to have its own unique pattern.

For example, in Ir, Joel's preterite form ("I went") is *fui*. This sounds completely different from his preterite tense for Hacer ("I did"), which is *hice*. And then that's different from the equivalent form of Poder ("I was able"), *pude*.

What do *fui*, *hice*, and *pude* have in common? Not a whole lot.

But look at the map. Ir, Hacer, and Poder are pretty far apart from each other. Suppose we look at two shops that are closer together.

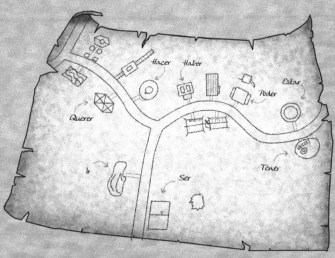

Compare these conjugations of Hacer and Querer:

quise / hice

quiso / hizo

quisiste / hiciste

querían / hacían

queríamos / hacíamos

These past tense forms should sound suspiciously similar. That's because these two verbs are closely related. Notice that Hacer and Querer are neighbors, facing one another across the street.

We're about to exercise our spatial imagination in order to memorize how these verbs are grouped together. As we do, we'll also be learning the names of a few more shops.

Imagine that you're Joel, and you want to take a flight around the neighborhood just to get some exercise and fresh air.

To start out, you fly out of the house and take a look down the street. To your right is Ser, and to your left is Ir.

As you fly along, you're going to have to make your first decision of the day: Right or left? As you approach the fork in the road, you see Haber to the right and Hacer to the left.

You feel more inclined to turn toward Hacer. Looking down that left-hand

street, you're greeted by Hacer, Querer, and a few other shops.

On the left side, beyond Querer, there's a gift shop called Dar. It's run by a woman who calls herself "darling". She sells and gives away novelty items, like musical cigarette boxes: The kinds of things you might buy as gifts for other people but that you would not be likely to buy for yourself.

The word *dar* means "to give". Note that it's next door to Querer, which means "to want" or "to love". Querer sells jewelry, which you might buy for someone you love. Both of these shops are associated with giving.

As Joel, you probably don't feel very generous, so you turn away from the left side of the street. Let's look instead at what's on the right side.

In the distance, there's a building called Decir. When Joel says "Decir", it sounds kind of like he's saying "the seer". The woman who runs it is a self-proclaimed prophetess, and everyone calls her "the seer".

Decir is a creepy place where the seer tries to tell people's fortunes. But instead of reading palms or a crystal ball, she tells them things based on what they say. When you enter Decir, you have to be careful what comes out of your mouth, because she'll judge every single word. The word *decir* means "to say".

Next door to Decir is Venir. This is another creepy place, but in a

different way. Venir is supposed to be a convenience store, but it's a little TOO convenient: Any time you walk by Venir, it tries to get as close to you as possible. It uses its wheels to roll as close to you as it can, and sometimes it actually follows you down the street. The person who runs it is nick-named "Near" because he always comes uncomfortably near to you, and *venir* means "to come".

To the right of Decir and Venir is another creepy store, Hacer, where live pigs are cooked and served.

Today, you don't feel like giving anything away or being creeped out. So you turn around to see what the other road has to offer.

To the left, the first shop is Haber. You have no interest in going there, because not only is this where the blind bear lives, today he seems to be practicing karate in the back yard.

Further down the road is Poder. This might be a good place for you to work out, but let's consider the other options first.

Between these two stores is Saber. Like Haber, Saber is run by a bear, but it's a different bear: The local mailman. Saber is the post office. But this bear is a very sad mailman, because nobody sends him any mail. So hc cries a lot, which gives him the nickname "sob bear" ("Saber").

Joel associates mail with knowledge. Whenever Joel gets a letter, he feels smart, because it's like he has new information to apply to his life. And he likes sending mail, because he feels like he's sharing his knowledge with other people. The word *saber* means "to know".

Haber and Saber are closely related. The bears are brothers, and both of them go around Yol to all the different stores and houses. But of course, the "Haber" bear likes to drink water from people's roofs, leaving them drier. "Sob bear", meanwhile, does the opposite: He usually leaves everything wet, because he cries all the time. In fact, his tears are what cause the back yard of Poder, next door, to be constantly muddy.

Also look down at the street that Haber, Saber, and Poder are attached to. The road has been worn down like a canyon, thanks to the rushing water of Saber's tears. Instead of a road, it's more like a U-shaped trench. If you're walking, you might find it hard to climb up to the shops on either side.

Haber, Saber, and Poder are to the left, but let's look to the right. Here we have two businesses that have very closely-related names: Poner and Suponer. Poner is a board game store and Suponer is a soup kitchen. These are both owned by Ner, the same eccentric old man who runs the toy shop. But Ner is often too busy with his toys, leaving his very young son to run Poner and Suponer.

Would you like to go into one of these shops? Let's consider whether it would be any fun.

At Poner, the most entertaining thing to do is to place chess pieces on the chess board. That may sound boring, but there's a special trick to it: If you do it right, the pieces magically get stuck and never move. Some people think this is fun. They say, "If you put a piece on the board right, it never moves!" But the word "never" is shortened to "ne'er": "The piece ne'er moves!"

The word *poner* means "to put". For example, "I want to put something here" would be **"Quiero poner algo aquí."**

Next door is Suponer, the soup kitchen. Here, there's really nothing fun to do except try to guess what's in the soup.

For example, you might say, "Why does this taste like a wet dog? I guess maybe you put chihuahua hair in here?"

Remember the stressed syllables "soup" and "ner", and you'll remember that the word *suponer* means "to guess" or "to suppose".

Look around again at these five shops,

and internalize the scene. Imagine yourself standing in front of Saber (the post office), facing the street. Look to your right at Haber, look to your left at Poder, look down at the muddy trench of a street, and look across the road at Suponer and Poner. From this angle, Suponer is to the left and Poner is to the right.

Next, you'll turn toward Poder and consider going in. But no, let's continue down the street a little further.

As the road curves to the right, something changes. The road is still a U-shaped ditch, but it's a bit more stylish, with some ultraviolet lights along the sides.

We're approaching the UV area. UV stands for "ultraviolet", but it also indicates something about the verbs we're visiting: Estar and Tener. They have a strange "uv" in the preterite tense (e.g. *tuve* and *estuvo*).

Now turn around and fly back to the fork in the road. Fly back home, past Ser and Ir.

You've just explored all the essential verbs in Joel's neighborhood!

But here's the thing. Even though you just did that whole exercise, I recommend that you do it again... but this time entirely in your imagination.

Close your eyes, put on your wings, and imagine yourself flying from Joel's front door down the street. See if you can remember every single shop, from Ser and Ir to Decir and then all the way to Tener and back to Joel's house.

If you can accurately remember where every single shop is, you're ready to explore the new stores' features.

Saber

We've learned the names of six new shops, but it's time to scratch past the surface to see what's inside.

Today Joel goes to the mailman because he's expecting a check. He lied to his rich uncle that he was having "financial difficulties". His uncle said he'd send him something.

When Joel picks up the envelope, the pandas crowd around him to find out what's inside. "How much did he send?" they ask enthusiastically.

This annoys Joel. Why is it their business? Anyway, he hasn't even opened the envelope yet. Sometimes he prefers to wait, savoring the excitement of not knowing. As long as he doesn't read the check, he can imagine that he's been sent a million dollars!

He hovers there silently while the pandas continue to push him:

"How much is it? Say! Say!"

Saber himself is curious too. He stops crying for a moment, and he joins in the chanting: "Say! Say!"

Joel bursts out: "I don't know!"

But to say this, he says *"¡No sé!"*

The word *sé* means "I know". When Joel says *"No sé"*, he means "I don't know".

Joel often equates the words "know" and "say". He's one to speak his mind, so for him, knowing something is often the same thing as saying it. For example, to say "I already know it", Joel says *"ya lo sé."*

Admittedly, this is a strange conjugation. It doesn't fit most of the first-person patterns that we're used to, such as *soy*, *estoy*, *voy*, *tengo*, *hago*, and *quiero*. Instead of "o" or "oy", it ends with "e". Haber and Saber, the two bear shops (which are right next to each other), are the only places where Joel's conjugation ends this way: *he* ("I have") and *sé* ("I know").

But other than that, Saber is actually a pretty normal shop. When Joel drops his envelope into a puddle of tears on the floor, the bear and the pandas all start crying, especially the bear, who sobs loudly. It's contagious: Joel begins to sob too. The conjugations are *sabe*, *sabes*, *saben*, and *sabemos*.

The past tense is very standard, and we don't even need a mnemonic for it. Remember *hacía*, *había*, and *podía*, the past-tense forms of the verbs close to Saber. They have the stress on "EEH-ah". The past tense of Saber is *sabía*, *sabían*, *sabíamos*, etc.; to say "I knew it", Joel says *"Lo sabía."*

If it helps, think of the stressed syllable as "bee". But in the future, we won't use mnemonics for every single form of new verbs, because they'll fit the normal patterns that we're already familiar with.

We've now learned all the common conjugations of Saber. But let's take a peek in the back yard.

Behind Saber, a bunch of apes dressed in mailman suits are playing in a pile of mail. One of them grabs Joel's soaked envelope and tears it into tiny pieces.

The stressed syllable "ape" represents that *sepa* is Saber's strange subjunctive. For example, "I want you to know" is *quiero que sepas*.

185

Poner

Joel is furious that his precious envelope has been destroyed.

Maybe if he finds his uncle, he can explain what happened, and his uncle will write him a check in person. But where will he find his uncle?

Looking across the street, Joel decides to go to Poner. Sometimes Joel's uncle goes there to play chess.

When Joel arrives at Poner, Joel doesn't find his uncle. However, he sees that Ner's young son is here, running the shop in Ner's absence. This gives Joel a new idea: Maybe he can take advantage of this boy somehow.

A price tag in the window says "Special chess pawn! 3.45 yen. Collector's item."

Joel decides to pull a trick on Ner's kid, who can't pronounce his Rs.

"How much is that chess pawn in the window? The one that says 'three forty-five'?"

The three-year-old responds, "Thwee fowty-five."

"What's that? How much?"

"Thwee fowty-five!"

"I'm sorry, I can't understand what you're saying."

The child is clearly frustrated. He decides to modify the price so that he can say it without any Rs:

"Two ninety-five."

"I'll take it!"

Joel is thrilled; he just saved 0.50 yen! But when he receives the pawn, he sees that it's from a very cheap, ugly chess set.

"This chess piece looks like an orangutan with holes drilled all through it."

It really does! It disgusts Joel, and he wants to get rid of it. He decides to put it some place where it won't be seen. He quietly says to himself, "I'll put this ugly thing where ugly pawns go: In the trash."

To say "I'm putting this here", he says **"Pongo esto aquí."**

The word **pongo** sounds ilke "pawn go", and it's how Joel says "I put" or "I'm putting".

Other forms of Poner in this room are pretty standard. The stressed syllable "pawn" applies to **pone**, **pones**, and **ponen**.

In the aisles of shelves, Ner allows a cat named "Puss" to knock over the merchandise and play with the chess pieces.

The most common past tense forms of Poner are *puse* for "I put" and *puso* for "he/she/it put". This is very similar to the stores across the street. Compare *puse* and *puso* (Poner) with *pude* and *pudo* (Poder).

As an example, "He put it there today" is *"Lo puso ahí hoy."*

In the back yard, some chess pieces float in a pool of mud. The subjunctive of Poner is *ponga*, based on *pongo*.

This is another pattern that you should get used to. We've learned several verbs that have a rogue letter G in the first person, such as *tengo* and *hago*. For each of these verbs, the G comes back in the backyard subjunctive form as well.

tengo / tenga

hago / haga

pongo / ponga

Any verb that has G in the first person will also have G in the subjunctive.

Poner's imperative is also very commonly used. Remember that

187

pon

Very often, the reflexive imperative is used: "Put yourself…" As an example, "Put yourself in contact with him" is *"Ponte en* contact *con él."*

Joel isn't interested in muddy chess pieces, but something else catches his attention: Ner's son is on the rooftop, trying to perform the chess trick that the Poner store is famous for. Remember, these chess pieces can magically get stuck to chess boards if the trick is performed correctly.

imperatives, like *vete*, *ten*, and *haz*, are always stored on the moving sidewalk beside the store.

As Joel leaves Poner, a man shouts to him: "Buy my pawn! Don't buy from Ner. My pawns are cheaper, because they're pawned second-hand."

This poor fellow is putting muddy chess pieces from the back yard on the conveyor belt, hoping that this will catch people's attention so that he can sell these dirty items at discount price.

The word here is simply *pon*, and it's an order: "Put…"

For example, "Put that here" would be *"Pon eso aquí."*

Ner's son shouts the magic word, "presto!" But he does it without pronouncing his R, so it sounds like *puesto*.

This is Poner's participle. For example, "He's put it here" is *"Lo ha puesto aquí."*

puesto

Suponer

As Joel leaves Poner, he glances at the soup kitchen next door.

The funny thing about Suponer is that it's conjugated exactly the same way that Poner is. So if you can remember each conjugation of Poner, you can remember everything about Suponer.

So we won't visit Suponer. Instead, we'll quickly do a review of all the conjugations of Poner, and then we'll add "soup" at the beginning.

First, here are all the conjugations we learned from Poner. Recall each scene from Poner as you look through these.

Present tense:

pongo / supongo

pone / supone

Preterite past tense:

puse / supuse

puso / supuso

Subjunctive:

ponga / suponga

Imperative:

pon / supón

Participle:

puesto / supuesto

Since Poner and Suponer are completely identical in their conjugations, we won't even look inside Suponer. Joel never goes there, because he associates soup kitchens with poverty, which disgusts him.

In other words, we don't need ANY conjugation mnemonics for Suponer.

We also won't worry about the meanings of these Suponer conjugations. Just remember that *suponer* means "to suppose" or "to guess", as in "I'm going to guess that it tastes like orangutan soup". We'll look at real-life examples of this verb near the end of this lesson.

Haber

While we're in the neighborhood, let's visit Haber again. He has a few more conjugations that we'll find useful.

First of all, remember that today we saw this mostly-blind bear doing karate in the back yard. The subjunctive of haber is *haya* (with a silent H, stress on "AY!"). This is something a bear might scream while doing blind kicks and punches.

Mud bricks have also begun to form in the ground, some of which he's trying to split with his kicks. Remember the bricks from the muddy back yard of Poder: In Yol, when mud sits in one place for a year, it turns into bricks. The word *hubiera* is the past tense subjunctive of Haber, just as *pudiera* is the past tense subjunctive of Poder.

Hubiera is a very common word in Spanish, one of the most important words of this lesson. But for now, just say the word a couple of times (with the stressed syllable "yer"), and remember that it's underground in Haber's back yard. We'll talk about how it's used later.

To the side of the store, as always, is an air conditioning unit. The conditional of Haber is *habría*, with the stressed syllable "Ría" as always.

Before we leave Haber, let's look inside really quickly. In addition to the animal skins hanging around the store, there's a stuffed owl in the merchandise area. When it's dark, this owl spontaneously hoots loudly. Most owls in Yol say "Hoo!", but this owl doesn't pronounce the H, so it says, "Ooh!"

The word *hubo* (stress: "ooh") is the most common preterite form of Haber. You'll see how it's used very soon.

Look Down

You might have noticed by now that there's an interesting abstract connection between the businesses in this neighborhood. The preterite tense always has a strange letter U in it: *puso* in Poner, *hubo* in Haber, *pudo* in Poder.

The path between the buildings is a trench that's shaped like the letter U. This path is what ties all of these buildings together. The designer of Yol (his name is Timothy) decided that these stores belong together because of the U in their preterite tenses.

This isn't trivia. These types of connections will become more and more important throughout the rest of the book.

Before continuing with this lesson, make sure to review what we've learned by mentally exploring Saber, Poner, and Haber again. Make sure you can remember what words are in each location.

Decir

We've just explored the part of the neighborhood that has a U-shaped trench. Now let's go back to the fork in the road and explore the businesses in the neighborhood of Hacer and Querer. Here, the street is much nicer; it's paved, with clearly-painted lane markers. These are curiously shaped like a capital letter I.

At the end of this street, on the right, is Decir, home of the seer who tells fortunes based on people's words.

Today, Joel goes to Decir with his friends. He tells the pandas, "Make sure not to say ANYTHING that can be misinterpreted. Keep it simple."

Personally, Joel expects to get a good fortune reading. As they walk in, Joel shows the pandas something he's brought for luck: A playing card.

"It's the ace of spades," he tells them. "I think it means good luck."

The seer hears this and shouts excitedly, "Did you say 'spades'? I know exactly what that means! A spade is a shovel. Joel, you are destined to DIG in my back yard for a thousand years!"

She gives Joel a shovel.

Meanwhile, the pandas remember Joel's advice to say only simple things. The simplest thing they can think of is a single letter.

They start yelling the letter "D" over and over. "D! D!"

"Ahh!" says the seer. "That's one of my favorite letters! But there's one letter I like even more…"

Joel thinks for a second. Apparently D is one of her favorite letters, because that's the first letter of "Decir". The only other letter he can think of is C.

All at once, Joel and his friends say, "C?"

Sure enough, those are the seer's two favorite letters: D and C.

In this scene, Joel's word is *digo* (stress "dig"). This means "I say".

Other words are *dice*, *dicen*, and *dices*, all of which have the stress on "D".

For "we say", the word is *decimos*, with the stressed syllable "C".

Compare these words with the present tense forms of Hacer:

digo / hago

dice / hace

decimos / hacemos

Decir takes Joel and the pandas to the "red room" for the preterite tense. Here she shows them a pile of hay and a hoe.

dije

dijo

"This is the best way to dig," she tells them. "Keep saying 'D', and use the hoe in the hay."

Joel starts digging in the hay with his shovel, and the lizard is given the hoe.

Here are the most common preterite forms of Decir:

dije (pronounced "D hay"): "I said"

dijo (pronounced "D hoe"): "he said"

Following the pattern that you learned at Hacer, you should be able to extend this to the other conjugations:

dijiste (like *hiciste*): "you said"

dijeron (like *hicieron*): "they said"

dijimos (like *hicimos*): "we said"

Focus on remembering *dije* and *dijo* for now.

Next, Decir throws Joel in the back yard and tells him to "dig!"… something he's completely unwilling to do. He sees several holes in the ground, showing that many former customers previously suffered this fate.

The subjunctive of Decir is *diga* (and the related *digan*, *digas*, etc.).

diga

di

Joel would rather not dig. He finds the moving sidewalk beside the store, which is decorated with the letter D. As he climbs onto the sidewalk, he yells to his friends, "If someone tries to enslave you, just say NO!" When Joel says "say no", he uses the imperative word *di*, pronounced like "D." It means "say" as an order.

More often than *di*, Joel likes to use the imperative *dile*, which means "say to him" or "say to her". For example, to say "Tell her that I'm not doing it," Joel says ***Dile que no lo hago.***

When Joel reaches the front of the store, he considers getting vengeance on Decir, using magic. He says, "I'll say what I want to say by using my magic wand." He pulls out his wand and uses the word *diré*, which means "I will say".

You might have expected the future tense to be "deciré", which would be normal. But this future tense word is unusually shortened, just like *haré* from nearby Hacer (which would otherwise be "haceré").

Joel chickens out, because he's not sure if his own magic would measure up to the seer's experience. So instead, he takes a sneakier, more ironic route: He flies up to the roof, carrying the shovel with him. Decir's roof is made of dirt, and Joel thinks it would be funny to use the seer's weapon, a shovel, against her.

He proceeds to dig a long ditch in Decir's roof until the dirt falls down inside the building, dirtying the seer's hair. Then Joel says, "There! I've said it." Finally, he ditches his shovel by dropping it in the ditch, and he flies quickly away.

The participle uses the stressed syllable "ditch": *dicho*. So to say "I have said it," Joel says ***Lo he dicho.***

Venir

As Joel walks back from Decir, the convenience store Venir rolls up to him on the path. The owner, Near, shouts out to Joel:

"You look like you're out shopping! Would you like to buy something?"

Joel doesn't want to buy anything, and he's annoyed that Near is being pushy. But Near continues: "Do you want a wallet or a hand bag?"

"No thanks, I already have one," says Joel. He tries to fly away. "I really didn't come here to buy anything."

"What about a suitcase?"

Joel suddenly listens. The idea of a suitcase makes him think about traveling around Yol in his blue car. He has become interested. "Hmm, maybe I do want a suitcase," he says.

As he turns around, the store unexpectedly appears around him, and something very strange happens.

Joel is in an X-ray machine.

Although he's eager to grab new customers, Venir maintains high security, with a complete X-ray scan of every entering customer.

The image of Joel in the X-ray machine is grotesque, with all his veins showing, along with the handbag that he keeps under his coat.

Venir is concerned. "You seem to have a handbag where most people have a heart," he says judgmentally.

But Joel is freaked out by all the veins. "Get me out of here!" he shouts, flying out of the machine and into the store.

The word for "I come" is *vengo*, with a stress on "vein". Imagine Joel coming into the store with all his veins showing.

Inside the store, instead of a price tag, each piece of merchandise has a Yen bill on it, labeling the item according to price. No wonder the security has to be so strong here! There's money all over the place.

This "Yen" represents the words *viene*, *vienes*, and *vienen*. (Meanwhile the word for "we come" sounds a lot like Venir itself, with the stress on "knee": *venimos*.)

In a separate area are some V-shaped umbrellas. These represent the most common preterite form of the verb: *vine* is "I came" and *vino* is "he/she/it came".

The other preterite forms start similarly, with the "V" sound at the beginning, but they stress different syllables: "knee" in the case of *viniste* and *vinimos*, and "air" in the case of *vinieron*.

These should all be very familiar verb forms to you based on the neighboring shops Hacer (*hiciste*, *hicimos*, *hicieron*) and Decir (*dijiste*, *dijimos*, *dijeron*). Practice saying these various forms of these verbs out loud and notice how similar they sound.

This similarity is also reflected by the present-tense Joel version of these words: *vengo*, *digo*, and *hago*. That funny letter G appears in the back yards of all these shops as well: *venga*, *diga*, and *haga*.

Dar

Darling's gift shop is the type of place you might walk in just for the environment. Pleasant items decorate the shop, including festive lights, colorful candies, and dozens of beautifully wrapped gifts.

Although the back of the room has the most merchandise, all of which appears as gifts shaped like the letter D, most guests prefer to sit in the main parlor-like entrance space, with all the pretty lights.

Unfortunately Joel is one of the few people who don't like going to Dar very much. Darling thinks he's super cute, and every time he comes, she squeezes his cheeks, calls him a "doll" or a "toy", and ties a colorful bow around his neck.

Everyone loudly exclaims, "d'awwwwwww!" in admiration of how cute this situation is. Joel blushes. Although he appreciates the affection, he really doesn't like to be put in this situation in front of the whole shop.

Joel gives the bow back to Darling, saying "I'm giving this back, because I'm NOT a doll or a toy." But instead of "doll" or "toy", Joel uses the word *doy*, which means "I give" or "I'm giving".

Meanwhile the affectionate "d'aw!" that everyone else uses represents the words *da*, *dan*, *das*, and *damos*.

As we've seen, the presents in the back room are shaped like the letter D. The preterite forms of Dar are based on the sound "D": "I gave" is *di*, "he/she/it gave" is *dio*, "they gave" is *dieron*, "you gave" is *diste*, and "we gave" is *dimos*.

197

Regular Verbs

Although we've learned six new verbs in this lesson, we haven't had to learn a ton of conjugations. That's because of the patterns that we've come to recognize.

Grouping these verbs together makes it very easy to find conjugations. It's pretty easy to find a past-tense form of Decir (such as *dijiste*) when you know it's going to rhyme with the equivalent past-tense forms of Hacer (such as *hiciste*). And Suponer and Poner are identical in every way except for the very beginning of the word. There's no reason to learn all their conjugations separately.

Now it's time for the best news yet: The rest of the verbs that we learn in this book are regular verbs.

That means that they ALL fit into one of two groups:

- Verbs that end in "-ar"

- Verbs that end in "-er" or "-ir"

That means that instead of being grouped together in clumps of two or three (like irregular verbs), ALL of these verbs are grouped together. If we learn how to conjugate just one "-ar" verb and one "-er/-ir" verb, we'll know how to conjugate hundreds and hundreds of more verbs, because they'll all follow the same patterns.

In short, the hard work is behind us. We're almost done learning complicated verb forms. Every new verb that we learn is going to be predictable.

For this lesson, let's learn just one verb of each type.

Hablar

To get to the regular verbs, we have to venture outside of this prime real estate near Joel's house, away from this little cluster of irregular verb shops, into realms we haven't explored yet.

Going to the west (left), beyond Decir, there's a very long street with shops on both sides of it along the edge of an enormous forest. This is where all the "-ar" verbs are stored. The first and most prominent shop we encounter is the Hablar shop, nestled shadily among some very tall trees. You'll notice that the entrance to this street along the edge of the forest has a decoration with an object blowing colorful letters out of it. That's because Hablar controls the entrance to the forest. You can't enter this street along the forest without thinking about Hablar and the idea of blowing letters.

"Hablar" is the word for "speaking" or "talking". We've just seen that *decir* means "to say", which indicates

specifically what you're saying; the seer is very particular about what people say and reading meaning into everything that people tell her. But as with the English terms "to talk" or "to speak", the Spanish word *hablar* just references the fact that you are speaking or talking, not specifically what's being said.

Hablar is a shop where Lar gives speaking lessons. But unfortunately, his lessons are extremely dull. He gives very boring lectures ("blah blah blah"), and he also teaches his students to give boring speeches. By his standards, it doesn't matter what people say; as long as you're "blowing out words", you're successful. So all of Lar's students just "blow out words" like Lar does. The word *hablar* means "to speak".

You may be able to guess the present tense versions of this word: *Hablo* for Joel, *habla* for the lizard, *hablas* for the owner, *hablan* for the pandas, and *hablamos* for "we speak". The stressed syllable of most of these sounds like "ah" (the first syllable), and the secondary syllable changes.

In Joel's case, he first says "ah", and then he simply blows out words boringly like Lar does: "Aaahhh- blow". The lizard says "ah", and then he somehow manages to say "blah", which is perhaps a slight improvement on "rah", though it's still very boring.

The rest of the words simply follow the normal pattern, but note that the first person plural *hablamos* has the stress on the second syllable "blah" instead of the first syllable "ah" (as is the case with most verbs).

Now let's go to the "red" area of Hablar's shop.

There's a window here, and the leaves from the forest outside are blowing into the room and hitting the lizard's face, interfering with its ability to try speaking. Instead of talking, the lizard starts simply blowing at the leaves to try to get them back out of the place. The word for "he spoke" is *habló*.

Note that the stress is on the last syllable here, "blow". Meanwhile Joel is extremely bored of Lar's nonsense, and he's often lulled to sleep by wind blowing through leaves, so he decides to lie down and take a nap while listening to the wind blowing. Joel's word is *hablé* (with the stressed syllable "lay").

A blast of wind hits Lar, and he shouts, "ah! blast it!" His word is *hablaste*, "you spoke".

The pandas try to imitate Lar, but they simply say his name over and over: "Lar! Lar! Lar!" Their word is *hablaron*, for "they spoke".

The last and easiest word is the first person plural, because it's exactly the same as the present tense: *hablamos*.

Meanwhile, the imperfect forms of Hablar are very easy. The stressed syllable is always "blah" because that's all that Lar says as he stands behind the counter: "blah blah blah". So we have *hablaba*, *hablabas*, *hablaban*, and *hablábamos*.

Outside the front, everything is exactly as you would expect it to be. "I will speak" is *hablaré*. "He/she/it will speak" is *hablará*. "We will speak" is just like Joel's version, *hablaré*, but with "mos" at the end: *hablaremos*. And then "you will speak" and "they will speak" are just the lizard's version with the normal modifications: *hablarás* and *hablarán*.

For the subjunctive, everything is much like the the present tense, except since they're in the woods, Joel lies down to take a nap. So the stressed syllable is "ahh", but the second syllable sounds like "lay": *hable*, *hablen*, and *hables*. For the group, the stress is "lay": *hablemos*.

Meanwhile the lizard tries to take a nap on the moving sidewalk to the side, indicating that the imperative is simply the same word as the lizard's present tense conjugation: *Habla*.

The unconjugated versions are also exactly what you'd expect. *Hablando* means "talking", as in "I am talking" (*estoy hablando*). On the roof, *hablado* is the participle meaning "spoken", as in "you have spoken" (*has hablado*).

The verb Hablar stands at the forefront of the long row of hundreds of shops in the woods, to the west of the neighborhood of irregular verbs. But if we go east, to the opposite side, we find something very different.

Deber

Just to the east of the irregular verb shops, beyond Estar and Tener, is a long street that runs along the Yol beach.

Something interesting about this street is that the shops on the left side are all in the dry sand, but the verbs on the right side are so close to the ocean that they often get wet, especially when the tide rises.

One of the most prominent shops is run by a bear named Deber.

A quick note: You may have noticed that all our verbs that have the stressed syllable "ber" are all different people; we had the big blind bear for Haber, the depressed postman for Saber, and now we have a female bear for Deber. She's the sister of the other two bears.

Deber is a money lender and debt collector. The verb *deber* can literally be used to mean "to owe", but it's used a lot where English speakers would use words such as "should" or "must". Basically it's a verb that expresses strong obligation to do something.

Deber is pretty strict and going to her store is a very stressful experience. If you ever go there a second time, you can be sure that she'll harass you about any money that you owe until you pay it all back.

The conjugations of Deber are extremely easy. We don't even need mnemonics for the normal present tense, because they're so regular: *debe* for the lizard (he must), *debes* for the second person (you must), *deben* for the pandas (they must), and *debo* for Joel ("I must"). The plural first person, "we must", is *debemos*.

To explain Deber's meaning a little bit more thoroughly, here's a quick example of how it's used. As we've learned before, to say "I have to be here", we would say *tengo que estar aquí*. But to make it stronger, we'd use "I must be here": *Debo estar aquí.*

Now how about the imperfect past tense? These are even easier. They all work the same way that Tener, Querer, and Hacer did: With a stress on "ía". So we have *debía*, *debías*, *debían*, and *debíamos*.

Now let's go to the back "red" area and learn the preterite past tenses, which are generally harder to learn than other tenses. Behind Deber's desk, she hangs a few bee's stingers that used to belong to previous debtors (bees that owed her money but didn't pay it back). If anyone is slow to pay Deber her money back, she uses these stingers for 'persuasion'.

To say "I owed" or "I needed" to do something, in the preterite tense, the word is *debí*, with a stress on "bee".

All of the other persons here have the letter "I" in their preterites. The lizard is *debió*, with a stress on the lettor O at the end (kind of like in Dar with *dio* and in Hablar with *habló*). The pandas' conjugation is *debieron* (much like *fueron*). The second person is *debiste*, like *fuiste*. And the plural first person is like Joel's conjugation in that it stresses the syllable "bee": *debimos*.

In the back yard, for the subjunctive mood, everything is just like the present tense except with the second vowel changed to the letter "A": *deba*, *debas*, *deban*, and *debamos*.

Lesson 10 Application:
Idioms

THE MANY VERBS that we studied in Lesson 10 have a plethora of associated idioms. We'll dive right in and practice using them, both in their simple uses and in their individual quirky phrasing tendencies.

Haber

We learned *haya*, the subjunctive, which often replaces *hay* in situations that normally take a subjunctive.

There isn't space.	*No hay lugar.*
Perhaps there's space.	*Tal vez haya lugar.*
I want that there be space.	*Quiero que haya lugar.*

The past tense subjunctive of Haber (underground in the back) is *hubiera*. As you can see, this word looks a lot like *pudiera* and other past tense subjunctives (*fuera*, *hiciera*, etc.).

Just like *fuera*, *hubiera* is used very often to indicate hypothetical situations. Consider these examples:

| If he were nice, he wouldn't go there. | *Si él fuera bueno, no iría ahí.* |
| If he had been nice, he wouldn't have gone there. | *Si él hubiera sido bueno, no habría ido ahí.* |

In the first case, we're using the present tense, but the past tense subjunctive *fuera* indicates something hypothetical ("if he were nice").

In the second case, we put that whole thing in the past. This is the most common use of *hubiera*.

This is actually pretty handy: You can use *hubiera* along with any participle to put any verb in the hypothetical mood. For example:

If she had been here…	*Si hubiera estado aquí…*
If she had had that…	*Si hubiera tenido eso…*
If she had gone there…	*Si hubiera ido ahí…*
If she had done this…	*Si hubiera hecho esto…*

You might find this easier than coming up with the past tense subjunctive of each of those verbs. Just use *hubiera* and then the participle. Here's a good example of both the past tense subjunctive (*hubieras*) and the conditional (*habría*).

| If you had wanted to do something bad, you already would have done it. | *Si hubieras querido hacer algo malo, ya lo habrías hecho.* |
| If he had wanted to do that, he already would have done it. | *Si hubiera querido hacer eso, ya lo habría hecho.* |

The idiom *una vez que* is used to mean "once this happens" or "once that happens". It is almost always followed by a subjunctive, because it indicates the future. Here's a simple example:

| Once she be here, we're going to do it. | *Una vez que ella esté aquí, lo vamos a hacer.* |
| Once they do it, we're going to leave. | *Una vez que lo hagan, nos vamos a ir.* |

To make a more complicated sentence structure, we can change that subjunctive verb to *haya* followed by a participle, meaning that something <u>will have happened</u>.

| Once the man has gone… | *Una vez que el hombre haya ido…* |

That is pretty advanced… We're talking about the hypothetical past of the future!

Look around the room that you're sitting in. Do you see brain matter on the walls and ceiling? No? Good, then your brain hasn't exploded yet. So let's just look at one more Haber example, this one using *hubo* for existence.

| But he couldn't, because there was a problem. | *Pero no pudo, porque hubo un problema.* |
| But I could, because there was no problem. | *Pero pude, porque no hubo ningún problema.* |

Saber

Let's start with several standard, simple uses of Saber:

I don't know why I called him.	*No sé por qué lo* I called.
They don't know why I called them.	*No saben por qué los* I called.

And how do YOU know that?	*¿Y cómo sabes eso tú?*
And how does she know my name?	*¿Y cómo sabe mi nombre ella?*

She always knows it all.	*Siempre lo sabe todo.*
Meanwhile they know it all.	*Mientras lo saben todo.*
Now we know it all.	*Ya lo sabemos todo.*

We knew that this would suffice.	*Sabíamos que esto* would suffice.
The knight knew that a war would suffice.	*El* knight *sabía que una* war would suffice.
The people knew that a good reason would suffice.	*La gente sabía que una buena razón* would suffice.

The preterite of Saber (*supe, supo*, etc.) is less common than the general imperfect past tense (*sabía*, etc.). But when someone suddenly knows something, as an event, the preterite can be used. It is basically a synonym for "realizing" something.

And how did the boy know that?	*¿Y cómo supo eso el* boy?
And how did the girl know this?	*¿Y cómo supo esto la* girl?
In this way I came to know that.	*Así yo supe eso.*

207

Venir

I come from another world.	*Vengo de otro mundo.*
She comes from another house.	*Viene de otra casa.*
We come from many places.	*Venimos de muchos lugares.*

Venir's imperative is very frequently used: *¡ven!* It simply means "come!" or "come on!"

All right, come on!	*Bueno, ¡ven!*
All right, come(plural)!	*Bueno, ¡vengan!*

I came to search for my friend.	*Vine* to search for *mi amigo.*
She came to search for her friends.	*Vino* to search for *sus amigos.*
Did you come to search for our friend?	*¿Viniste* to search for *nuestro amigo?*

How nice that you're coming with me!	*¡Qué bueno que vengas conmigo!*
How nice that you all are coming with me!	*¡Qué bueno que vengan conmigo!*

Poner and Suponer

Supongo is used to mean "I guess…" or "I suppose…"

I suppose so.	*Supongo que sí.*
I suppose that they're around.	*Supongo que están por ahí.*
I guess that he went there just afterwards.	*Supongo que fue ahí justo después.*

The other forms of Suponer are actually pretty rare, except that the participle, *supuesto*, is used in a common idiom. The phrase *por supuesto*, literally "by supposed" or "by supposition", is often used to say "of course!"

Of course!	*¡Por supuesto!*

Meanwhile, Poner is used in many idioms to mean some pretty strange things.

As one example, if you want to "set" one person "against" another person, making them enemies of each other, you might *poner* them *en su contra*, literally "put them in their against".

He was able to set them against him.	*Los pudo poner en su contra.*
He was able to set her against me.	*La pudo poner en mi contra.*

When Poner is used reflexively, which is very common, it can mean several things. One easy way to think of it is that Ponerse refers to "getting" a certain way.

For example, you might "get" yourself to a place or attitude:

Get over here.	*Ponte aquí.*
They got over here.	*Se pusieron aquí.*
We got happy.	*Nos pusimos felices.*

Or you might "get thinking", or "put yourself to thinking", as they say in Spanish:

He set himself to think.	*Se puso a* think.
I'm getting thinking.	*Me pongo a* think.
We have started thinking.	*Nos hemos puesto a* think.

Dar

Dar often uses both an indirect object and a direct object. Imagine that you're giving a gift to a friend. The gifted item itself is the direct object, and the person who receives it is the indirect object.

And I can give you money.	*Y te puedo dar dinero.*
And they can give us those things.	*Y nos pueden dar esas cosas.*
And it might give him certain problems.	*Y le puede dar ciertos problemas.*

Someone's going to have to give me something.	*Alguien va a tener que darme algo.*
The children are going to have to give us something.	*Los hijos van a tener que darnos algo.*

Stop, I already gave you enough reasons.	*Basta, ya te di suficientes razones.*
All right, they already gave me a thousand ideas.	*Bueno, ya me dieron mil ideas.*

Excuse me, have you(formal) already given me the money?	*Perdón, ¿ya me dio el dinero?*

Here's an imperative use. The imperative of Dar is simply the lizard conjugation, *da* (as is the case with most verbs, actually). Now, this can be combined with an indirect object to indicate to whom something is given; *dame algo* is "give me something" and *danos algo* is "give us something".

Give me something and I'll read it.	*Dame algo y lo* I'll read.
Give her something and she'll read it.	*Dale algo y lo* she'll read.
Give us some things and we'll read them.	*Danos algunas cosas y las* we'll read.

Dar is used in some idioms. One of the most common is *me da lo mismo*, which literally means "it gives me the same". Spanish speakers use this to say "I don't care; it's all the same to me".

Another way to say this is *me da igual*, literally "it gives me equally".

I don't know, it's all the same to me.	*No sé, me da igual.*
I don't know, I don't really care.	*No sé, me da lo mismo.*

Decir

Decir is a funny verb. Like Dar, it generally takes both indirect and direct objects. The thing that you say is considered a direct object, and the person that you're telling it to is an indirect object.

However, one or the other is often omitted. In our first example, the person, *le*, is used in the infinitive *decirle* ("telling her"). But the thing that's being told is being implied; the direct object is not stated in this sentence.

He wouldn't go there, to her house without telling her.	*No iría ahí, a su casa sin decirle.*
He wouldn't go there, toward that place without telling you.	*No iría allí, hacia ese lugar sin decirte.*
He would almost do that, during the night without telling me.	*Casi haría eso, durante la noche sin decirme.*

In this next example, the direct object is stated as a *que* phrase rather than a noun. The indirect object, *le*, is the person being told something, and the thing that's being said is "that I'm sorry".

I have to tell him that I'm sorry.	*Le tengo que decir que* I'm sorry.
We have to tell them the truth.	*Les tenemos que decir la verdad.*
He has to tell me that he loves me.	*Me tiene que decir que me quiere.*

Here's a similar sentence with both an indirect object and a direct object, the latter as a *que* phrase. But one of the variations uses *la verdad* instead of the *que* phrase, demonstrating that the direct object can simply be a noun if it makes sense in context.

He told me that he didn't want to see me again.	*Él me dijo que no me quería* to see again.
She told us that she didn't want to see us again.	*Ella nos dijo que no nos quería* to see again.
They told him the truth.	*Ellos le dijeron la verdad.*
We told them that we loved them.	*Nosotros les dijimos que los queríamos.*

Here are some simple uses of Decir conjugations, now with direct objects but without stating the indirect objects:

The man isn't saying it.	*El hombre no lo dice.*
I'm not saying it yet.	*No lo digo aún.*
My friends aren't saying it.	*Mis amigos no lo dicen.*

In the next example, the indirect object happens first, and then the direct object is an entire quote instead of a noun or a *que* phrase.

I told him, "I'll help you."	*Le dije, "Te* I'll help."
She'll tell him, "I'll help them."	*Le dirá, "Los* I'll help."
They told me, "He'll help her."	*Me dijeron, "La* he'll help."

She had already told him that soon she would have to leave.	*Ya le había dicho que pronto tendría que irse.*
He had already told her that he would first have to leave.	*Ya le había dicho que primero tendría que irse.*
I had already told you that I would never, ever have to leave.	*Ya te había dicho que nunca jamás tendría que irme.*

Decir's imperative, *di*, almost always gets an indirect object appended to the end.

OK, tell me, what do you want?	*Bueno, dime, ¿qué quieres?*
OK, tell us, what do you all want?	*Bueno, dinos, ¿qué quieren?*
OK, tell her, where does she have to go?	*Bueno, dile, ¿adónde tiene que ir?*

What else do you want that I tell you?	*¿Qué más quieres que te diga?*
What else do you(plural) want them to tell you?	*¿Qué más quieren que les digan?*
What else do you(formal) want that we tell you?	*¿Qué más quiere que le digamos?*

This next example involves the idiom *hay quien*. When Spanish speakers say *hay quien*, it means "there are those who". (The literal translation is "there are who".)

This phrase is followed by a singular verb (a "lizard" conjugation). For example, "There are those who have a lot of money" would be *hay quien tiene mucho dinero* (literally "there are who has much money").

There are those who say that nobody is there.	*Hay quien dice que nadie está ahí.*
There are those who say that they don't ever come back.	*Hay quien dice que no* they come back *nunca.*

Hablar

Hablar is most commonly followed by *de* [a topic] or *con* [a person]. For example, "we're talking about that" is *hablamos de eso*. "We're talking with our parents" is *hablamos con nuestros padres*.

Today I talked with Miguel.	*Hoy hablé con Miguel.*
Meanwhile they talked with Isabella.	*Mientras hablaron con Isabella.*
Still, he talked with me.	*Igual, habló conmigo.*

Sometimes Hablar is followed by *sobre* instead of *de*, though it's not as common.

They were talking about that from the morning to the night.	*Hablaban sobre eso desde la mañana hasta la noche.*
He was talking about me from the afternoon to the night.	*Hablaba de mi desde la tarde hasta la noche.*
She was talking about him all day.	*Hablaba sobre él todo el día.*
We were talking about her at home.	*Hablabamos de ella en casa.*

As you can see, "she spoke about him" would be translated as *habló de él*. But if "she spoke about how she loved him", we're basically joining two sentences together: "she spoke" and "she loved him". In these cases, we always need a conjunction. This is why it's very common to use *de que* after Hablar; roughly, *hablar de que* means "talk about how".

She talked about how she loved him a lot.	*Habló de que lo quería mucho.*
You talked about how you loved her only a little bit.	*Hablaste de que la querías muy poco.*
We talked about how we loved them so much that we would do it.	*Hablamos de que las queríamos tanto que lo haríamos.*

Remember that to use a negative imperative, such as "don't talk to him", you don't use any actual imperative form; instead, you use *no* followed by a subjunctive.

Don't talk to me.	*No me hables.*
Don't talk to me (all of you).	*No me hablen.*
Don't talk to him yet.	*No le hables aún.*

Deber

We generally think of Deber as being equivalent to "must", indicating a very strong sense of obgligation.

He must find the money.	*Debe* to find *el dinero.*
I must go to a different place.	*Debo ir a otro lugar.*
We must have the biggest house of all.	*Debemos tener la mayor casa de todas.*

But what if instead of saying "he must do this", we wanted to say something slightly softer, like "he should do this"?

In these cases, we still use Deber, but we normally use the conditional version of the word: *Debería hacer esto.*

You should come in because I love you.	*Deberías* come in *porque te quiero.*
You shouldn't come in like that because it's scary.	*No deberías* come in *así porque* it's scary.
They should do that somewhere else.	*Deberían hacer eso en otra parte.*
He shouldn't do this if she's here.	*No debería hacer esto si ella está aquí.*

Dialogue Assignment

In Lessons 10-12, we're going to focus on a new dialogue. It's between Nicolás, who is reading a book, and his sister Lucía, who wants him to come and play with her.

Of course, you should also continue to study the Sofía/Laura dialogue, which you'll find in full at the end of the book. But for now, let's hear about this dialogue.

Nicolás is reading a book about kid who, himself, is reading several different short stories. The kid in the book can actually physically enter these stories that he reads, which is why Nicolás likes this book so much. Nicolás is describing this to Lucía.

Right now, let's study the part of the dialogue where Nicolás is describing the second "story" that the kid enters. The kid steps into a story about an absent-minded police officer. As Nicolás is about to describe, this officer is trying to solve a mystery that only the kid can help him solve.

The Kid Who Enters Stories

Nicolás – Well, in the second part he's in a story where a policeman is worried because he has to find a very important man's money and it's very hard because he only has seven hours to do it.

Nicolás - *Pues, en la segunda parte está en una* story *donde un* policeman *está* worried *porque debe* to find *el dinero de un hombre muy importante y es muy difícil porque sólo tiene siete horas para hacerlo.*

Lucía – Why does he have so little time?

Lucía - *¿Por qué tiene tan poco tiempo?*

Nicolás – It happens that it was six days that he was working on that case, and the man, who had a lot of power, had told him that if he didn't find it in a week, he could forget about his job.

Nicolás - It happens *que hacía seis días que estaba* working *en ese* case, *y el hombre, que tenía mucho* power, *le había dicho que si no lo* he found *en una semana* he could forget *de su trabajo.*

Lucía – And did he like his job a lot?

Lucía - *¿Y le* was pleasing *mucho su trabajo?*

Nicolás – Tons. The story says that since they were boys he and his brother wanted to be policemen. They would talk about that from morning until night, every day. Though his brother became a doctor, he did what he always had wanted.

Actually, he didn't know what to do if he were to have to quite his job. And he was one of those people that until they do things they can't think about other things. And, as such, he almost goes crazy.

So, when he got there, the boy asked the policeman if he had already gone back over his steps in order to see if he had forgotten about something. At first it seemed not so to the policeman. But when he got thinking, he realized that something very important had happened to him.

What happened was that he found the money behind the house of the guy! Of the same one that was telling him that if he didn't find it he would end up without a job! In the end the boy was right; the policeman had been at man's house many times and hadn't seen the most important thing.

The guy wanted to do something mean to him because when they were boys they had had a problem and, as he was a little crazy, he hadn't been able to forget it.

Nicolás - *Mucho, la* story tells *que desde que eran* children *él y su* brother *querían ser* policemen. *Hablaban sobre eso desde la mañana hasta la noche, todos los días. Aunque su* brother *se hizo doctor él hizo lo que siempre había querido.*

En verdad, no sabría qué hacer si tuviera que give up *su trabajo. Y era de* those people *que hasta que no hacen las cosas no pueden* to think *en otras. Y, como tal, casi* he goes *loco.*

Entonces, cuando he arrived, *el* boy *le* asked *al* policeman *si ya había* gone back *sobre sus steps para* to see *si* he had forgotten *algo. Al* policeman *primero le* it seemed *que no. Pero cuando se puso a* to think he realized *que le* had happened *algo muy importante.*

¡Lo que happened *fue que* he found *el dinero atrás de la casa del tipo! ¡Del mismo que le decía que si no lo* he found, he would end up *sin trabajo!* In the end *el* boy *tenía razón, el* policeman *había estado en la casa del hombre muchas veces y no había* seen *lo más importante.*

El tipo quería hacerle algo malo porque cuando eran children *habían tenido un problema y, como estaba un poco loco, no lo había podido* to forget.

LESSON 11

Practice Right

You'll never grow out of imitating native Spanish speakers.

We've spent the last few lessons expanding our freedom of Spanish expression. But let's not get carried away. We want to sound more and more like native speakers, so we need to keep sticking closely to the exact way that they form sentences.

Let's build good study habits that balance speaking, listening, reading, and writing, all while focused on solid, native-created materials.

Lesson 11 Theory:

Don't Practice Wrong

"It is easier to prevent bad habits than to break them."
- Benjamin Franklin

HAVE YOU ever had a nightmare about embarrassing yourself on stage?

Imagine that you're trying to learn a song to perform in concert, accompanied by a large orchestra. The song is in Hungarian, a language that you don't know, but you spend three weeks preparing it in the privacy of your home.

One week before the big day, you get together with the orchestra to have a rehearsal together. After a few successful run-throughs, the conductor dismisses the instrumentalists, but then he calls you over for a private conversation:

"I think you're getting this one line wrong."

"Oh! Am I misreading the notes?"

"No, the notes are right, but the correct meaning is 'I wish I knew the way'. You've switched the syllables around. What you've been singing means 'my hovercraft is full of eels', which I don't think the Hungarians in the audience will appreciate."

How embarrassing. You've spent three weeks training yourself to sing the lines incorrectly!

You still have a whole week before the concert, but unfortunately, it's going to be very difficult for you. It's practically impossible to un-train a habit. Even if you try to practice it correctly all week, the concert might not go as planned. In the pressure of live performance, your brain is likely to glide along the smoother track that you've been training for much longer.

The Tragedy of Practicing Wrong

In good accelerated learning, you're making mistakes AND learning from them. Any time you make an error, you should recognize what you did wrong and then immediately re-do it correctly.

When this is the goal, every time you make a mistake and then correct it, you are more likely never to make that mistake again.

But note that this assumes that all your mistakes are being corrected so that you are improving from them.

Unfortunately, most people who practice a language make errors that pull them down rather than lifting them up. The more often you make a mistake WITHOUT correcting it, the more often you'll make that same mistake. Then it will become a habit.

Let's use an example that may be relatable:

Have you ever tried to imitate someone else's handwriting?

I grew up with several brothers and sisters, but we all knew each other's writing. I used to play games where I would write messages and try to disguise whom it was from.

Eventually I learned that I couldn't do it. I found it impossible to imitate someone else's style effectively. I might try for hours to pass off a paragraph as if it were written by my sister, but nobody was ever convinced. My own handwriting always showed through.

Why is it so hard to change your handwriting?

The answer is simple: Strongly engrained habits.

If you're like me, you've been writing for most of your life, almost as long as you've been speaking. Every single time you make a stroke with a pen, you're reinforcing your own style. You're building on muscle memory you've been practicing your whole life, and that muscle memory is extremely difficult to retrain. It can take hours of practice just to change the way you write a capital letter P so that it's not obvious that your own hand did it.

Language is very similar. You've been saying certain things the same way your whole life, without even thinking about it. Those habits are engrained, as if in your muscle memory, and they're very difficult to change.

The more you say things like "I did it" and "we're getting there", the more they become a natural part of you. Native English speakers say these phrases all the time, and they can say them in their sleep.

Now, what do you say in Spanish all the time?

What are the phrases that are becoming so natural that you can say them in your sleep? And are you absolutely sure that they're correct?

Or is there a chance that you are training errors into your speech?

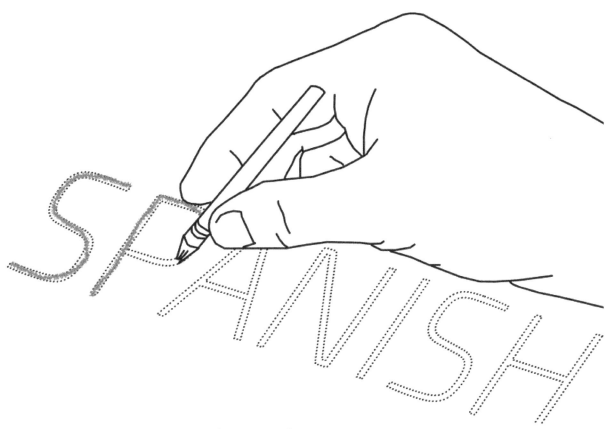

Imagine that a friend of yours is learning English. You've invited her to stay in your home for a few days while she practices with you. She appreciates your patience in listening attentively and helping correct her errors and lack of clarity.

But you can tell that she has some very bad English habits. It's hard to convince her to change her wording on certain idioms. In fact, while she is in bed one night, you hear her muttering in her sleep phrases like "oh no, I have did the mistake again" and "I am here since three days".

These errors are marks of a non-native speaker. They can be endearing at times, but they often make it hard to communicate. If you want to work toward sounding like a native Spanish speaker, you need to avoid the pitfall of making errors into habits.

Bad habits don't die easily. Once you start speaking or writing a certain way, it's almost impossible to change.

For example, many beginning students confuse the verbs Ser and Estar, and they end up frequently using erroneous phrases such as *"es aquí"* instead of *"está aquí"*. The problem escalates: If you say *"es aquí"* enough times, it will become automatic so that you're not even thinking about that phrase.

Later, when you're taught that this is wrong (a native speaker might have trouble understanding the phrase), you'll want to try to correct yourself.

But it will be very difficult. Since you've been saying this erroneous phrase by default, without thinking about it, you won't even be able to identify your error when you make it unless you start forcing yourself to slow down and check every single thing you say.

That's why I don't let my students speak bad Spanish when they're starting out. Practicing errors (without immediately correcting them) is a tragic mistake that's very difficult to reverse.

Fortunately, you can prevent these mistakes through an accelerated learning tactic that you've already been practicing: The tactic of learning phrases as chunks.

Language Chunks

One of humans' essential learning tools is "chunking".

As described by Daniel Coyle in The Talent Code, all training involves turning tiny elements into larger "chunks" of information. The brain quickly learns to process these chunks not as strings of little pieces, but a as single unit.

In language learning, it works like this:

(1) We learn to put letters together into words, such as **estoy** and **verdad**. Eventually, instead of seeing individual letters (e-s-t-o-y), you can glance at the word, and you

recognize it as a single entity.

(2) We learn to put words together into phrases, such as **ya no lo son** and **¿por donde estás?** Eventually, with a lot of language training, you can hear most phrases in the language and recognize them (instead of having to piece together the meaning word by word).

Children raised in Spanish-speaking homes have spent their entire lives "chunking" phrases together. They've heard hundreds of thousands of sentences in their native tongue, and the core sentence structures and phrasings are now so second-nature that they flow out of them even in their sleep, with no phrasing errors.

"Yo lo soy."

But if you've been practicing wrong, it's like learning a Hungarian song with the wrong words. You're likely to keep singing your errors by habit.

That's why it's important to get those things right from day 1. Once you're saying the core language essentials perfectly, without thinking about them, you can spend your conscious thinking on other nuances of your speech.

Too many students are convinced that that they have to speak Spanish as much as possible from the very beginning, even if it means making mistakes at first.

This is a very dangereous route.

Sure, it's important to speak as soon as possible, but you want to make sure you're doing it right. How hard is it to make a habit of saying *"dónde está"* from the very beginning?

But if you start off saying *"dónde es"*, un-learning that mistake will be harder (and much more frustrating) than simply learning it correctly in the first place.

"Wait," you might be saying. "Are you saying that we can't make any mistakes at all? How are we supposed to learn anything if we're in constant fear of making mistakes?"

Well that's not quite my point. There are some mistakes that are fine to make. Even native-speaking children make mistakes that are easily corrected later. We don't always correct a 3-year-old's grammar when she says "I didn't found it"; she'll learn this later on. That's not a grave error; it's the type of mistake that native speakers themselves often make, and those are permissible when you're starting to learn a language.

But there are some errors that native speakers would never make. For example, native English speakers never confuse the verbs "to make" and "to do", even as young children (we never accidentally say "I did a mistake" or "I'm making my exercise"). However, most Spanish speakers who are learning English end up getting mixed up on those verbs all the time.

It's similar when you're learning Spanish. Native speakers never confuse ser and estar. Never ever. Not even three-year-olds.

But many students make these mistakes simply because they have fallen into a common trap: The arbitrary rule of "speaking in Spanish at all costs". They are more interested in hearing their own voices saying Spanish words than in spending a little time making sure those words are correct.

Luckily, there's a very easy way to make a good habit of speaking correctly: The rule of imitation.

When you mimick things that native speakers say, you can be confident that you're not training yourself in rookie errors.

So to get Spanish truly into your voice, you need to say perfect Spanish sentences aloud, as much as possible.

Emphasize the Dialogues

For some reason, many Spanish students don't understand the value of speaking from scripts. They use most of their study time on vocabulary and writing, but they skim over or completely ignore the limited-vocabualry dialogues.

If you want to speak fluently, you HAVE to keep imitating native speakers. Don't just imitate words. Imitate entire sentences.

We require our students to memorize both of the dialogues that you find at the end of this book. This amounts to about 15 minutes of scripted Spanish dialogue, which is a lot! But it's because dialogue memorization is one of the most effective tools we've implemented.

Memorizing these scripts ensures that you're constantly reviewing all the essential vocabulary and grammar of the Spanish language, very succinctly, all at once. You don't have to review this entire book. Just go through a couple of entertaining conversations.

Besides, saying these dialogues over and over, in entire phrases, will make your speech smoother and smoother. You'll quickly become comfortable delivering a wide variety of entire sentences, using all your essential words and idioms.

These two dialogues give you all the essential phrases and sentence structures in Spanish, with confidence that you're training your brain in the right way. Once these patterns are automatic, entire phras-

es will be automatic "chunks" to your brain. In other words, you'll be able to rattle off entire Spanish phrases almost without thinking.

That's an exponential increase in skill! All from just practicing speaking the essential phrases, over and over.

Not only that, but these sentences teach you abstract expression, which is much more valuable than simple label vocabulary. You'll be able to express complex things even without thousands of words, and you'll know that you're doing it correctly, with confidence.

Later, when you learn more vocabulary, you'll be able to use it very easily, because you're already speaking all kinds of Spanish sentences fluently.

Lesson 11 Vocabulary:

Nouns!

W E'RE GOING TO go through Joel's house, one room at a time, filling them with over 100 nouns. Let's dive straight in, starting with his hall (pictured on the next page).

Physical Nouns

Hanging from Joel's ceiling, we find the most common <u>substances</u> he talks about: Water, light, and fire.

On the left side, the chandelier gives light via some very loose light bulbs, and Joel's word for light is *luz*. Meanwhile, just in case the light bulbs get too hot, this chandelier is created with several built-in water taps, sort of like fire protection sprinklers, occasionally spraying out a blue-green watery substance that Joel calls "aqua" or *agua*.

On the right, a wig is dangling down and producing flames and smoke. Joel's word for "fire" is *fuego* (stress on "wig").

Behind the stairs, Joel keeps pictures of animals. In particular, on the right he has a pear-shaped picture of a dog, which he calls a *perro*.

In front of the stairs, Joel has a table where he keep all the foods that can't be found in the kitchen, mostly for daytime snacks. On the left above the table, he has posted a sign that says "Come eat!". His word for food is *comida*.

Along the right edge of this table, Joel has wrapped some small cans of food in Yen bills. His word for "goods", meaning things that you own or sell (such as "canned goods"), is *bienes*. ("A good" is *un bien*.) Admittedly, this may seem a bit weird since his adverb for "well" is *bien* but his adjective for "good" is *bueno*. And yet *bien* is the noun.

Further back to the left is the door to the kitchen. But this "door" is made of cloth; it's basically a curtain. When Joel is bored, sometimes he likes to wrap himself in this door and say,

"Look! I'm wearing the door!" For this reason, his word for "door" has the stressed syllable "wear": *puerta*.

Among the pink coasters on the left side of the floor, one item stands out: A tiny piece of furniture shaped like a comma. Sometimes Joel is too tired to fly or even to crawl upstairs, so he rests on this tiny comma-shaped bed for the night. His word for "bed" is *cama*.

Upstairs, on the balcony, Joel has a suit of armor that holds a weapon. The weapon is difficult to identify, though it is shaped kind of like a human arm. Joel's word for "weapon" is *arma*.

The window on the right side of the room shows the weather outside. But it's a special window that exaggerates the weather depending on the time of day. For example, as the sun comes up on a clear day, the window displays a calm, smooth scene. But if there's any rain at all, the window turns into a violent display of shapes and colors as the day goes on; it looks scariest at sunset during a storm.

Joel's word for "weather" is *tiempo*. This is a bit odd, as we think of *tiempo* as "time". But out here in the hall it has a different meaning. For example, "good weather" is *buen tiempo*.

In front of the window, falling from the *dinero* bag, is a shower of US dollars. Joel is disappointed: "I wanted Yen, not dollars!" His word for "dollars" is *dólares*.

Below these dollars, on the table, is Joel's telephone. This telephone's receptor is made from a leaf. Joel feels a little uncomfortable whenever he speaks on the phone, because his mustache brushes against the leaf and it tickles him. His word for "telephone" is *teléfono*, with the stress on the syllable "lef".

On the same table is a drill. When Joel bought this drill, the first thing he did was go home and stick it through the table. Although it got stuck and he was never able to get the drill out of the table again, Joel was impressed that it had the ability to put holes in things so easily. Joel declared, "That's a keeper!" His word for "equipment" is *equipo*, pronounced "eh-KEEP-o".

On the floor in the walkway is a toy car. This car is much smaller than the "real" cars that he keeps outside, but he likes to drive around the house in it once in a while. Since it's a remote control car, he also likes to surprise his guests with it. He can even program it to drive at them automatically when they first open the door, just to startle them. His word for "car" is *auto*.

Family Room

Joel's uncle has made an appearance. Joel has always liked his uncle, because he always makes him happy by bringing him tea. Joel calls his uncle his *tío*.

Actually, Joel occasionally calls other people tío in a casual way, using it kind of like the word tipo. (This use of *tío* is common in Spain.)

Let's also look at the relationships between some of these people.

We've already talked about the parent-child relationships here: Parents are *padres* or *papás*, and children are *hijos*.

Those are vertical relationships. But what about the horizontal relationships, such as between parent and parent or between brother and sister?

First of all, notice how Joel's parents look into each other's eyes lovingly. This "spouse" relationship gives us the words *esposa* and *esposo*, which mean "wife" and "husband".

But the horizontal relationship between Joel and his sister is not so positive. In Joel's world, siblings fight constantly, and they basically need a referee to keep them from killing each other. A man stands between them, holding up his hands. Because this <u>man</u> represents the relationship between Joel and his sister, Joel's word for "sister" is *hermana,* and his word for "brother" is *hermano* (stress on "man" in both cases).

Stage

On the window above the stage we find an interesting tracing of a human. When the sun hits this "person", it glows yellow. This represents Joel's general word for "person", which is *persona* (stress on "son").

Notice that this tracing is only on the left side of the window. Strangely, the word for "person" is always feminine, no matter whether the person is male or female. So "a person" is always *una persona*. This word is also commonly plural: "Several people" is *algunas personas*.

On the right side of the window, Joel represents the only two alternatives that he knows to "persons", besides animals: Spirits.

One is a "devil". It has horns and amazing abs, because Joel imagines that a devil must be strong. His word for this is *diablo*, with a stress on "ab".

In addition to that, we have a group of circles, like the letter O drawn several times. Joel can't imagine what a god looks like, so he simply represents it with "O"s. His word for "god" or "God" is *dios*.

The walls on either side of the stage store pictures of groups of people. We've already learned *la gente* to mean "the people". Some other groups might be "the family", "the class", "the police", and "the team".

On the left side, Joel has posted pictures of the categories of people that he might recruit as actors.

One category is family. He has a picture of a happy family sitting down and eating a meal. For him, the concept of "family" is basically equivalent to a bunch of people eating a meal together, so this is how he always represents it. Consequently, his word for "family" is *familia*, with a stress on "meal".

Another category is "class". We simply have a picture of students sitting in a classroom, and the word for "class" is *clase*.

A final category is "police". Joel displays a group of policemen, all blindfolded so that they can't see what they're doing. "The police", as a group, is *la policia* (stress on "see").

On the right side, Joel advertises two very dark plays that he wants to put on.

One is called "The Team". In this, a band of men with electric drills run around terrorizing people. This represents the word *equipo*, which looks and sounds like the word that we learned in Joel's hall, but when it's used to refer to a group of people, it means "team".

Finally, below the *equipo* poster is a picture of a bunch of people about to be hit by a wave. Joel is imagining an upcoming play where this group of people, basically an enormous family, is suddenly eliminated by a tsunami. This represents the word *pueblo*. (The word is pronounced PWEB-lo, but remember that Joel's B and V sound identical, so the stressed syllable sounds like "wave".)

Pueblo essentially means "people", but in a different sense from *gente*; whereas *gente* generally refers to any group of people, *pueblo* tends to refer to a people group, such as all the people of a nation.

Now let's go to the stage itself, where we see many new actors in Joel's current play.

Opposite the *señor* and his mansion is a similar mansion. This one is where the formal, wealthy women live. There are two of them: An older *señora* and a younger *señorita*.

In general, señora means "Mrs." and señorita means "miss". But just like señor, these words tend to indicate dignity or status; for example, sometimes parents may tell their daughter to behave like a señorita ("act like a young lady!").

Between these two ends of the stage, Joel has positioned a long line of kids.

Almost all of the younger people are in chicken costumes. This represents the word *chico*, which means "kid" or "child". This word has some variations: *chicos* means "boys" and *chicas* means "girls". This word can refer to boys and girls of all ages, or sometimes *chicos* simply means "guys", as a very informal word for any group of people.

However, the children are behaving differently based on their ages. The youngest kids have fallen on their knees and torn their costumes, hurting themselves. Since all the young kids have a way of hurting their knees, Joel calls them *niños* (or *niñas*).

Meanwhile, the older, teenage *chicos* are dancing and singing "chacha! chacha!" Joel finds this very annoying, and he tends to dislike teenagers in general, so they don't usually make it into his plays. He calls a

teenager a *muchacho* or a *muchacha* (stress on "chacho" and "chacha").

The only person who's not in a chicken costume is the baby. Joel has basically no experience with babies, except that he has seen moms (*mamás*) and dads (*papás*) holding them. Since he pronounces his words *mamá* and *papá* with a stress on the final syllable, he does the same with his word for baby: *bebé*.

Meanwhile, the village idiot in the play is standing behind this line. His main role is to say "yo, yo, yo" over and over as he tries to hit a fly on his forehead. Joel's word for "idiot" is *idiota* (stress on "yo").

At the end of the *señor* porch, we find several professions that Joel finds interesting.

Joel has organized these people by his concept of importance. On the top are what Joel considers royalty: A king

234

and a president. Lower down are a "master" and a "boss".

At the top, a ray of light is shining on the king, so Joel's word for "king" is *rey*. The president sits next to him sadly, feeling silly because he's wearing a wig with a huge dent in it. The word for "president" is *presidente* (stress on "dent").

The "master" sits awkwardly, trying to speak to the people below them, but all that comes out is "um… um…" Joel's word for "master" is *amo*.

Lower down, the "boss" is a chief who wears feathers on his head and gives orders grumpily. Joel calls this man "Chief Head Feathers", or *jefe* for short (sounds like the beginnings of the words "head feathers"). The word *jefe* means "boss" or "chief".

Each of these rulers has a person serving beneath them.

The *jefe* is trying to give orders to a doctor, but the doctor is messing up. He's trying to heal a teddy bear, but instead he's accidentally torn the toy. Feathers fly everywhere (in Yol, teddy bears are stuffed with feathers). Joel's word for "doctor" is *doctor* (stress on "tore").

Meanwhile the *amo*, saying "um…", is trying to give directions to a captain, but the captain is not listening. This captain is enormous, and the *amo* feels helpless to give him any orders, because he seems very powerful. Besides, he weighs so much that he is breaking the stage. This captain must weigh a ton. Joel's word for "captain" is *capitán* (stress on the last syllable, which sounds a little like "ton").

Part of the reason that the *presidente* is sad is because someone has blindfolded the police officer that he's in charge of. The *presidente* doesn't know what to do about it. Joel's word for "policeman" is *policía*, with a stress on "see" because the policeman can't see (like the ones in the poster).

Below the king, with the light shining on him, is a "knight". This knight has been preparing for this position for a long time: He's been basking in the presence of the king for an entire year, and now that the year is over, he's officially a knight. (Apparently that's how it works in this imaginary world.) Joel's word for "knight" is *caballero*, with a stress on the syllable that sounds like "year", because of this "year" of standing in the king's light.

Note that the word *caballero* is common because it means not only "knight", but also "gentleman" in some cases.

Before we move on, I recommend immersing yourself in this scene to make sure you can remember all the words. Imagine that you're really there, feeling the shape of the president's dented wig and the texture of the policeman's blindfold. Pace between the steps of the *señora* and the *señor*, high-fiving all the *chicos* along the way, meanwhile avoiding bumping into the *hombre*'s mule.

Having Feels for Dinner

Although Joel eats casually throughout the day, he has some interesting superstitions about dinner in particular. He always has dinner in the dining room, and this room is almost a sacred place for Joel. Everything must be done with extreme care and perfect ritual.

As you can see, Joel sits at the left end of the table, and his food is served to him on the right end. Before eating, Joel insists that everyone who is here must "pass the peace pipe" around the table. That way, there will (supposedly) be great peace during dinner. In fact, the more times they pass it around, the more peace there will be. The word for "peace" is *paz*.

Joel strictly forbids swearing at the dinner table. Personally, he doesn't have a problem with swearing in general, but during dinner he thinks it's bad luck. Good luck, however, comes from wearing a green shirt that says "Don't swear! Bad luck!" The word *suerte* (stress on swear) means "luck".

When it's finally time to eat, despite the general "peace" that Joel has promoted, he has trouble controlling his feelings. He is emotionally very unstable at the dinner table. All his feelings become exaggerated.

For example, if a servant carries in a plate of food, Joel becomes immensely affectionate. Even though the man who's carrying in the food is not special at all, Joel feels extreme affection for him in the moment, simply because he's carrying in food. Sometimes in these moments Joel bursts out saying the word *"Cariño!"*, which means "affection" but sounds kind of like "carry in" ("ca-REEN-yo").

Let's look at what this servant brought and why it made Joel so happy. Apparently it's a cooked goose. Joel finds geese annoying, but he feels a lot of morbid pleasure when he sees them dead. So when this goose appears at the table, cooked and ready to eat, Joel experiences great pleasure. The word for "pleasure" is *gusto*.

But nearby is something that terrifies Joel. A bunch of disembodied human heads float in a jar. These heads give Joel an enormous sense of fear, and his word for "fear" is *miedo* (stress almost sounds like "head").

Finally, let's come to Joel's word for "love". Joel doesn't think about love and affection the way that most people do. He felt the most affection (*cariño*) when someone carried in a dead goose for him to eat. But the more extreme word, "love", can only be attained by providing Joel with "more" of these things that give him pleasure. To the right of the dining room table, you can see that more and more dinner supplies are in store (in the shape of a heart), and that's where Joel's most positive emotion is stored up. Give him more and more, and he'll experience the feeling that we identify as love. His word for "love" simply stresses the syllable more: *amor*.

All of these words can be used after the verb Tener or Dar. To say "I have affection", you say *tengo cariño*. "I'm afraid" is *tengo miedo* (literally "I have fear"). To say "It gives me pleasure", you can say *me da gusto*, and "it gives me luck" is *me da suerte*.

Kitchen: Refrigerator

The first thing we encounter in the kitchen is the refrigerator.

The refrigerator is divided into two parts: The freezer on top and the main part of the refrigerator below. On top, we've already learned *verdad* (on the left) and *acuerdo* (on the right), both of which are commonly used after the word *de*.

As you can see on the next page, there are a few new things in the freezer: Some pictures of Joel's dad's wings, a frozen tiny whale turning around, and on the right, a picture of an "H", like a helicopter landing pad.

The Vs represent the word *veras*, which is a lot like the word *verdad*. The phrase "*¿de veras?*" simply means

237

"really?"; it's basically a more casual version of "*¿de verdad?*"

The whale turning around represents the word *vuelta*. The whale seems to be chasing its tail, as if it wants to go back to where it was. (Well, if it were alive, that is. It seems to be frozen in the middle of the "redo" action.) The word *vuelta* (stress on "whale") means "return", but its most common use is in the phrase *de vuelta*, which means "once again".

Meanwhile the H is a bit funny. Joel has painted this here to represent the word *hecho*, which as a noun means "fact" or "act". For example, *un hecho* can mean "an act". But this word's most common use is in the idiom *de hecho*, which means "in fact".

Practice using these words with *de* before them, and then proceed to the refrigerator:

Below the freezer, in the refrigerator itself, are nouns that tend to have the word *de* <u>after</u> them rather than before them.

The refrigerator is where Joel likes to do experiments on birds. He likes to put them in the refrigerator and see how long they can survive. For example, the sparrow in the middle of the refrigerator has been here for several weeks. It keeps asking Joel, "How much longer do I have to wait in here?", and Joel keeps telling it, "Just be patient and wait, little sparrow. You'll be in a better place soon. Just wait."

The word *espera* means "wait", as a noun. It often is followed by the word *de* when you're referring to what you're waiting for; for example, when you're waiting for food, you might say that you're in *espera de comida*.

As you can see, the sparrow is shouting **"ayuda!"** What she's saying is, "Help! Joel, I thought <u>youda</u> helped me by now! Or chef! I thought at least <u>YOUDA</u> helped me!" The word *ayuda* means "help". For example, "the help of a friend" would be *la ayuda de un amigo*.

Below the bird is a sideways egg carton. Unfortunately, all the eggs fell out of the egg carton, which makes Joel upset; instead of having eggs, he only has a <u>lack</u> of eggs, because they all fell out. The word *falta* (stress on "fall") means "lack". For example, "a lack of food" is *una falta de comida*.

This sparrow is always looking for a way to get out of the refrigerator. A formation of water vapor in the refrigerator gives her an idea: Maybe she can hide in this formation, and when Joel opens the refrigerator door and doesn't see her, she can burst out of it before he knows it. This would be a great <u>way</u> to get out.

The word *forma* sounds like it should mean "form", but more commonly it means "way". So "a way of doing it" would be *una forma de hacerlo*.

There's a synonym for this word: Notice that the "form" of vapor looks kind of like Ner (from the Tener shop).

The word *manera* means "manner" or "way". So it's also common to say *una manera de hacerlo*.

Below this is a pair of spoons. The sparrow sees these as another opportunity to escape: Maybe if she tries to play a "tune" on the spoons, it will distract Joel for a moment and she'll be able to escape. Actually, this almost worked once; the bird clacked the spoons together, and Joel suddenly tuned out for a moment and said, "Oh, that tune reminds me of the tunes that my dad used to play!" The bird saw this as a great opportunity, but unfortunately Joel collected himself and slammed the door. The sparrow missed her chance.

The word *oportunidad* has the stressed syllable "dad", with a secondary stressed syllable "tune" (op-or-TUNE-i-DAD). *Una oportunidad* means "an opportunity" or "a chance". For example, "a chance of doing it" is *una oportunidad de hacerlo*.

239

Kitchen: Shelves

In the cabinet with the *idea* light bulbs and the *razón* sun, somebody has stuck gum all over one of the shelves. This made Joel extremely angry when he found out: "Gum in my kitchen? Whose fault is this?" he demanded. At that moment, the chef made an enormous, guilty-sounding gulping noise: "Culp!" (In doing so, he swallowed the gum that he was chewing.) When Joel heard that, he immediately knew who was to blame. "It's your fault! The blame is yours!"

Joel's word for "blame" is *culpa*. For Joel, "being guilty of something" is the same as "having the blame of something", or *tener la culpa de algo*.

In a shelf on the right side, the chef has hung some aromatic tea bags, simply for the scent. The chef told Joel, "The scent of this tea helps me to cook better." Joel responded, "That doesn't make any sense..." but then he smelled the beautiful aroma and he changed his mind: "OK, you're right, that makes sense."

The word *sentido* (which sounds like "scent-TEA-doe) means "sense". For Joel, something that makes sense actually <u>has</u> sense; for example, "that makes sense" is *eso tiene sentido*.

These tea scent bags are held up by a mini-figure of Dare from the Poder shop. This represents *poder*, which as a noun means "power" or "ability".

Dare is also holding a very thick, heavy notebook that says "plan" on it. This contains many plans that Joel has for making more money. The word *plan* is a cognate meaning "plan".

In a nearby shelf above the *problema* hat, Joel has installed a steering wheel and a couple of levers. These "controls" don't really do anything, but they give Joel comfort: He likes to feel like he has control. The word *control* is a cognate; *tener control* means "to have control".

On the door of this cabinet, Joel has a big yellow sign that says, "*¡Cuidado!* Wet paint!" This direction is actually aimed at his dad: He is tired of his dad taking things from the cabinets (even though they're things that his dad lent to him). He is trying to scare his dad away, and his word for "carefulness" has the stressed syllable "dad". The idiom for "being careful" is *tener cuidado* (literally "having carefulness").

Practice going through all these shelves, using the verb Tener before each word. Then we'll move down to the wall below them.

Kitchen: Wall

Things written into the kitchen wall represent nouns that are commonly combined with the verb Dar. On the left side, Joel has decorated with some Christmas lights, shaped like another whale. Just like the whale in the refrigerator, this whale seems to be turning around backwards. This represents the word *vuelta*, which means "turn".

It may seem strange that the word for "turn" is used with Dar. But that's normal in Spanish: Instead of "making a turn", you always "give a turn", or *dar una vuelta*. Actually, *una vuelta* can mean "a walk" as well as "a turn" (even though whales can't walk), so be prepared to see it used both ways.

Next to the whale leans a coin, with a list of prices on it. One of the funny things about Yol is that most of the money is in bills, but itemized lists of money (such as bills and account summaries) are written down on metal coins. In this case, Joel has taken money from various investors, and their account information is on this coin. The word *cuenta* (stress sounds kind of like "coin") means "account".

Cuenta is an important word mainly because it is used in some common idioms, particularly along with the verb Dar, as we'll see soon.

Now check out the right wall below the shelves. Joel and his chef don't use recipes. Instead, they use three simple steps for every meal. These three steps are written on the wall above the counter, and Joel likes to talk about "passing over" each step. Whenever he completes a step, he says "OK, we passed that step! Let's pass on to the next one." His word for "step" is *paso*.

CUENTA:

Paso 1: Gather Food
Paso 2: Cook Food
Paso 3: Put Food on Coasters

Kitchen: Counter

On the counter we've seen things that Joel can "do": "I do the work" is *hago el trabajo*, and "he did me a favor" is *me hizo un favor*.

You might be surprised at some of the other things that Joel can "do" or "make": He can "make a deal", "make a question", and in some cases, "make case". This may seem odd, because in English we don't "make" a question, we "ask" a question. But Joel uses the verb Hacer with everything on the counter.

On the left side of the counter, near the *cuenta*, are a bunch of tiny "goons", all carrying clubs. These goons keep asking Joel very difficult questions. In particular, one of Joel's investors is apparently very suspicious of how Joel is using the money. He has sent his goons to find out if it's true that Joel wasted 10,000 Yen on a robot pony, when he agreed to use that money to start a business. Joel thinks that the questions that these goons pose are very uncomfortable. In general, Joel refers to a question as a *pregunta* (stress on "goon").

To the right, where the stove is, Joel's tiny animatronic pony trots around happily, carrying a suitcase. This was part of a deal that he made with the chef: The chef didn't want Joel's romping toy in the kitchen, because the "clip clop" of its hooves is very distracting, but Joel agreed only to let it trot around on the stove to avoid leaving black hoof prints on the nice green counter. This "deal" that they made is referred to as the *trato* (stress on "trot").

Note that although the word *trato* generally means "deal", it can also be used to mean "treatment" in some cases. Joel insists that the pony must be treated very gently and carefully; for example, a stove burner should not be lit when the pony is on top of it.

But why is the pony carrying around a suitcase? This is full of the papers that Joel has prepared for his lawyers. He's drawn up an entire case for why he should be allowed to have a toy trotting pony in the kitchen, and why it was a good investment. The word *caso* means "case", and this word is used in a variety of ways as we'll learn soon.

Kitchen: Inside the Island

Inside the kitchen island, we encounter a couple of nouns that usually have the word *en* before them. (See the next page for the full image.)

There's a tiny pathway through the island, leading to a minuscule doorway. This is actually a prank that Joel plays on guests: He has them start walking down the path, but then it gets smaller and smaller, and they aren't able to fit through the tiny door at the other end. They always end up saying, "That's so mean! This isn't a real path, and it doesn't go anywhere!"

The word *camino* (stressed syllable "mean") means "path", "route", or "way". For example, "on the way" is *en el camino*.

To the left, Joel keeps a virtual reality headset that he lets his guests play with. He only does this so that they won't bother him, especially his dad, who loves virtual reality but also likes messing with things in Joel's kitchen. The word *realidad* means "reality"; it sound similar to the English word, but the stress is on the syllable "dad" at the end. For exmaple, "in reality" would be *en realidad*.

Kitchen: Other

We've already stored dozens of abstract nouns in various places in the kitchen, depending on what words they tend to be used with. But on top of the island in the middle, we store more general abstract words like *cosa* that are commonly used in a variety of ways.

The window in the island gives Joel a very nice view of anyone who happens to be inside the island below him. Joel always feels very important when he looks out a window at anyone or anything below him. He calls the view a *vista* because he thinks it's a grand kind of word, and it makes him feel special.

But Joel wants this *vista* (view) to be reserved for him only and protected from anyone else. In order to keep it safe, he has surrounded the window with things that look like insect wings, just for security. These wings remind him of the security that his own dad used to make him feel as a child, and his word for "security" is *seguridad* (stress on "dad").

To help prevent people from trying to hop over the wings of *seguridad*, he has posted some interesting items that he hopes will distract people.

243

One says, "Word lab! Danger, do not enter; words are being invented here." Joel has been told that words are very dangerous, and that laboratories are dangerous, so he thought that this would scare people away. Joel's word for "word" is *palabra* (stress "lab").

The second is simply a long list: "*Lista.* Read this list before proceeding." Joel's word for "list" is *lista*.

But the third and strangest thing that he posted is a wanted poster: "Wanted! Gary." Apparently Gary is a "bad guy" who is wanted for starting a war. The reward is 1 million Yen. Of course, this interests guests greatly (if they don't realize that it's fictional). But now it has confused even Joel's mind, and every time he thinks of a "war", he calls it a *guerra* (pronounced "GEHR-rah").

On the right side of the counter is a record player with a record that has a drawing of Joel and the chef, just like in the freezer. This is a recording of a funny conversation between Joel and the chef, where they had an argument and Joel actually won the argument (mostly because he threatened to kick the chef out of the house). Joel is obsessed with this memory, and he listens to it over and over. His word for "a memory" is *un recuerdo*.

Partly underneath the record player is a powdered wig. This is for a game that Joel likes to play: He puts the wig on different people and laughs at them. Any time a guest asks "Can we play a game?", Joel says "Yes!" and then subjects them to this embarrassment. Since this is the only game that Joel knows how to play, he calls every game a *juego* (stress on "wig").

Now it's time to go upstairs. Let's leave the kitchen through *la puerta*, and proceed up the stairs (past *el perro*), across the balcony (past *la arma*), and through the big double doors on the left into the ballroom.

Ballroom

On the left side of the ballroom, in the space of floor unoccupied by mints, a man is lying down and sleeping. According to Joel, a new man lies down here every week. Each man wakes up and leaves after seven days, when the next man comes to replace him. This represents the word *semana* (stress on "man"), which means "week".

Between the man and the vase, Joel has put up some Easter decorations, including chocolate bunnies and colored eggs. Joel's biggest party every year is held at Easter. He also leaves some of the decorations up year-round because it's too much hassle to change them every time. Although Joel holds informal gatherings all the time, he always looks forward to his big Easter party, and so for him, each party is just a reflection of Easter. His word for "party" is *fiesta* (stress on "esta", which sounds kind of like "easter").

On the right side of the room, we see Joel's clock. The minute hand of this clock is shaped like a slimy newt.

Instead of ticking steadily, this newt moves all of a sudden every minute, making a slippy squeaking sound as it does. Joel's word for "minute" is *minuto*, with a stress on "newt".

Joel loves measuring time in minutes, hours, days, and weeks. However, he thinks months are stupid. They aren't proper measurements of time, because they're of differing lengths. Some months are 31 days long, and others are only 28 or 29 days. What a mess! How is that useful for measuring time?

To reflect this, Joel keeps a home-made calendar on which he's scribbled out every page, because he thinks months are a "mess" in terms of tracking time. His word for "month" is *mes*.

Behind the temple, Joel has a relic from a former life: A sad, small piece of broken-down furniture slumps in the corner. This represents the word *pasado*, which means "past" (and has the stressed syllable "sad").

A piece of grain from the baker's stand has found its way to the ballroom, sitting on top of one of the mints. This grain used to ring loudly, like the ones in the plaza, but this one has lost that ability and sits there uselessly. When *entonces* is used as a noun, it refers to a specific period of time (usually in the past).

Library

Joel has only been to school one day in his entire life. He hated it. Right after going to school, he went home and wrote a book that talks about what a horrible place school is. The entire book is shaped like a face that's crying loudly, or "wailing". In fact, whenever Joel thinks about the idea of going to school, he almost wants to "wail". His word for "school" is *escuela* (stress on "wail"). Not many people have bought Joel's book, but he proudly displays a copy on his shelf.

A spot of fluffy mud is sitting on top of Joel's book about school. During Joel's only day at school, he was taught that Planet Earth is made of mud and air. They were required to create a model by shaping fluffy mud into a circle. Joel was embarrassed when his classmates took his own circle of mud and put it on Joel's head, saying, "Look at Joel! He's wearing a tiara!" Joel shudders when he remembers that day, and he has put this "tiara" made of earth on top of his book about school so that he can remember how awful it was. His word for "Earth" is *tierra*.

As a quick note, remember that we have our word for "the world" on the right: *el mundo*. But *la tierra* represents "the earth". These two words basically mean the same thing, though *el mundo* sometimes refers to the people in the world and *la tierra* tends to refer to Earth as a planet and what it's made of (such as dirt or mud).

Joel sometimes builds cities out of Legos in the library. He loves large cities, because he thinks that they're powerful and wealthy. However, one sad day, his careless dad knocked over his Lego city. Joel was very angry, and he thought about suing his dad for destroying his creation. "Sue dad!" he shouted in anger. His word for "city" is *ciudad*.

To the right of this, Joel has also created a much smaller town out of Legos. It's modeled to look like the tiny town that Joel was raised in as a baby bee. But Joel hates small towns. He likes to pretend that this little town is in big trouble: A wave of water is about to wash over it, destroying the town. To enact this, Joel splashes water from a small cup on this incredibly small town. Then he laughs: "Hahaha! You silly small town! You'll never survive a wave of water!" His word for "town" is *pueblo* (the same word as is used for "people"), with the stress on "wave".

Above the *pueblo*, Joel has a painted ladder that is used for accessing books on the top shelves (when he doesn't feel like flying, of course). As you can see, this word is right next to the *parte*

window, and like the window, it's divided in smaller parts. Joel calls this ladder his *lado*.

The word *lado* is very much like the word *parte*, in that it's used to mean "place" right after indefinite adjectives (such as *otro*, *cada*, or *muchos*). So "another place" could be *otra parte*, or it could be *otro lado*.

The tallest book that Joel owns on this large bookshelf is a book about hospitals. This book is so tall that it takes up the height of two shelves. Joel imagines that hospitals must be tall too, and so his word for "hospital" is *hospital*, with the stress on "tall".

A few misshapen pies are sitting on top of some of the books on a lower shelf. This is the geography section of Joel's library; the different countries are represented by different books. But Joel's pie crusts are made with yeast, and the yeast is causing the crusts to run down in front of the different countries, covering up their names in varying amounts. Joel refers to a "country" as a *país*, a word that sounds kind of like "pies" but has an emphasis on the ending, which sounds like "yeast": "pa-YEES".

Meanwhile, there is some empty space on one of the shelves. This area of the shelf has green bumps all over it. Joel doesn't know what these bumps are, so he doesn't put any books here, for fear of infecting them with "warts". Instead, he plays with some of his toys here, pretending that it's a little bedroom instead of a bookshelf. The word *cuarto* is used to mean "room" or "bedroom".

Speaking of which, let's turn around and go into Joel's bedroom.

Bedroom

Joel often crawls into his bedroom extremely tired from flying all day. When he does so, all he cares about is getting into bed comfortably.

The *poco* yen bills on the floor are sometimes nice for poking his feet and reminding him of his wealth, but when he's tired, he doesn't want to be poked. So as you can see, he's left a pair of socks near his bed, providing something softer to step on. This represents the word *par*, which means "couple".

Par and *poco* are used in similar ways to talk about small amounts of something. For example, Joel might have "a little bit of money", *un poco de dinero*, or he could have "a couple dollars", *un par de dólares*.

Remember that Joel's bed itself is used to represent parts of something. We've seen before that the blanket on the left side of Joel's bed is divided into *partes*. But on the right side of the bed, it's punctuated with dots or "points" instead. He calls these points *puntos*. He doesn't like sleeping in the *puntos*, so he usually sleeps in the *parte* half of the bed.

Between these is a dotted line down the middle, as if to divide the lanes of his bed. Joel calls this *el medio*, which means "the middle".

Still, the right side of the bed is important. Joel has a small ladder on the right side of his bed, for climbing in when he has no energy to fly. The word *lado* means "side" (although we've seen in the library that it also sometimes means "place").

There's a nail at the end of Joel's bed. In fact, when Joel thinks of the "end" of something, he thinks about this nail. His word for "end" is *final*, with the stress on "nal" (like "nail").

For some reason, this nail is pinning a fish's fin to Joel's bedpost. The word *fin* also means "end", though it's used slightly differently (mostly in idioms).

Now let's look at Joel's two nightstands, which represent aspects of something. Any person or object has many aspects: They have a life (*vida*),

a name (*nombre*), and a type (*tipo*), as we've seen before. They're also likely to have a death, a form, a story (or a "history"), a number, and a position. We're about to cover these words.

On the lefthand nightstand, the *vida* lamp has emitted a large amount of steam. But this steam clings together in a funny vague shape, almost identifiable as the shape of a person, but not quite. Whenever Joel looks at this, he thinks of the word *forma*, which means "form".

Leaning against the lantern is a book that Joel sometimes likes to read as a bedtime story, when he's not too tired already. This book is simply the story of Joel's life, or his "history", so he calls this his "bedtime history". Joel's word for "story" or "history" is *historia*. (The word may look like the English word "history", but the stress is on story).

Beneath the lantern and the book is a T-shirt. This is a shirt that Joel would

never want to wear, because it reminds him of his mortality: It has a big picture of a skull on the front, which is a symbol of death. Every time Joel throws the shirt out, it keeps appearing again, right here under the *vida* lamp and the *historia* story book. Sometimes when Joel is half asleep, he thinks that he can hear the skull quietly saying "Wear me… wear me…"

Not only that, but the skull glows slightly at night, just like the lamp does, so it's always present. They seem bound to each other in a mysterious way; Joel has concluded that he can't get rid of the shirt without also getting rid of the lamp, which he is unwilling to do.

The word *muerte* (stress on wear) means "death". In Joel's world, you can't have life (*vida*) without also having death (*muerte*), no matter how hard you try.

On the right side of the bed, the teapot that the gnome is holding is Joel's alarm clock. Every morning it brews a different type (*tipo*) of tea, which is exciting to Joel. But he also likes to look at the clock on the side of the teapot. The numbers on the clock are Roman numerals, and whenever Joel thinks of the word "number", he pronounces it as *número* (which sounds kind of like the word "numeral").

Meanwhile, remember that the gnome doesn't have a name (*nombre*). Nevertheless, it does have an identity. The gnome is very proud to be Joel's teapot holder, because previously, he was just the wastebasket holder. He didn't like his previous position, but his current position suits him very well. As you can see, another, smaller gnome now has the lower position of holding the wastebasket. Joel's word for "position" is *puesto* (stress on <u>waste</u>).

Bathroom

Adjacent to Joel's bedroom is the bathroom, where we store words for body parts.

On the left side of the room, we see Joel's toilet and his sink. Check out the base of Joel's toilet, which is shaped like a human head. The word *cabeza* (stress on "base") means "head".

Now look at the mirror above Joel's sink. As you know, Joel loves his blue car. He thinks it's the prettiest thing he owns, and consequently uses at as the standard by which beauty is measured.

But he's also a bit of a narcissist. When he looks at his own face, he likes to think that it looks beautiful. To represent this, he always draws

an outline of his blue car over his face, in the mirror, to make his face's reflection more beautiful. There is now a permanent blue car outline on his mirror.

The word *cara* (with a stress on "car") means "face".

When Joel was growing up, he was always told to "wash the hands! wash the hands!" As he's grown older and more mature, he's come to see the wisdom in "washing the hands". After using the bathroom, he always washes a pair of human hands. As you can see, he keeps two man's hands in the sink for washing. The word *mano* means "hand".

Note that this word *mano* is feminine, even though it ends with the letter O.

So you would say *las manos*, just as you would say *la cara* or *la cabeza*.

The man's hands in the sink seem to be bleeding: They're pouring out a greyish substance with the consistency of sand. Joel concludes that all blood probably looks like this grey sand, and so he refers to blood as *sangre* (which sounds like "sand grey").

On the right side of the room, we have Joel's shower and bathtub. Nowadays, Joel always takes showers rather than baths, because the bathtub has a body in it. Joel doesn't know where this body came from (or at least he doesn't remember), but he doesn't want to call anyone to remove it, because if the police come to his house, they might suspect him of crimes that he may or may not have committed. Meanwhile,

Joel calls this body a "corpse", or as he puts it, a *cuerpo*. The word *cuerpo* means "body" (whether the person is alive or dead).

The body in the bathtub pretty much looks like a skeleton, but it still seems to have a heart, though this heart is bright and shiny like the sun. Whenever Joel thinks about someone's heart, he thinks of this body's heart, and he imagines that each person's heart looks like the sun. The word for "heart" is *corazón*.

A giant, ghostly, apple-shaped head appears next to the shower whenever Joel is bathing. It floats there staring angrily at him until he finishes, and then it vanishes. The word *ser*, as a noun, means "being"; to say "my being" Joel says *mi ser*, and "a strange being" is *un ser extraño*.

While showering, Joel uses weeds to clean out the insides of his ears. Since he gets pieces of the weeds stuck in his ears, he calls his ears his *oídos*.

Meanwhile, he washes his eyes with two O-shaped hoses, specially designed for bees' eyes. He refers to his eyes as his *ojos* (which sounds like "O hose").

Lesson 11 Application:

Labels

"With great privilege comes great responsibility."
-unknown

IN MY EXPERIENCE, every aspiring Spanish speaker is eager to learn nouns. And for good reason! Now instead of describing things with pronouns (*esto, eso*, etc.), you can actually say what they are (*la comida, el pueblo*, etc.).

However, this also comes with a huge challenge. Now that you know these nouns, you need to learn some special ways to use them.

We have dozens of idiomatic uses to learn in this lesson, so hang tight. If you can master these, fluency is around the corner.

Physical Nouns

For the most part, the physical nouns that we learned in the hall are basically simple labels: You can easily use them exactly as their equivalents would be used in English. However, note that in some cases cases, such as the following one, it's common to put definite articles (usually *el* or *la*) before the noun, even when we wouldn't in English.

He liked to play with fire.	*Le* it was pleasing to play *con el fuego.*
He liked to play with light.	*Le* it was pleasing to play *con la luz.*
He liked to play with the dog.	*Le* it was pleasing to play *con el perro.*
He liked to play with the weapon.	*Le* it was pleasing to play *con la arma.*

It has everything, even a bed for you.	*Tiene de todo, hasta una cama para ti.*
It has everything, even some weapons for them.	*Tiene de todo, hasta unas armas para ellos.*
It has everything, even a door for her.	*Tiene de todo, hasta una puerta para ella.*
It has everything, even a car for us.	*Tiene de todo, hasta un auto para nosotros.*
It has everything, even a telephone for you.	*Tiene de todo, hasta un teléfono para ti.*

So there was neither food nor money.	*Entonces no había ni comida ni dinero.*
So there was either equipment or other goods.	*Entonces había o equipo u otros bienes.*

The weather is nice right now.	*El tiempo es bueno ahora.*
The dog is under the bed right now.	*El perro está bajo la cama ahora.*

You're about to see something strange: The phrase *el agua* doesn't seem to make sense. Isn't *agua* feminine, on the left side of the hall? Why are we using the masculine article *el*?

This strange exception to the rule happens because *agua* starts with the letter A. Spanish speakers avoid saying *la agua* and instead use the incongruent *el*. However, *agua* is indeed a feminine noun (for example, "the correct water" would be *el agua correcta*, using a feminine adjective).

They had to find the water.	*Había que* find *el agua.*
They had to find the weapon.	*Había que* find *el arma.*
They had to find the dog.	*Había que* find *el perro.*
They had to find three dollars.	*Había que* find *tres dólares.*

The phrase *la puerta de atrás* means "the back door" (literally "the door of back").

Through the back door.	*Por la puerta de atrás.*
Through the front door.	*Por la puerta de adelante.*

Does your friend have a very large car?	*¿Tu amigo tiene un auto muy grande?*
Does your friend have a very small dog?	*¿Tu amiga tiene un perro muy pequeño?*

Speaking of a "very small dog", here's a fun trick that can apply to most Spanish nouns: Take the word *perro* and change the -o to -ito. Suddenly instead of "dog", you have "little dog" or "doggy".

Beforehand we had a little girl dog.	*Antes teníamos una perrita.*
I gave my dog a little house.	*Yo le di a mi perro una casita.*
Beforehand my dog had a tiny little bed.	*Antes mi perro tenía una camita.*

The -ito/-ita trick is technically called "diminutive", but it's often used to create a term of endearment for someone very close and familiar to you. For example, many names can easily be transformed into a nickname this way; Ana becomes Anita, Luna becomes Lunita, and so on. (Just don't do this to someone when you first meet them.)

Family Members

I know that his wife is here.	*Sé que su esposa está acá.*
I know that your husband is here.	*Sé que tu esposo está acá.*
I know that my uncle is here.	*Sé que mi tío está acá.*
I know that her sister is here.	*Sé que su hermana está acá.*

Other People

The persons of that story, the boy, his family, the president, and his wife.	*Las personas de esa historia, el niño, su familia, el presidente, y su mujer.*
The person of that city, the kid, his family, the captain, and his wife.	*La persona de esa ciudad, el chico, su familia, el capitán, y su mujer.*
The girls of that city, the woman, her family, the boss, and his wife.	*Las chicas de esa ciudad, la señora, su familia, el jefe, y su mujer.*

But, thank God, the kid was able to find the way.	*Pero, gracias a Dios, el niño pudo* to find *la manera.*
But, thank God, the mother was able to find the baby.	*Pero, gracias a Dios, la madre pudo* to find *el bebé.*
But, thank God, the girl was able to find her brothers.	*Pero, gracias a Dios, la muchacha pudo* to find *sus hermanos.*

The boy finds himself with a girl.	*El niño* finds himself *con una chica.*
The gentleman finds himself with a young woman.	*El caballero* finds himself *con una señorita.*
The girl finds herself with an idiot.	*La muchacha* finds herself *con un idiota.*

As if he were their master.	*Como si fuera su amo.*
As if he were their king.	*Como si fuera su rey.*
As if he were a baby.	*Como si fuera un bebé.*
As if he were their boss.	*Como si fuera su jefe.*

Some occupations can be modified to be feminine. For example, *el doctor* can turn into *la doctora* if the doctor is a woman.

| Both are doctors and policewomen and also they play on important teams. | *Las dos son doctoras y policías y también* they play *en equipos importantes.* |

Any "group" noun (represented on the posters on the wall) typically gets a singular article.

And does anyone else in the family know about this?	*¿Y alguien más en la familia sabe sobre esto?*
And does anyone else in the class know about this?	*¿Y alguien más en la clase sabe sobre esto?*
And does anyone else in the team know about this?	*¿Y alguien más en el equipo sabe sobre esto?*

Feelings

Normally it's easy to use the dining room words: Simply use a conjugation of Tener and then the word. For example, "I have affection" is ***tengo cariño***, and "I'm afraid" is ***tengo miedo***. But here are a few more uses for these words.

Feelings are often "had", using the verb Tener, but they can also be "given", using the verb Dar.

At first it gave her much fear.	*Primero le daba mucho miedo.*
At first it gave her much pleasure.	*Primero le daba mucho gusto.*
At first it gave her much luck.	*Primero le daba mucha suerte.*
At first it gave them some peace.	*Primero les daba algo de paz.*

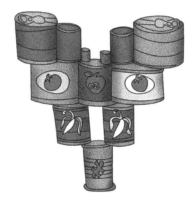

Doing something "with affection", or ***con cariño***, simply means doing it "nicely". Of course, you can also do something with other emotions, but ***con cariño*** is one of the nicest ways to do something.

If you had done it with affection, I would have done it.	*Si lo hubieras hecho con cariño lo habría hecho.*
If you had done it with love, I would have done it.	*Si lo hubieras hecho con amor lo habría hecho.*
If you had done it with fear, I would have done it.	*Si lo hubieras hecho con miedo lo habría hecho.*

The exclamation ***¡Qué suerte!*** is often used to mean "what luck!"

What luck! Thanks so much!	*¡Qué suerte! ¡Muchas gracias!*

Abstract Nouns with "De"

We have many words in the kitchen, but they're very neatly organized for you based on how they tend to be used in a sentence.

The nouns in the refrigerator are associated with the preposition *de*, though in two different ways: The ones in the freezer compartment at the top of the refrigerator are usually preceded by *de* (e.g. *de verdad* and *de acuerdo*), and the ones in the main part of the refrigerator are typically followed by *de*. Let's start in the freezer.

The idiom *de veras* is pretty much the only way that *veras* is used. It's generally used as an exclamation of almost-disbelief: "Really??" "*¿De veras?*"

Really? Thanks!	*¿De veras? ¡Gracias!*

The idiom *de hecho* literally means "of fact", but it's equivalent to the English idiom "in fact":

In fact, my parents are telling me that I have to leave.	*De hecho, mis padres me dicen que me tengo que ir.*
In fact, the policeman told him that he would have had to leave.	*De hecho, el policía le dijo que habría tenido que irse.*

The idiom *de vuelta* is used to mean "again", but in the sense that someone has "returned" to do something. For example, "I want to go to Colombia again" could be *quiero ir a colombia otra vez*, but native speakers are more likely to say *quiero ir a colombia de vuelta*, emphasizing the idea of <u>returning</u>.

I want to go to Colombia again.	*Quiero ir a Colombia de vuelta.*

The lower, main part of the refrigerator contains nouns that are usually followed by *de* (e.g. *oportunidad de* and *ayuda de*). In the following sentence, look at the noun before *de* and practice switching it out with other refrigerator nouns.

There wasn't a way to do it.	*No había forma de hacerlo.*
We found the way to do it.	We found *la manera de hacerlo.*
There was an opportunity to do it.	*Había una oportunidad de hacerlo.*
We told them that there was a lack of food.	*Les dijimos que había una falta de comida.*
He told you that there was the help of friends.	*Te dijo que había la ayuda de amigos.*

Remember that Joel likes to use the preposition *a* to indicate moments in time. To say that someone is in a moment of waiting for something, he uses the phrase *a la espera*, which we translate as "in waiting".

| It's kind of difficult to stay for so long in waiting for that. | *Es medio difícil* to stay *tanto tiempo a la espera de eso.* |
| It's kind of difficult to live for very long in lack of that. | *Es medio difícil* to live *mucho tiempo a falta de eso.* |

The idiom *le hace falta* means that something is missing for someone; literally "it makes him/her a lack" (although the subject "it" isn't really anything in particular).

This idiom always takes an indirect object (*le, les, te, me, nos*). In the sentences below, this idiom has been translated into English in several different ways to demonstrate how differently the same expression can be presented in English.

It's missing a lot.	*Le hace falta mucho.*
It isn't missing anything.	*No le hace falta nada.*
We need a couple more years.	*Nos hace falta un par de años.*
You're still in need of a lot.	*Te hace falta mucho.*
Food is lacking for them.	*Les hace falta la comida.*

Abstract Nouns with "Tener"

In that sense, one has to be careful.	*En ese sentido uno tiene que tener cuidado.*
In that sense, one has to have a plan.	*En ese sentido uno tiene que tener un plan.*
In that sense, one has to have the ability.	*En ese sentido uno tiene que tener el poder.*

They might not have control.	*Pueden no tener control.*
They might not make sense.	*Pueden no tener sentido.*
They might not be at fault.	*Pueden no tener culpa.*

Abstract Nouns with "Dar"

The words on the wall are associated with Dar ("to give"), and this requires some explanation.

First of all, note that Joel doesn't like walking much. He prefers to fly.

Any time he has to take actual steps, with his feet, he feels like he's "giving" something, because it's so much effort.

In English, we say that someone "takes" a step, but in Spanish, it's always "give" a step (*dar un paso*).

It gets stranger: Joel would never "take a walk". Instead, he would "give a turn" (*dar una vuelta*). Yeah, I know that's weird, but I guess when he takes walks, he usually just goes around in circles, turning constantly.

They went to take a walk.	*Fueron a dar una vuelta.*
We went to take a few steps backwards.	*Fuimos a dar unos pasos atrás.*
Let's take a walk around the city.	*Demos una vuelta por la ciudad.*

OK, that covers *paso* and *vuelta*. But what is *cuenta* doing here on the wall? When do you "give account", and is that so common?

Well, yes, but not in the way you might expect. *Cuenta* is usually something that you give yourself.

When you "give yourself account of" something, you're "realizing" something. That may seem really complicated, but you'll hear native speakers use it all the time. The idiom is *darse cuenta de que*.

Take some time to get used to these examples. In these cases, I've underlined the idiom so that you can focus on that part. (The phrase after *que* can be any statement that you would "realize".)

I realized that there wasn't anyone around.	*Me di cuenta de que no había nadie por ahí.*
She realized that the thing was nice.	*Se dio cuenta de que la cosa era buena.*
Do you realize that you're not there anymore?	*¿Te das cuenta de que ya no estás allí?*
They realized that there was a new person in the city.	*Se dieron cuenta de que había una nueva persona en la ciudad.*
She was realizing that there was someone in the house.	*Se daba cuenta de que había alguien en la casa.*
I'm realizing that it's not true.	*Me doy cuenta de que no es verdad.*

Abstract Nouns with "Hacer"

The nouns on the counter tend to be associated with Hacer.

But notice that *cuenta* is leaning against the wall, so it seems to be both on the wall and on the counter. That's because it's often used in an idiom that uses Hacer, as well as the *darse cuenta* idiom we just learned. The idiom uses a *de* in between: *hacer de cuenta*. It means "pretend" (literally "make of account"), and it's followed by *que* and then the sentence that you're pretending.

They're pretending that they're brothers.	*Hacen de cuenta que son hermanos.*
Let's pretend that these two are friends.	*Hagamos de cuenta que estos dos son amigos.*
I'm pretending that it's the devil.	*Hago de cuenta que es el diablo.*
Are you pretending that you're God or something?	*¿Haces de cuenta que eres Dios o algo?*

The word *trato* can mean "treatment", but when associated with Hacer, it means "deal".

| Let's make a deal. | *Hagamos un trato.* |
| Let's ask a question. | *Hagamos una pregunta.* |

The word *caso* can be used without Hacer to mean "case", in pretty much any way you would use the abstract word "case" in English.

| In that case she wouldn't do it. | *En ese caso no lo haría.* |
| In this case it's better to have a plan. | *En este caso, es mejor tener un plan.* |

263

But when *caso* is used along with Hacer, it has to do with "obedience". The idiom is *hacerle caso a alguien*, literally "to do case to someone". For example, *le hace caso al policía* literally translates to "he does case to the policeman". This idiom generally means to "pay attention" to someone, "obey" them, or follow what they say in general.

Do you follow what your mother says?	*¿Le haces caso a tu mamá?*
I obey my parents.	*Yo les hago caso a mis padres.*
You have to listen to the police.	*Hay que hacerle caso a la policía.*

Abstract Nouns with "En"

The words inside Joel's island are typically preceded by *en*.

They know that they are on the way.	*Saben que están en el camino.*
They can't know that they don't live in reality.	*No pueden saber que no* they live *en la realidad.*

General Abstract Nouns

The words on the island counter are pretty easy to use; you don't have to remember to combine them with a specific preposition or verb. They're straightforward labels.

Still it's a nice memory.	*Igual es un buen recuerdo.*
Still it was a good word.	*Igual era una buena palabra.*
Still it would be a nice view.	*Igual sería una buena vista.*
Still it was the same war.	*Igual era la misma guerra.*
Still it will be a new list.	*Igual será una nueva lista.*
Still it would be a nice game.	*Igual sería un buen juego.*

I'm not able to say it with words.	*No lo puedo decir con palabras.*
I can't say it without a list.	*No lo puedo decir sin una lista.*
I can't say it during this war.	*No lo puedo decir durante esta guerra.*

There's just one idiom to learn here: "point of view" is *punto de vista*. It is often said that someone is "under" a point of view.

With that point of view then, it's very bad.	*Bajo ese punto de vista entonces es muy malo.*
With that point of view, then, it's a fairly nice city.	*Bajo ese punto de vista entonces es una ciudad medio buena.*

Time Nouns

A month ago I talked with Ignacio.	*Hace un mes hablé con Ignacio.*
Three minutes ago I talked with my parents.	*Hace tres minutos hablé con mis papás.*
Two weeks ago I talked with her uncle.	*Hace dos semanas hablé con su tío.*

At that time the king was young.	*En ese entonces, el rey era joven.*
At that party my friends were mean.	*En esa fiesta, mis amigos eran malos.*
In the past the doctor was very nice.	*En el pasado, el doctor era muy bueno.*
In the past, she had lived in another story.	*En el pasado, había* lived *en otra historia.*

Locations

The phrase *cualquier lado* means "any place". Practice switching out *cualquier* with other indefinite adjectives (and *lado* with *parte*).

We can go to any place.	*Podemos ir a cualquier lado.*
We were able to go to many places.	*Podíamos ir a muchos lados.*
She wasn't in any place.	*No estaba en ningún lado.*
She wasn't in any place.	*No estaba en ninguna parte.*

I'm in the country. I had to leave Argentina.	*Estoy en el país. Me tuve que ir de Argentina.*
I'm in the city. I had to leave my hometown.	*Estoy en la cuidad. Me tuve que ir de mi pueblo.*
I'm in the hospital. I had to leave my room.	*Estoy en el hospital. Me tuve que ir de mi cuarto.*

Parts of Things

Put yourself here to my side.	*Ponte aquí a mi lado.*
Put yourself here at the middle.	*Ponte aquí al medio.*
Put that here at this point.	*Pon eso aquí a este punto.*
Put the word there at the end.	*Pon la palabra ahí al final.*

Practicing switching out the "aspect" nouns, like "number", "type", "life", "death", "story", and "position":

Death is better than that.	*La muerte es mejor que eso.*
The position has more than that.	*El puesto tiene más que eso.*
The number is greater than that.	*El número es mayor que eso.*
The story is better than that.	*La historia es mejor que eso.*
The form is something else.	*La forma es algo más.*

Now let's look at three idioms that are commonly used at the end of a spoken description. You might say these in a conversation as your last sentence before it's the other person's turn to speak.

The idiom ***de todas formas*** is used to mean "regardless" or "one way or another". You'll often use it after you've described a situation, but you're now summing up with the important part.

One way or another, I came to look for him.	*De todas formas, **lo** I came to seek.*
One way or another, I have her.	*De todas formas, la tengo.*
One way or another, I see you.	*De todas formas, **te** I see.*

The idiom *al final* means "in the end". (Remember that Joel likes to use *a* to represent a specific point in time, so it's literally "to the end" or "at the end".)

In the end the kid was right.	*Al final el niño tenía razón.*
In the end it was nothing.	*Al final no era nada.*

The idiom *en fin* is often used to sum up or conclude a story. It's roughly equivalent to "anyway" or "in a nutshell".

Well, anyway, that's the story.	*Bueno, en fin, esa es la historia.*
Well, anyway, that's what it was.	*Bueno, en fin, eso es lo que era.*
Well, anyway, that's my question.	*Bueno, en fin, esa es mi pregunta.*

The idiom *un par de* is used just like the phrase "a couple of" in English; it represents a very small number, usually 2 (or an estimated 2 or 3).

A couple of houses from the school.	*Un par de casas de la escuela.*
A couple of steps from the house.	*Un par de pasos de la casa.*

Parts of People

Joel has high respect for body parts.

As such, he usually glorifies them with the word "the": "Don't touch the wings!" "Be careful with the hands." It's rare to hear a Spanish speaker say "your hands" or "my hands"; instead it's almost always "the hands".

Gotta be careful with the hands.	*Hay que tener cuidado con las manos.*
Gotta have control of the head.	*Hay que tener control de la cabeza.*

I want to play with the serious-faced woman.	*Yo quiero to play con la mujer de cara seria.*
I want to talk with the light-eyed girl.	*Yo quiero hablar con la chica de ojos claros.*
I want to say it to the man with strong hands.	*Yo se lo quiero decir al hombre de manos fuertes.*
She wasn't in any place.	*No estaba en ninguna parte.*

The boy with his great head managed to find the way.	*El niño con su gran cabeza pudo* to find *la manera.*
The woman with her great heart managed to convince her daughter.	*La señora con su gran corazón pudo* to convince *su hija.*
The knight with his noble blood was able to transform the country.	*El caballero con su sangre* noble *pudo* to transform *el país.*

Although the word *ser* as a noun can describe a person's "being", as in "my being" (*mi ser*), it can also refer to an unknown creature or "mysterious being".

| A being that isn't from Earth? | *¿Un ser que no es de la tierra?* |
| A body that isn't a person's? | *¿Un cuerpo que no es de una persona?* |

The idiom "give me a hand" is equivalent between Spanish and English.

| Can you give me a hand with this? | *¿Puedes darme una mano con esto?* |
| Someone's going to have to give me a hand with a lot of things. | *Alguien va a tener que darme una mano con muchas cosas.* |

Writing Assignment

We're near the end of Volume 2, which means you need to be keenly aware of your own weaknesses.

Nouns aren't terribly difficult to integrate into your vocabulary, but you want to make sure you're focused on the most tricky uses of these nouns. Search the dialogues for difficult sentences, and write variations on those sentences until you're extremely comfortable with the phrasal structures. You want to be able to say these phrases comfortably in a conversation, with your own meaning.

Dialogue Assignment

The sentences in this portion of the dialogue will help you to diagnose your own weaknesses, both in speaking and in comprehension.

Look for the most difficult sentences here and ask yourself: "Would I even think to say that?" If the answer is no, then you should work on those sentences to make them second-nature.

In this part of the dialogue, Lucía is asking Nicolás about the book he's reading. If the boy in the book is able to stay in the stories, what's the theory behind this? Can the boy get back out of the stories if he wants? And what are the advantages and disadvantages of living inside a fictional story, if one chooses to stay inside the story?

"¿Y Yo Puedo Ir?"

Lucía – Can one stay at any moment?

Lucía - *¿Uno puede* to stay *en cualquier momento?*

Nicolás – Actually, I'm not sure. It seems so; I don't yet quite understand because I haven't arrived at the end. Still, if it's possible, I think that there might be problems.

Nicolás - *En verdad, no estoy seguro.* It seems *que sí, todavía no* I understand *bien porque no* I've arrived *al final. Igual, si se puede,* I think *que puede haber problemas.*

Lucía – What problems?

Lucía - *¿Cuáles problemas?*

Nicolás – I think that if one stays in the story too much time then everyone gets old, but the one doesn't. So the friends die.

Nicolás - I think *que si uno* stays *en la historia demasiado tiempo entonces todos se hacen viejos, pero uno no. Entonces los amigos* die.

Lucía – I don't wish that for anyone! Under that point of view, then it's very bad to live in a story; better to pass through many without staying in any.
Nicolás – Sure, of course, I think the same. While one is a short time then he doesn't have anything bad; it's more,

Lucía - *¡No le* I wish *eso a nadie! Bajo ese punta de vista entonces es muy malo* to live *en una historia, mejor* to pass *por muchas sin* staying *en ninguna.*
Nicolás - *Claro, desde ya, yo* think *lo mismo. Mientras uno esté poco tiempo entonces no tiene nada de malo, es más,*

269

it's really nice! One can meet kings and strange things, and afterwards go along his way. It's important that one know when it's time to leave in order not to stay. Still, in the end, I think that it's kind of difficult to stay so much time in waiting for things to happen; after a while surely one wants to leave.

Lucía – And does anyone else in the kid's family know about this?

Nicolás – That he enters in stories? No! Everyone would think that he's crazy.

Lucía – You're right, this book is the best! It just has everything.

Nicolás – Right?? I told you so. We need more books like this that are so good.

Lucía – And when you read those stories, do you also enter those worlds?

Nicolás – I suppose so… I wasn't able yet, but I'd like it! Sometimes I think that if I read them again and again, at some moment I'm going to be able to enter. When I can enter, I hope to go to the best place of all.

Lucía – To where?

Nicolás – To where Olivia is!

Lucía – Do you even know where she is?

Nicolás – No, but I'm going to look for her.

Lucía – And do you know anyone who knows how to enter?

¡es muy bueno! Uno puede meet reyes y cosas extrañas, y después continue su camino. Es importante que uno sepa cuando es momento de irse para no querer to stay. Igual, al final, I think que es medio difícil to stay tanto tiempo a la espera de que things happen, luego de un tiempo seguro que uno quiere irse.

Lucía - ¿Y alguien más en la familia del niño sabe sobre esto?

Nicolás - ¿Que he enters en las historias? ¡No! Todos would think que está loco.

Lucía - Tienes razón, ¡este book es lo más! No le hace falta nada.

Nicolás - See? Te lo dije. We need más books así de buenos.

Lucía - ¿Y cuando tú read esas historias también you enter a esos mundos?

Nicolás - Supongo que sí… Todavía no pude, ¡pero quisiera! A veces I think que si los I read una y otra vez en algún momento voy a poder to enter. Cuando pueda to enter, I hope ir al mejor lugar de todos.

Lucía - ¿Adónde?

Nicolás - ¡A donde está Olivia!

Lucía - ¿Siquiera sabes dónde está?

Nicolás - No, pero la voy a seek.

Lucía - ¿Y do you know alguien que sepa cómo to enter?

Nicolás – No, I don't know anyone who has entered a book. But it has to be possible; I'm going to read until I can.

Lucía – And can I go?

Nicolás – Of course! Do you seriously want to go? If I enter, someone is going to have to give me a hand with many things. It could be you.

Lucía – Definitely!

Nicolás – All right, come on! But then you would have to read as well.

Lucía – It would make my day!

Nicolás – All right, tell me, what do you want to read?

Lucía – I don't know, it doesn't matter to me. Give me something and I'll read it.

Nicolás – Look, over there there are many books, which are all really good.

Lucía – Let's see… Where?

Nicolás – Over there, by the bed. Do you see them?

Lucía – Yeah, I see them. Which is best?

Nicolás – I like all of them, you can take whichever… unless you want us to read this one together.

Lucía – Really? Thanks!

Nicolás – You're welcome. Get over here by my side, we'll read like this.

Nicolás - *No, no* I know *nadie que haya* entered *en un libro. Pero se tiene que poder, voy a* read *hasta que pueda.*

Lucía - *¿Y yo puedo ir?*

Nicolás - *¡Por supuesto! ¿En serio quieres ir? Si* I enter, *alguien va a tener que darme una mano con muchas cosas, puedes ser tú.*

Lucía - *¡Claro que sí!*

Nicolás - *Bueno, ¡ven! Pero entonces tendrías que* read *tú también.*

Lucía - *¡Sería lo mejor de mi día!*

Nicolás - *Bueno, dime, ¿qué quieres* to read?

Lucía - *No sé, me da igual. Dame algo y lo* I'll read.

Nicolás - Look, *allí hay muchos* books, *los cuales son todos muy buenos.*

Lucía - Let's see… *¿Dónde?*

Nicolás - *Allá, por la cama, ¿los* you see?

Lucía - *Sí, los* I see, *¿cuál es mejor?*

Nicolás - *Me* are pleasing *todos, puedes* take *el que sea… a menos que quieras que* we read *este juntos.*

Lucía - *¿De veras? ¡Gracias!*

Nicolás - *De nada. Ponte aquí a mi lado, así* we'll read.

LESSON 12

Have Adventures

It's time to leap into fluency.

If you've genuinely mastered the previous 11 lessons, you're just about ready to immerse yourself in the Spanish-speaking world and call yourself a fluent speaker.

But before you do, let's make sure you're truly ready to take wing. Never forget the fundamentals, and make sure that you use your new freedom to improve, not deteriorate.

Let's have some adventures.

Lesson 12 Theory:

Have Adventures

"TIME TO MOVE to Argentina!" I thought I had done everything right. I knew 2000 words and how to use them. I had practiced with several conversational dialogues until I could recite them flawlessly. I had spent countless hours in Spanish conversation with my native-speaking teachers online.

My three-month reservation would have me staying in downtown Buenos Aires. As my airplane crossed the equator, I felt on top of the world.

I took a taxi from the airport into the heart of the city. After 30 minutes on winding roads, the car turned onto one of the most incredible streets I'd ever seen:

9 de Julio, which runs straight through the entire length of downtown.

The driver dropped me off on the west edge of this street, pointing me toward my Airbnb apartment a few blocks away. My adventure began!

…Then I started getting lost.

Within a few days of living in Buenos Aires, I managed to shatter almost all of my confidence.

(1) I couldn't read my Airbnb house rules without a Spanish-English dictionary.

(2) I could hardly order coffee and understand what my server was saying.

(3) I lost direction multiple times, once even finding myself stranded in one of the shadiest areas of the city without knowing where I was.

When #3 happened, I made up my mind: I had to change my habits in order to survive.

One afternoon I sat down and studied a map of Buenos Aires. In just 90 minutes I forced myself to memorize all the names of the major streets in the center of the city.

But perhaps more importantly, I changed my

walking habits. Instead of meandering along the little streets throughout the city, I began sticking to the giant avenues that define the landscape. I often went out of my way to use the large, central streets instead of taking obscure shortcuts.

Suddenly the map fell together in my head. After that point, I never got lost in Buenos Aires again… or in any other large city I've visited.

And my Spanish confidence grew exponentially at the same time, thanks to the exact same strategy.

9 de Julio

9 de Julio (literally "9th of July", Argentina's independence day) is the widest street in the world.

The street is intimidating for pedestrians. Measured from edge to edge, the crossing distance is longer than an entire city block. With about 15-20 lanes (depending on how you count them), it can take a few minutes to cross at rush hour.

But even though it's an extremely challenging street, I chose to walk along this avenue as often as I could, for one essential reason:

It gave me a view of the entire city.

Not quite literally; *9 de Julio* is surrounded by tall buildings (it's essentially the Times Square of Buenos Aires). But once I knew how to navigate this street, I found that I could navigate all 8 neighborhoods of downtown Buenos Aires, simply by using this enormous avenue as a reference.

At the same time, my Spanish improved because I was able to find my *9 de Julio* in the language.

Instead of simply losing myself in conversations with all the locals that I met, I spent part of every day focusing strictly on the essentials of Spanish. When I went walking, I turned on Spanish dialogues and spoke along. I wrote in Spanish frequently. I communicated with my tutors regularly.

And thanks to this, my conversations with locals were fruitful and rewarding. I developed friendships that would last for years afterwards, entirely in Spanish.

This is a paradox. Why was I so successful if I was avoiding "immersing" myself most of the time? And how did I get to know the map of Buenos Aires better than my own hometown if I spent half my time on just one street?

Obviously, if I had ONLY walked on Nueve de Julio, I would have had a very boring time in the city.

And if I hadn't communicated with locals frequently, my entire time in Argentina would have been wasted.

However, my time also would have been wasted if I spent my entire visit getting lost. I was only able to make progress because of a healthy balance between immersion and fundamentals.

If you've mastered the course to this point, you're almost ready to immerse yourself in

Spanish. Volume 3 of this series will be in Spanish, not English.

But before I stop feeding you any more English, I'm going to leave you with two essential rules of Spanish immersion.

Rule 1: Don't Get Lost.

If you get in over your head too often, you might feel discouraged with yourself.

So it's important to remind yourself of how much you know, every single day. Get into your comfort zone and sharpen your foundational skills each day before you explore new territories.

Spend at least a few minutes every morning on the essentials of three language areas:

<u>Vocabulary, phrase practice, and writing.</u>

(1) For vocabulary, you should balance learning new vocabulary with reviewing fundamental vocabulary. In both cases, you should be able to <u>list words from memory</u> each day. For example, you should right now be able to write down all the conjugations of Dar from memory, organized by tense, without much trouble. Or maybe all the subject and object pronouns you know, organized by function. Do this exercise every day, focusing on the vocabulary that you know *should* be second-nature to you by now.

(2) "Phrase practice" means saying Spanish phrases out loud. You should be speaking sentences from the course dialogues until they come naturally to you. Make sure you're saying everything properly, and repeat these sentences until

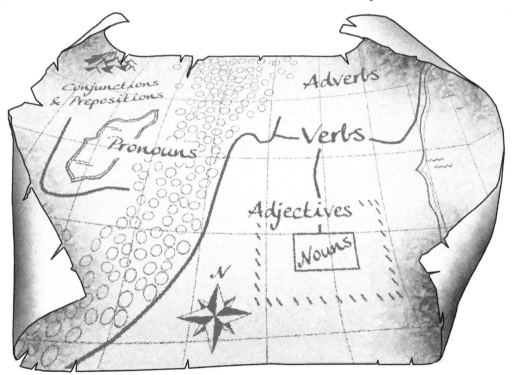

you can say them without thinking about English at all. (If you're an Accelerated Spanish member, you can record yourself at SpanishIn1Month.com and get personal feedback from me and my team.)

(3) Writing is extremely important. I have my coaching students write every single day. Using dialogue sentences, along with the sentence-building skills you learned in Lesson 8, you should be able to express almost anything in Spanish. Write at least 15 sentences every morning, using any new vocabulary or grammar that you're trying to perfect. Then send them to a native speaker to get feedback on how you're doing.

Every language learner needs to work on all 3 areas in their personal study, no matter how advanced they are.

But of course, everyone's schedule and goals are somewhat different, so this has to be customized based on your situation.

Let's use an example.

Imagine that you have a full-time job in Houston. Every morning you have about 1 hour to study before you have to leave for your 30-minute commute to the office.

Let's also say that you've finished Lessons 1-12 of this course, and you're feeling pretty good about it. You still have a little trouble with some of the conjugations of the more complicated verbs, and you want to get a little better at saying certain phrases and idioms.

Here's what your morning schedule might look like one day:

Morning study:

- 15 minutes: Try to write down all the conjugations of Dar, Decir, and Venir, and check yourself against the book.

- 15 minutes: Look for all the instances of Dar, Decir, and Venir in the course dialogues. Read these sentences out loud to reinforce them and to parctice speaking them smoothly.

- 30 minutes: Write variations on these sentences, and send your writings to your coach for corrections.

On-the-go study for the commute:

- 20 minutes: Listen to a new, more advanced dialogue that you're working on, trying to speak along. Pause every time you have trouble speaking along with a use of Decir or Dar; rewind and try again.

- 10 minutes (only relevant if you're on a train rather than driving): Quiz on your smart phone to review new phrases and vocabulary you've been learning, focusing on the trickiest ones.

Evening routine:

- 50 minutes: Have a Skype call with a native-Spanish-speaking friend, talking about the subject you've been practicing. For the first 25 minutes, don't use English at all. Have your friend correct any errors you make, and write down the correct versions of those sentences.

- 10 minutes: Review those sentences to enforce the habit of speaking them correctly. Repeat them to yourself before you go to bed so that they stay in your long-term memory.

As you can see, this routine includes not only learning new material, but also returning to the fundamental dialogues in this book. This will keep you from losing your way, even while you continue to branch out.

Use the essential dialogues as your *9 de Julio*. Make sure you know how to express your most important thoughts, and then, when you feel safe again, go out and explore some more!

Rule 2: Don't Settle.

Make sure your comfort zone keeps getting bigger. Never lose sight of what is fundamental, but don't be satisfied with staying there.

As long as you know the way, feel free to branch out. But be careful! Expanding into new territory is an easy way to get overwhelmed or to introduce bad habits. Remember the principle of imitation to keep you out of trouble when you begin branching out.

What exactly should you be imitating? Let's get into that.

As mentioned in Lesson 7, you need to be able to express your own thoughts in idiomatic Spanish.

Imagine that you're in Julia's position:

Hi, my name is Julia. I was born in New York City and have always lived here. I just moved to a new apartment with my dog, Snoop. I work as a financial advisor helping people manage their investments and achieve their goals.

On the weekends, I like to take Snoop to the nearby parks. Since I don't have a car, I ride my bike everywhere. I also love to eat at amazing restaurants with friends. I mainly eat vegetables, but once in a while,

I will indulge in tacos when my friends do.

Unfortunately when I'm with Spanish speakers I cannot understand them, and I am hesitant to speak myself for fear of making mistakes and embarrassing myself. One of the pleasures I get is listening to Latinos communicating with one another. They seem to get along famously! However, they speak too fast for me to pick up hardly any of the words. My primary goals are to be able to understand spoken Spanish and express myself in a way that others can understand me.

Many of these phrases are things that Julia is likely to say frequently. Wouldn't it be nice if she could simply rattle those sentences off, without even thinking about it?

To help her with this, my team and I provided her with a Spanish translation:

Hola. Me llamo Julia. Nací y he vivido toda mi vida en la ciudad de Nueva York. Recién me mudé a un nuevo apartamento con mi perro, Snoop. Trabajo como consultora

financiera y ayudo a las personas a administrar sus inversiones y alcanzar sus objetivos.

Los fines de semana, me gusta llevar a Snoop a los parques cercanos. Ya que no tengo auto, voy en bicicleta a todas partes. También me gusta comer en restaurantes muy buenos con amigos. Principalmente como vegetales, pero de vez en cuando me doy el lujo de comer los tacos cuando lo hacen mis amigos.

Desafortudanamente, cuando estoy con los que hablan español, no los entiendo bien, y no estoy decidido a hablarlo yo mismo por miedo a cometer errores y avergonzarme. Uno de mis placeres es escuchar a latinos comunicarse entre ellos. ¡Parece que se llevan muy bien! Sin embargo, hablan muy rápido y casi no puedo entender ninguna de las palabras. Mis objetivos principales son ser capaz de entender el español hablado y expresarme de forma que los demás me puedan entender.

After some practice, Julia now can say any of these sentences fluidly, knowing exactly what she's saying. This makes her extremely confident in starting conversations in Spanish: Confident that she's not practicing errors; she's actually practicing flawless Spanish.

Of course, in order to learn this, there were a few words that she had to learn in addition to the words from the Accelerated Spanish course (such as the words for "bicycle", "vegetables", and "financial advisor"). But obviously these are words that are very important to her, personally (not arbitratry stock words like "elephant" and "purple").

To become conversationally confident, Julia worked this personal script, as well as the limited-vocabulary dialogues, into her daily practice routine. She used focus and worked closely toward mastering these sentences, and her daily efforts paid off.

Time To Explore

Once you're oriented, you're ready to explore.

If you truly know your way back downtown from anywhere, then have some adventures! Go off to the awesome Congreso building, or even all the way to the beautiful suburbs.

For now you're probably going to have to spend a while on the dialogues from this course. Get to know Sofía, Laura, Nicolás, and Lucía as if they're your best friends.

But as you grow more and more familiar with these stories, you'll find that you won't need to review them quite as often. Eventually you'll be able to get down to listening to them them only a couple of times a month.

Once you can understand every sentence in those dialogues as well as you can understand English, congratulations: It's time to take the plunge into careful, intentional immersion.

Lesson 12 Vocabulary:
Regular Verbs

WE'VE LEARNED ALL the verbs in the "irregular" neighborhood near Joel's house. We've also been introduced to one regular verb on the beach, Deber, and one regular verb in the woods, Hablar.

We're going to learn about 45 new verbs today. But we don't have to learn conjugations! That's because the verbs along the beach are conjugated like Deber, and the verbs along the woods are conjugated like Hablar. So we'll basically just learn the infinitive of each verb we encounter.

Although the woods and beach are very different, the two separate verb paths follow some similar trends. In each case, there's more business and urban development to the south (nearer to Joel's house), but as we proceed north, things get more quiet.

Starting from Hablar and Deber, let's follow both paths northward and see how they're similar.

We begin by going to the beach.

Deber has already been introduced to us as the first shop here. This is in an area where there is very little else; it's a unique spot where buildings are connected to each other by skywalks.

Across the street from Deber is Seguir (pronounced "seh-GEAR"), a repair shop for segway scooters. As you can see, people are driving their scooters around in the skywalk. Seguir provides the parts (such as gears, belts, and gyroscopes) necessary for keeping a scooter going.

Seguir means "to continue" (or sometimes "to follow"). This verb is commonly followed by a gerund; for example, "to continue being a doctor" is *seguir siendo un doctor*, and "to continue doing that" is *seguir haciendo eso*.

Meanwhile, Deber is also normally followed by a verb, although it's usually followed by an infinitive: "I must be a doctor" is *debo ser un doctor*, and "I must do that" is *debo hacer eso*.

Now that we've seen what's next door to Deber, let's cross the irregular verb area and go over to the woods to see what is happening in Hablar's neighborhood.

Ar Verbs: Amusement in the Woods

After all this time that we've spent in Yol, you may have have a burning question: Where do most of the people actually live? Joel has an enormous house at the south end of our map, but the rest of the people must live somewhere.

Well, most of them live in apartment buildings on top of some of the shops. The Hablar shop, for example, has several floors of flats above it.

The woods around Hablar are prime real estate. Many people go by here, and it's a thriving community; there are tall buildings and public transportation to handle the masses.

There are a few neighborhoods here, each with a distinguishing appearance. In Hablar's neighborhood in particular, all the shops have fancy awnings over their windows, which look suspiciously like the top of the carousel from the amusement park.

Next door to Hablar is Joel's own office, which is called Trabajar. Joel claims that he's a very "hard" worker. What he means by that is that he goes to his office about once a week, and as soon as he thinks about working, he says "That's too hard!" and leaves. *Trabajar*, with a stress on "hard", is the word for "to work".

This office is connected with Dejar, a pawn shop that Joel owns. If you want to borrow even a small amount of money from Dejar, you have to leave your most prized possession as collateral. Most people find this very <u>hard</u> to do, but there are enough poor people in Joel's neighborhood that his business manages to swindle them out of some fantastic possessions. The word *dejar*, with a stress on "hard", means "to leave" or "to leave behind".

Actually, a lot of things in this neighborhood are "hard", even just walking down the street. As you can see, Joel is sleeping outside his office, a broken-down pawned car is outside Dejar, and just next door, a bunch of buckets of tar are blocking the way.

The buckets of tar belong to the local manners school, Tratar. The motto of this store is "Try to treat everyone nicely." Students are given a bucket of tar to balance on their heads, and if they mess up and spill tar on anyone, they are expelled. (As you can see, the awning is splashed with some tar. Students are expelled almost every day.)

The word *tratar* means either "to try" or "to treat", depending on the context. Keep in mind the phrase "try to treat everyone nicely" for Tratar.

All four of these verbs, Hablar, Trabajar, Dejar, and Tratar, are most commonly followed by *de*. We'll see why soon, but for now, just remember the colorful awnings, and imagine Joel flying out from under them, shouting "day!", just like at the carousel.

The next neighborhood has public transport available: Small carousel-style horses move along, allowing people to get a break from walking. However, this is a small neighborhood, so these horses don't really go very far. In fact, right now there are only two businesses open in this neighborhood: Entrar on the left and Pensar on the right.

Entrar is a secret society of reptiles. You have to say a password in order to get in, and only reptiles know the password. Joel sees the lizard going in all the time, but he himself has never been able to guess the password. The word *entrar* (with a stress on "rar", which is the password) means "to enter".

Meanwhile, Pensar is a shop run by the "Tsar". The Tsar does not really have any political power in Yol; he did once, but he never got anything done because he's as lazy as Joel (and less resourceful). Now he runs a few shops in Yol, where he is just as productive in business as he was in power.

At Pensar, he tries to sell pens. He insists that if you have a pen, everyone will think that you're smart, or at least that you're thinking. His marketing method is to sit on the street in front of his shop, holding the pens out and telling the passersby, "Buy a pen! People will think that you're thinking!" (This is not very effective in anything except marking all the carousel horses with pen ink.)

The word *pensar* means "to think". Note that both Pensar and Entrar are commonly followed by *en*; for example, "to enter a house" is *entrar en una casa*, and "to think about a house" is *pensar en una casa*.

If you go through this carousel horse neighborhood and don't jump off your horse, you'll end up being dumped onto a watery slide that takes you through the next neighborhood. In this neighborhood,

rather than *en*, verbs tend to be followed by *a*.

The first one we encounter is a shop run by Dar, whom we met in the irregular verb neighborhood. Here she has a "lifesaving" shop where she tries to sell lifejackets and life preservers to people who are going past on the slides. She mostly tries to sell these to the birds who go by. They normally ignore her, since they can naturally float just fine, though she shouts out "I'm just trying to help you!" The word *ayudar* (stress on Dar) means "to help".

In the adjacent shop is Llamar, a sign shop run by a llama named Mar. Any new business has to buy a fin-shaped sign from Mar.

However, Mar is a bit of a bully; his rage and strength have victimized many Yol residents who have crossed him. He tries to stay professional in his store, but he gets angry very easily; for example, if a customer calls him a "lama" (pronounced LA-ma) rather than a

287

"llama" (pronounced YA-ma), he pours out his rage on the sign that he's selling them, "marring" the sign beyond recognition. The word *llamar* (pronounced "ya-MAR"), means "to call". This is the word used when you're referring to what someone is called.

The slides end at two shops: Llegar on the left and Jugar on the right.

Whoever slides into Llegar is greeted loudly with a shout: "She got here!"

The owner of Llegar is an old granny who loves giving out prizes to little girls, especially little girls who are brave enough to slide past all of the shops in this neighborhood. But she's blind, so she doesn't realize that half of the people who slide in are guys, not girls. The word *llegar* (which sounds like "yeh-GAR" or "jye-GAR", kind of like "she got here") means "to arrive".

On the right side at Jugar, we find another old woman. She wants young boys to come and play, because she

288

has a bunch of games, but they're all designed for little boys. For example, she likes playing a blindfold game, and normally she's still wearing the blindfold every time a guest arrives. So every time someone arrives, in order to find out if it's a boy who wants to play a game, she always says, "Who got here?", or as she pronounces it, *jugar*. The word *jugar* means "to play".

Let's continue past the slides where the ground becomes level. The last neighborhood in this noisy urban area only has one business: Contar, a business that offers to pave people's driveways with tar in creative ways. Their motto is "Make your driveway count"; they pave driveways with very high-quality tar, and they claim that they can use the tar to help your driveway "tell a story". They think that makes them sound very important, although in reality their version of a "story" usually just looks like an elaboration on a hopscotch design.

The word *contar* has two meanings: It can mean "to count", or it can

mean "to tell" in the sense of telling a story. Think about a driveway with hopscotch to remember the double meaning.

Joel normally zooms past this store in a neighborhood on a train. This train looks a bit like a roller coaster, and it zooms away from the city toward the shops we'll find in the country.

Er Verbs: Amusement at the Beach

When we go over to the east side of the city, the busy urban area by the beach is laid out in a manner somewhat similar to the city area we just visited in the woods.

First, we encounter a neighborhood of buildings where the carousel-style awning is standard. However, there's only one shop here: Salir.

Salir sells airplane tickets. But it has a major problem: The business sits on the right side of the street, halfway in the water; when the tide comes in, Salir is often flooded with water all the way up to the awning. In these cases, the owner flies out in a Learjet, shouting "OK it's time to lear!" (He means "leave", but because it's a Learjet, he says "lear".)

Salir means "to exit" (or "to leave", or "to go out"). It is most commonly followed by *de*, e.g. *salir de la casa*.

The next neighborhood uses carousel horse transport. On the left side are Vivir, run by a prankster clown, and Creer, run by a crayfish who loves seafood.

Vivir is strange, because if you're innocently going by on a carousel horse, the horse might spontaneously veer off of its public path and actually go inside the store. If that happens, you've fallen into Vir's trap.

Many guests have fallen prey to this; they beg, "Can we get out now, Mr. Vir?" Vir always responds: "No! Your horse veered toward me, so now you live here! Hahahaha!" The word *vivir* means "to live". For example, "to live in Madrid" is *vivir en Madrid*.

Creer is a seafood shop with very foul air. In fact, it almost violates health code; the crayfish who owns the shop is required to wrap all the food in paper. Otherwise the smell would simply be far too strong.

However, there's a problem: He now doesn't know what's in each package, and neither do the guests. All he can say is something like, "Based on the smell, I believe this is a marlin head." Then he charges each customer based on what he "believes" the product is.

The word *creer* (with a stress on "air") means "to believe", or "to think", usually in the sense that you think something is the case. For example, "to believe in God" is *creer en Dios*, while "to believe that this is good" is *creer que esto es bueno*.

If you go down the water slide that follows this neighborhood, the only shop you encounter is Volver, which sells teleport devices. Well, it <u>would</u> sell teleport devices if it were successful. But it's not. It's a bit of a failure. Usually what happens is that guests slide in via a revolving door, and then very quickly, they are thrown back out. The revolving door moves extremely fast, sometimes throwing the guest back into the slide before they even entered the store.

Volver means "to return", often meaning returning to do something you already did. So "to return to that place" is *volver a ese lugar*.

Er Verbs: Parking Lot by the Beach

After this busy downtown beach area, we come to a small, plain-looking neighborhood that doesn't have a counterpart in the woods.

Here we find some verbs that are normally used by themselves, without any kind of object or prepositional phrase afterwards.

This is an area where beachgoers can park. The main features here are food trucks and other wheeled businesses that serve tourists.

On the left side is Suceder, an auto insurance company run by Dare. He convinces tourists that cars are often struck by lightning here (which isn't true), and he charges 100 Yen to give them special lightning insurance, "just in case that happens".

The word *suceder* (stressed syllable "der" but with a secondary syllable "soos", which sounds kind of like "Zeus") means "to happen". For example, "That happened" is eso sucedió.

Just across from Suceder is Morir, a funeral hearse. The owner, "Moe Rear", charges 50 Yen to carry away any dead bodies, for example when someone drowns in the ocean or gets struck by lightning. But he's not a huge fan of dead bodies; he always emphasizes, "The body goes in the REAR of the truck, not the front." *Morir* means "to die".

Next door is Dormir, a dormitory for meerkats. In Yol, the meerkats usually have an easy time burrowing and sleeping underground, but here at the parking lot, there is no place to burrow. So this van provides some nice tunnel-like compartments where the meerkats can sleep. Joel sometimes comes by to listen to the little animals snoring in their funny voices, though he tries not to get too close because he's afraid of all mammals. *Dormir* means "to sleep".

The last business in this neighborhood is Valer, a souvenir shop for beachgoers that primarily sells Russian nesting dolls. One of their most popular toys looks like a fish, with smaller and smaller fish inside of it, each of them more beautiful than the last, until there's a solid gold toy fish in the very center. Tourists love this kind of toy, because as you take away the layers, it seems to get more and more valuable.

Valer is an interesting verb that means "to be valuable". This is actually pretty common in Spanish, and you'll become familiar with many uses before long.

293

Ar Verbs: Countryside Shops

Beyond the bustling southern part of the city, the north is more tranquil. There are very few apartments, and the shops here are mostly independent buildings.

In the woods, there's a very large hill that accommodates quiet shops very nicely. However, this is the neighborhood that houses more verbs than any other; a hike up and down the peak brings us past over a dozen businesses.

All of these businesses on the hill are very commonly used with a direct object. (Think of the hill where the shepherd sings a hymn and leads Joel to covet his tea.) We'll use a simple recurring sentence example for all of these verbs: *la [action]*. This sentence structure is identical to *la tengo* or *la*

quiero, but now with the 13 new verbs that we'll learn on this hill.

At the base of the hill is an area where the trees have been burnt by a forest fire years ago and still haven't recovered.

The first shop is in a large tree that was severely damaged by the fire. The owner, Scar, set up a woodburning shop inside the tree. (He actually calls it a "woodscarring" shop.) However, the entrance is very hard to find. The entrance is through a crack, or "scar", in the tree, and visitors are expected to "seek the scar" before entering. Very few end up finding it.

Buscar means "to seek" or "to search for". As an example, "he searched for her" is *la buscó*.

Next door is another tree shop, this one with a door that is easy to find. The interior of the tree has been turned entirely into charcoal, and the owner sells charcoal pencils that make funny squeaking sounds when used. Theoretically, if you listen closely to these squeaky pencils, you can hear them telling the story of the forest fire. However, this requires very close, attentive listening.

Escuchar means "to listen". "He listened to her" is *la escuchó*.

The next shop is a small tent that is run by Dar's father Vincent Dar, whom everyone calls "Old V. Dar". He is a very forgetful man; he tries to sell holiday decorations such as Christmas lights, but he continually misplaces his merchandise. Consequently, he hasn't made enough revenue to upgrade his tent to a full shop.

Olvidar means "to forget". "He forgot her" is *la olvidó*.

The llama, Mar, has a couple more stores where the hill begins to get steeper (on the next page). One is a Valentines-Day-themed shop where he sells signs that have love messages. However, most of these are beaten up or broken, evidence of Mar's uncontrollable temper.

Amar means "to love". "He loved her" is *la amó*.

The second store sells large mugs. Mar sells these mugs because he thinks that the messages on them can serve as signs. However, most of the mugs just say "Take me!" on the side. They have very large handles so that they're very easy to pick up.

Tomar means "to take". "He took her" is *la tomó*. However, this verb is very rarely used with people; it really refers to "taking" in the sense of taking something in the hand, or sometimes in the mouth; for example, if a boy drank some water, someone might say *la tomó* to mean "he drank it" (the water). Just remember a mug associated with Tomar; both meanings are tied to this image.

Next door to Tomar is Extrañar (pronounced ex-tran-YAR), the "yard" store, which sells sod to the residents of the forest. As you can see, there's

a small clearing around the store, though all the sod around the store has died. There's a backstory to this: The local forest grew up within the last 50 years; previously, there was much more grass, and people had grassy yards. But unfortunately, yards are not a realistic hope for the future of this area. The store is meant to be very nostalgic, and their motto is "We miss yards! Bring yards back!"

Extrañar means "to miss". "He missed her" is *la extrañó*.

Disculpar is a sport shop owned by the con man. Supposedly, he sells frisbees and golf balls. But all of the supplies here are made of chewed gum. In fact, if anyone comes into the store with gum in their mouth, the con man trips them so that it falls out of their mouth. Afterwards, he always says "Oh sorry!" or "Please forgive me!" but then he turns the gum into more merchandise.

Disculpar means "to excuse". "He excused her" is *la disculpó*. (You might also notice that this has the syllable "culp" in it, like *culpa* from the kitchen meaning "blame" or "guilt".)

The next three shops are owned by the lizard: Mirar, Esperar, and (across the street) Encontrar. These are all built into a steep part of the hill, and all three are mostly underground; the lizard loves dark places and caves. (Note that the stressed syllable of all of these shops sounds like "rawr!")

Mirar is the lizard's primary business, where he sells mirrors. But he's not very successful. Because of the darkness of the store, the guests usually can't even see the mirrors that they want to buy. And then if the lizard turns on a light, there's a new problem: He ends up staring in the mirror, looking at himself in endless fascination with his reflection until he forces himself to turn the light off again.

Mirar means "to look at" or "to watch". "He looked at her" is *la miró*.

Esperar is the lizard's underground bird sanctuary. He knows that Joel likes to experiment on birds by putting them in the refrigerator. So the lizard provides a place for them to hide from Joel. If birds are afraid of Joel, they wait here and hope that he doesn't find them.

Esperar means "to wait" or "to hope". "He waited for her" is *la esperó*.

Speaking of finding things, the lizard has another underground shop to distract Joel. Encontrar across the street has the tagline, "Find the lizard!" Guests search through a series of tunnel mazes, and their only clue for where to go is the lizard saying "Rah!" over and over. As they get closer, the sound gets louder, and when they finally find the lizard, he shouts "Rar!", as if to say "You win! You found the lizard!"

Encontrar means "to find" or "to encounter". "He found her" is *la encontró*.

Beyond the lizard's shops, the sun blazes hot on a flatter stretch of ground, slightly melting the tar of the road in front of Matar and Necesitar.

Matar, like the lizard's shops, is mostly underground. But it's for a completely different reason: Matar provides illegal entertainment. Hot tar is poured in the windows, and high-paying guests are invited to use the tar to kill animals. It's very ugly.

Matar means "to kill". "He killed her" is *la mató*.

Next door, Necesitar is a more friendly shop, where instead of being used to kill animals, the tar from the road is collected in buckets and sold. In fact, Necesitar is closely associated with Contar, but it serves a different market: Contar sells tar to wealthy individuals who are paving their driveways luxuriously. Necesitar sells tar to the public at much cheaper rates, and their tagline is "You need tar!" In Yol, tar is used to make anything watertight: Roads, roofs, boats, and bathtubs. Tar really is a necessary substance, and that's why it is sold for such cheap prices here.

Necesitar means "to need". "He needed her" is *la necesitó*.

As the ground becomes level at the base of the hill, we encounter a toll booth. If you travel over the entire hill, you must pass through Llevar (pronounced yeh-VAR) and be taxed on whatever you brought with you. This is the only neighborhood with a toll booth, but it's implemented because of how far the road goes. Anything you brought with you, including your clothes, is taxed at 20%, payable immediately before proceeding.

Llevar (stress sounds kind of like "far") means "to bring". "He brought her" is ***la llevó***.

After the hill, we come to a railroad crossing. All of the verbs in this neighborhood are commonly used with indirect objects, such as le, but the railway divides the neighborhood into two categories.

On the nearer side, we encounter verbs that often use both a direct object and an indirect object. As examples in English, we might say "I asked him something", rephrased as "To him I asked something." Here "to him" is the indirect object (***le***), and "something" is a direct object.

In fact, "to ask" is our first verb: Preguntar is a business that serves expecting mothers. A pregnant lady comes in and asks, "Is the baby a boy or a girl?" and the response is to paint the answer on the lady's belly.

Preguntar means "to ask". For example, "I asked him something" is ***le pregunté algo***.

The next shop is often visited by the same women. In Desear (pronounced "deh-seh-AR"), women make wishes for their future baby. However, all of their wishes have to begin with the letter R. They might wish that he be "royal", or that she should have "radiance", or that he be a "reincarnation", or that she have "reliability".

The word *desear* means "to wish". It's often used to wish something for someone else. For example, "I wish you all a good day" is ***les deseo un buen día***.

On the further side, we find some very strange verbs.

As you can see, all of these shops are in tree houses above the ground. You can't access them directly from the road, and these verbs are associated with indirect objects, but not direct objects. This creates a strange grammatical effect, one that we pretty much don't have in English. (For the grammar nerds, these verbs are often referred to as the *afectivos* or "affective" verbs, because they refer to how the subject affects someone.)

The first is a treehouse restaurant called Gustar. This is a five-star restaurant (unlike Hacer, the 1-star restaurant near Joel's house). There's a very simple reason why this restaurant is so successful: Their motto is "We aim to be pleasing." The verb *gustar* means "to be pleasing".

A couple of strange things about this word:

First of all, it's always used with dative objects. For example, "It is pleasing to her" is *le gusta*. "It was pleasing to them" is *les gustaba*.

Second, this word is how the English word "like" is usually translated. In English, we tend to say "He likes the food." But Joel always insists that the food is the one doing the action: "The food is pleasing to him," or *le gusta la comida*.

This is a strange grammatical construction that almost never occurs in English, but there are actually several verbs that work this way, so it's very important.

Another of these stores is the verb Importar, which buys special imported goods, dips them in tar, and sells them at exorbitant prices. As you can see, this store is at the top of a very high tree, making it the highest store in the neighborhood. Tar drips down onto the other shops, but they don't mind; it's such a classy, important store that everyone is grateful to be rained on by their special tar.

The word *importar* means "to be important" or "to matter". For example, "The food is important to her" is *le importa la comida*.

This sentence is a bit more familiar to English speakers than *le gusta la comida*, but as you can see the sentence structure is the same in both cases. Practice switching out Importar and Gustar in that sentence.

Below Gustar, in the same tree, is a place called Bastar. Guests who climb down from Gustar have to go by Bastar, which sells expensive take-out boxes if they have any leftovers. The server always asks the guests two questions "Did you eat enough?" and "Did that meal do the trick?"

Bastar means "to be enough" or "to do the trick". For example, "that food was enough for her" is *le bastó esa comida*. (Spanish speakers use this interesting verb pretty often, and we'll look at more uses later.)

A few trees further on, we find a more negative shop, Preocupar. This is one of the con man's golf shops; at this one, he sells golf clubs. Anyone who enters is immediately scared into buying something: They climb up the ladder and enter the shop, and he quickly tells them, "You're going to fall out of the tree if you don't buy one of these golf clubs for balance!" (It's almost true, too, because the tree sways back and forth in the wind, nearly dumping the guests out.) The customers quickly buy one of his golf clubs to keep from falling, and then the con man adds, "Good choice! That club will help you make par on any golf course."

The verb *preocupar* (stress on "par") means "to be worrisome". For example, "the food worries her" is *le preocupa la comida*.

It's a little strange that the con man has a store here, because this is the most elite store neighborhood in Yol. But apparently the con man has swindled enough money to pay the exorbitant rent.

The owner of this real estate is the Tsar, the same lazy owner of Pensar. He sits in his real estate office at the end of the neighborhood, simply watching people pass by. He tries to make sure they all look worthy of his wealthy neighborhood, but he doesn't leave the building, and he never lets anybody in. He simply sits here, watching people pass by and watching things happen.

The word *pasar* (stress on "tsar") means "to pass" or "to happen". For example, "This happened to her" is *le pasó esto* (using the same structure as *le gusta la comida*).

Practice using Gustar, Bastar, Importar, Preocupar, and Pasar interchangeably, putting an indirect object before the verb in each case.

We have one more verb neighborhood in the woods. After we pass by Pasar, we find a bridge over a stream, which is just like the reflexive stream from the countryside.

Here we find three verb shops: Casar and Quedar on the left and Sentar on the right.

Casar is the floating Justice of the Peace office where couples can get married. The Tsar officiates these weddings, if he happens to decide to leave his Pasar office.

The word *casar* means "to marry". However, note that this word is almost always reflexive: To say "he's getting married", you would say *se casa*, and "I'm getting married" is *me caso*.

Quedar is another business, floating on the same boat. Here, Dar sells very special glowing darts: If you throw them into the water, they stay exactly where you threw them, floating on the surface of the water and never moving.

Quedar means "to remain". This verb actually means various things, but the most common use is as a reflexive verb that means "to stay". For example, "He's staying here" is *se queda aquí*.

"I'm staying there" is *me quedo ahí*.

Sentar, on the other side of the bridge, is a foot therapy operation. The business just looks like a bunch of floating seats; the theory is that once you're seated, the fish in the stream will nibble your feet therapeutically.

Sentar means "to seat". The most common use is as a reflexive verb: *Sentarme* is "to seat myself", and *sentarse* is "to seat herself". (Nobody in Yol says "sit down"; they always say "seat yourself".)

Er Verbs: Countryside Beach Shops

Just like the "Ar" verbs in the woods, the "Er" verbs along the beach get quieter as we go north. After the parking lot area, we come to a hill in the form of a rocky cliff along the

beach. The verb shops here are used just like the ones we encountered on the hill in the woods: They are normally accompanied by direct objects.

The first store at the base of the hill is Comer, owned by a horse named Mary. She is a health-conscious mare obsessed with seaweed, and she invites female horses to come and eat the green goodness that washes up on the shore. There aren't many horses in Yol that like seaweed, so she has a very niche business.

Comer (stress on "mare") means "to eat". For example, "he ate it" is *lo comió* or *la comió* (remember that *comida* is feminine, so the *la* here may refer to "food").

A little further up is a bookstore in a cave. This store is called "Leer", and it's run by the crayfish who owns Creer. The funny thing about this cave is that the ocean breeze blows through it in such a way that it turns the pages of the books every single minute. This means that customers have to read at a steady pace; they're forced to move on to the next page because of the salty air that blows through the store.

Leer (stress on "air") means "to read". "He read it" is *lo leó* or *la leó* (remember that *historia* is feminine, so the *la* here may refer to a story).

The next shop is Ver, a glass lens shop that produces telescopes, microscopes, and reading glasses. The glass that Ver uses is the clearest glass in Yol, made from the tiny sand that blows up the hill; the motto of the store is "Very Clear!" As a demo item, a telescope stands on the roof so that customers can see far out over the ocean or across the city.

The word *ver* (think "very clear") means "to see". "He saw her" is *la vió*.

On the right side of the path is Oír, an ear doctor's office that looks suspiciously like Ir (from near Joel's house), but rounder. This place is run by Ir's brother, Oliver, who goes by

"O. Ir"; he is much more sane than Ir, and he genuinely helps people to understand their ears and to hear better.

Oír means "to hear". "He heard her" is ***la oyó***.

The stores next to Oír, low down on the right side of the cliff, are subject to the rising tide. They're kind of hard to get to, and few people really ever go to the other two beyond Oír.

Conocer is a speed dating shop for beachgoers. It's owned by Ser, but actually she secretly has this business because she has no friends (nobody likes Ser) and she is desperate to find ways to get to know people.

Conocer means "to meet" or "to be acquainted with". Generally, it means "get to know" a person or a place; if you you meet a person, that's *conocer*, or if you're getting familiar with a city, that also is *conocer*. As an example, "he met her" is ***la conoció***.

If nobody shows up to Ser's speed dating events, she cries and goes next door to Entender. This is where Dare (from Poder) tries to offer counseling to people in distress. His version of "counseling" is to put on an understanding face, which he calls his "tender face", and simply listen to their problems. His most regular customer is Ser. If Ser comes over and cries and talks about her worries for an hour, Dare simply says, "I understand". (He never really says anything other than that.) Then Ser is happy and goes home, and Dare congratulates himself on being such a "tender", understanding counselor.

The word *entender* means "to understand". "He understood her" is ***la entendió***.

Beyond this hill, we encounter a railroad crossing, just like we did in the woods. For some reason, this railroad runs straight into the sea.

Here we find one verb that is used with both direct and indirect objects: Parecer. Parecer is run by Ser, but it's only open for a few hours a week

(usually after she's been at Conocer and Entender). Here Ser provides hair styling. But she's a one-trick pony; she only knows how to part people's hair directly down the middle, just like the con man's. Anyone who visits Parecer walks out with a middle part and questioning looks from others: "That guy looks a lot like the con man!"

The word *parecer* (stress on "ser", secondary stress on "par") means "to seem". If something seems like something else, then it *parece* something else. "It seemed to me like a dog" is *me pareció un perro*.

Nearby, the stream crosses our path and meets the ocean. Floating in this stream is an office belonging to the local psychotherapist, Tir (pronounced "tear", as in "he shed a tear").

Unlike Dare, Tir is a true certified psychiatrist. Supposedly he is really good at serving his patients, because he doesn't simply try to "understand" them (like at Entender); he truly tries to *feel* their pains. This can be a bit of a problem, though. He feels very strongly for his patients, sometimes even more than they do. So he ends up crying a lot throughout the day, and it often puts his floating office in danger of sinking because his empathetic tears amount to such a large volume of water. (Especially when Sob Bear visits.)

Sentir means "to feel". This word is normally reflexive; for example, "She felt happy" is *se sentió feliz*.

Before you do anything else in Spanish, make sure you can recall the names of all the shops we learned today. Walk through the woods, one neighborhood at a time. What shops are on the left and what shops are on the right? Do the same along the beach. Write down each infinitive as you go past them in your imagination.

Then proceed to the next section, and we'll learn about some quirks that many of these new verbs have.

Lesson 12 Application:
Verb Fluency

W HEN YOU LEARN more than 45 new verbs, you have to make sure you can use them properly! Native speakers use them flawlessly, without thinking about them. So how do we get there?

This will come to you in 3 distinct phases, not by trying to learn all the nuances at once. Our application lesson on the next several pages is extremely in-depth, but don't get overwhelmed! I recommend learning to use our new verbs in these 3 stages:

(1) Infinitives

Practice using just the infinitive forms of our new verbs, using *tenguo que* [infinitive]. For example, *tengo que hablar, tengo que trabajar, tengo que dejar*, and so on. For the "reflexive" verbs, use the reflexive word *me* before the phrase: *me tengo que quedar, me tengo que casar, me tengo que sentar*, and at the beach, *me tengo que sentir*.

Step through all of our verbs, and make sure you can *think* the basic meaning of each verb as you say these phrases. Get as comfortable with that as possible.

(2) Stock Sentences

Scan the next several pages for the highlighted sentences. Practice them until you can say them smoothly, knowing what you're saying (the quizzing resources at Spanishin1Month.com will be helpful here). Don't worry about any uses of these verbs beyond their use in the stock sentences.

(3) Idiomatic Use

Finally, proceed by turning through all of the next 24 pages carefully, absorbing everything through active work. Write your own sentences with each verb, including all their most nuanced uses.

This may take a few days or even weeks of practice. If you get frustrated or lost, go back to just practicing the infinitives for a while. Ensure that you know the verbs at their essence. Then jump back into learning the idioms.

Regular Verbs That Are Irregular

I kind of lied to you earlier.

I've called all the verbs in Lesson 12 "regular" verbs.

Well, that's _mostly_ true.

You probably noticed that we put some verbs on the "left" side of the paths and other verbs on the "right" side (based on the idea that Joel is flying north, as he usually does when following these streets).

Well, the verbs on the left side are all regular. They're conjugated exactly like Hablar (in the case of the woods) or Deber (in the case of the beach), with some extremely slight variations.

However, any verbs that occur on the right side of a street have some significant exceptions. Fortunately, those exceptions fall into some standard categories.

Take Jugar for example. You would think that the present tense would be "jugo"/"juga"/etc., but since it's on the right side, it's actually *juego*/*juega*/etc..

Basically, an extra E vowel has been added to the <u>stressed syllable</u>. This is because Spanish speakers don't like stressing "U" all by itself in a verb. They prefer the sound of a stressed "ue" sound.

Spanish speakers also don't like the stressed "O" sound all by itself; they tend to replace it, also, by a stresse "ue".

And they also don't like the stressed "E" sound all by itself. It gets replaced by "ie", in fairly predictable ways.

These changes apply to the verbs Pensar (*pienso*/*piensa*), Contar (*cuento*/*cuenta*), Encontrar (*encuentro*/*encuentra*), Sentar (*siento*/*sienta*), Volver (*vuelvo*/*vuelve*), Entender (*entiendo*/*entiende*), and Sentir (*siento*/*siente*).

If you practice saying these conjugations a few times, emphasizing the stressed syllable in each case, you'll get used to the patterns.

Salir and Oír do a "G" thing that you've seen before, in Hacer (*hago*), Decir (*digo*), and Tener (*tengo*). There's an inexplicable G in some of the conjugations: Specifically, the <u>first person present tense</u> (which is just one form) and ALL of the subjunctive forms.

Salir present tense:

salgo, sale, sales, salen, salimos

Salir subjunctive:

salga, salgan, salgas, salgamos

Oír present tense:

oigo, oye, oyes, oyen, oímos

Oír subjunctive:

oiga, oigas, oigan, oigamos

Make sure you become familiar with this pattern. If the first person present tense has this strange change, that change applies to all the subjunctive forms as well.

Conocer does the exact same thing, but this time with "zc" instead of "g".

Conocer present tense:

conozco, conoce, conoces, conocen, conocemos

Conocer subjunctive:

conozca, conozcas, conozcan, conozcamos

And then Seguir, to the right of Deber, is one of the weirdest verbs. You would think that the present tense would be sego/segue, but the letter E turns into a letter I: *sigo*/ *sigue* (pronounced "SEEG-o" and "SEEG-ch").

Seguir present tense:

sigo, sigue, sigues, siguen, seguimos

Seguir subjunctive:

siga, sigas, sigan, sigamos

All of the exceptions that I've described only apply to the present tense and the subjunctive tense. Any other conjugation of our regular verbs will be normal.

`

Hablar, Trabajar, Dejar, and Tratar

Let's go through all the verb neighborhoods one at a time and look at all the common uses of each verb. In each case, try to become really familiar with the idioms, and write your own variations on these sentences. This is how you truly get comfortable actually USING these verbs, as you'd do in a conversation.

The verbs in Hablar's neighborhood are all often followed by *de*. However, the *de* is used in different ways for the different verbs; there is no single sentence structure that applies to all these verbs, so we'll have to talk about each one separately.

In the case of Hablar, the *de* is usually followed by a noun (whatever you're talking about):

We're talking about my story.	*Hablamos de mi historia.*
I talked about tomorrow.	*Hablé de mañana.*

Trabajar is also usually followed by *de* and then a noun. The noun will typically be what you are in your work (such as "police officer").

You work as a police officer?	*¿Trabajas de policía?*
He was working as a doctor.	*Trabajaba de doctor.*
She will work as a doctor.	*Trabajará de doctora.*

Dejar can mean a couple of things. First of all, when used with *de*, it means to stop doing something.

Stop doing that!	*¡Deja de hacer eso!*
Stop reading!	*¡Deja de leer!*
I'm going to stop being so mean.	*Voy a dejar de ser tan mala.*
She stopped saying those things.	*Dejó de decir esas cosas.*

But sometimes Dejar means "let". In these cases, it gets a direct object before it and then a verb (infitive) after it.

They're letting you do this.	*Te dejan hacer esto.*
Are you letting me enter?	*¿Me dejas entrar?*
They haven't let her eat.	*No la han dejado comer.*
You wouldn't have let me enter.	*No me habrías dejado entrar.*

Tratar also has multiple meanings, as indicated by the institution's motto, "try to treat everyone nicely"; it can mean either "to try" or "to treat".

Tratar means "to treat" when it's used in the simplest way possible, with a direct object:

Do they treat you well?	*¿Te tratan bien?*
Why do you treat me like this?	*¿Por qué me tratas así?*
I treat him better than that!	*¡Lo trato mejor que eso!*

When it's followed by *de* and then a verb, it means "to try". Memorize the highlighted example:

Try to read fast!	*¡Trata de leer rápido!*
They try to read fast.	*Tratan de leer rápido.*
They were trying to do it like this.	*Trataban de hacerlo así.*

But when Tratar is reflexive, it means something complicated: It refers to what something is about. For example, "the story is about a little girl" would be *la historia se trata de una niña*.

It's about a girl.	*Se trata de una chica.*
It's about a little boy.	*Se trata de un niño.*
The story is about a large family.	*La historia se trata de una gran familia.*

Once you're comfortable with these idioms:

"he talks about that": *habla de eso*

"she works as a doctor": *trabaja de doctora*

"he stops doing it": *deja de hacerlo*

"she's letting me do that": *me deja hacer eso*

"he treats her well": *la trata bien*

"she tries to do it": *trata de hacerlo*

"it's about this": *se trata de esto*

…then you're ready to move on to the next neighborhood!

Entrar and Pensar

Spanish speakers don't think "about" things as often as they "think on things" (*pensar en cosas*).

They can't think about others.	*No pueden pensar en otras.*
I can't think about anything else.	*No puedo pensar en nada más.*
You can't enter the house?	*¿No puedes entrar en la casa?*

When Pensar is used right before another verb, it means someone's thinking about doing something.

They're thinking about getting married.	*Piensan casarse.*
He's thinking about getting married to the daughter.	*Piensa casarse con la hija.*
She's thinking about sleeping soon.	*Piensa dormir pronto.*
We were thinking about eating soon.	*Pensábamos comer pronto.*
I'm thinking about leaving later.	*Pienso irme más tarde.*

Next, the horses that are transporting us will dump us down the slides into the next neighborhood.

Ayudar, Llamar, Llegar, and Jugar

The verbs on the downhill "waterslide" slope in the city are commonly followed by the preposition *a*. Llegar is followed by *a* because, for Joel, people don't "arrive <u>at</u>" a place, they "arrive <u>to</u>" a place; for example, "arrive at the house" is *llegar a la casa*. Meanwhile, Jugar is followed by *a* when we talk about what game we're playing; for example, "to play football" would be "*jugar a* football".

She arrives in the country.	*Llega al país.*
He's playing these games.	*Juega a estos juegos.*

As far as Llamar goes, it probably seems natural that you would call "to" someone (*llamar a alguien*). But it's used in other ways as well. The idiom *llamar a la puerta*, literally "call to the door", is used to mean "to knock".

Afterwards they knocked at the door.	*Después llamaron a la puerta.*
Afterwards they arrived at the door.	*Después llegaron a la puerta.*

A very handy idiom: If you're meeting someone, it's normally polite to ask what they "call themselves" rather than what their name is.

What's your name?	*¿Cómo se llama usted?*
She was called Luna.	*Se llamaba Luna.*
Is he called Santiago?	*¿Se llama Santiago?*

Ayudar uses *a* if you're "helping someone do something". For example, although "he helps her" is simply *la ayuda*, "he helps her do it" is *la ayuda a hacerlo*. As you can see, the *a* is used right after Ayudar and right before the other verb.

I'm helping her to do it.	*La ayudo a hacerlo.*
He helps her find her house.	*La ayuda a encontrar su casa.*
They helped me play.	*Me ayudaron a jugar.*

Let's look at one more idiom using Llegar. The word *por*, when combined with some verbs, means that it's "yet to happen" or in the future. For example, *está por llegar* means "it's yet to arrive". (You can do this with Venir as well, meaning "it's yet to come".)

The best is yet to arrive.	*Lo mejor está por llegar.*
The best is yet to come.	*Lo mejor está por venir.*

Contar

The verb Contar is the only verb in its neighborhood, but it keeps itself company pretty well. Contar can mean many different things.

First of all, it can simply mean "count", as in counting with numbers:

| The child knows how to count from 1 to 100. | *El niño sabe contar del uno al ciento.* |

It also means to "count" in the sense of "being relevant"; for example, "that doesn't count":

| That doesn't count. | *Eso no cuenta.* |
| No, these things don't count. | *No, estas cosas no cuentan.* |

In English we also use the verb "count" to mean "rely", as in "you can count on me!" This happens in Spanish too, but instead of "count on", the idiom is "count with" (*contar con*).

To remember this, notice that the means of transportation in this neighborhood is a roller coaster track. This reminds Joel of the con man from the roller coaster. Joel is extremely untrusting, and in general, he doesn't think he can "count <u>on</u>" anyone. In fact, Joel thinks of "counting on someone" as a complete "con". So remember to follow Contar with *con* in the idiom "count on me".

| You can count on him. | *Puedes contar con él.* |

There's one more common use of Contar. Remember that the tar sold in Contar is used to make a driveway "tell a story", as they say. Well, that's because Contar can mean "tell a story". In fact, this is possibly the most common use of Contar; it's related to the idea of "relating a story" or "giving an account".

He told me his story.	*Me contó su historia.*
She was telling us the story of her life.	*Nos contaba la historia de su vida.*
He told me that he had lived a very strange life.	*Me contó que había vivido una vida muy extraña.*
The story tells that they wanted to be policemen.	*La historia cuenta que querían ser policías.*

In these cases, it's used just like Decir. In general, Decir is used for quotes and short facts, whereas Contar is used for entire stories.

"Direct" Hill in the Woods

Our largest verb neighborhood is the one with 13 "Ar" verbs that take direct objects. Here's one of the simplest ways to practice these verbs:

First he wanted to look for it.	*Antes quería buscarlo.*
First she wanted to listen to her.	*Antes quería escucharla.*
First he wanted to forget it.	*Antes quería olvidarlo.*
First she wanted to love him.	*Antes quería amarlo.*
First he wanted to take it.	*Antes quería tomarla.*
First she wanted to miss him.	*Antes quería extrañarlo.*
First he wanted to forgive him.	*Antes quería disculparlo.*
First she wanted to watch him.	*Antes quería mirarlo.*
First he wanted to wait for her.	*Antes quería esperarla.*
First she wanted to find her.	*Antes quería encontrarla.*
First he wanted to kill him.	*Antes quería matarlo.*
First she wanted to need it.	*Antes quería necesitarlo.*
First he wanted to bring it.	*Antes quería llevarla.*

In the next example you'll see a funny phrase, *el que sea*. This is a lot like *lo que sea*, which means "whatever it is", but *el que sea* (or *la que sea*) means "whichever it is".

You can take whichever.	*Puedes tomar el que sea.*
You can look for whichever.	*Puedes buscar la que sea.*

Let's remember something strange about direct objects in Spanish: When the direct object is a person, it gets an extra *a* before it. Compare these two examples:

I'm seeking money.	*Estoy buscando dinero.*
I'm seeking my friend.	*Estoy buscando a mi amigo.*

In both sentences, the structure is the same, and the noun at the end is a direct object. But since *mi amigo* is a person, it gets an extra *a* before it.

Let's get some more experience with this. On the next page, we'll practice this sentence again, but this time switching out various direct objects. Some sentences will use a non-human object (which will simply be a noun) and some will use a person (which will get an extra *a* before it).

I'm seeking the party.	*Estoy buscando la fiesta.*
I'm seeking the doctor.	*Estoy buscando al doctor.*
I'm seeking the story.	*Estoy buscando la historia.*
I'm seeking my mother.	*Estoy buscando a mi madre.*

Now let's try combining Decir with these verbs. When someone <u>tells someone to do something</u>, the order is in the subjunctive mood. Try out the subjunctive versions of your new verbs:

Tell her to take it.	*Dile que lo tome.*
Tell him to forgive me.	*Dile que me disculpe.*
Tell her to meet me.	*Dile que me encuentre.*
Tell them to wait for me.	*Diles que me esperen.*
Tell her to forget me.	*Dile que me olvide.*
Tell them to look at me.	*Diles que me miren.*

When Esperar is used to hope that something be the case, this always results in a subjunctive:

I hope it's tall.	*Espero que sea alto.*
I hope she doesn't need it.	*Espero que no lo necesite.*
I hope he doesn't kill it.	*Espero que no lo mate.*
I hope they aren't seeking me.	*Espero que no me busquen*.*

New idiom: When it's difficult to hear someone, it's common to use the word for "listen" instead of "hear". For example, "Can you hear me?" is "*¿Me escuchas?*"

I can't hear you very well.	*No te escucho muy bien.*
Do you hear me?	*¿Me escuchas?*

*Notice that the spelling of some words is a little strange. They're still pronounced as normal, and the quirks of spelling are there to keep the words from being mispronounced.

*For example, the letter C becomes a problem in certain verbs. In Buscar, the first person, **busco**, works just fine, because you have a hard C before O. But the subjunctive, **busce**, would sound like "busse" because the C is always "soft" before the letter E. So it's changed to a Q: **busque**, pronounced "bus-ke". The basic sound pattern, **busco/busque**, is still normal.*

The imperatives for Mirar, Escuchar, and Esperar are often used as interjections.

Look, over there there are many.	*Mira, allí hay muchos.*
Listen! Over there there are many.	*¡Escucha! Allí hay muchos.*
Wait (all of you), over there there are many.	*Esperen, allí hay muchos.*
Let's listen!	*¡Escuchemos!*

Extrañar does a funny thing sometimes. Usually, you're going to "miss" a direct object that's simply a person, place, or thing, such as *extraño a mi madre* or *extraño la cuidad*.

However, sometimes you'll "miss" a fact, or something that used to be the case. For example, "I miss us doing things together". That phrasing doesn't work in Spanish; instead, you'll replace the noun with a *que* phrase. This would phrase it as "I miss that we do things together", or *extraño que hagamos cosas juntos*.

Actually, you can do this with other verbs as well, such as Amar ("I love that we do things together"). With both Amar and Extrañar, you're expressing how you feel about a certain fact, so there will be a subjunctive verb after the *que*.

I miss us doing things together.	*Extraño que hagamos cosas juntos.*
I love us doing things together.	*Amo que hagamos cosas juntos.*

Llevar can mean "take", as in "I'm taking the water far away", but it can also mean "wear". Generally, Llevar has to do with the idea of bringing something along some sort of distance.

They had to find the water and take it far away.	*Había que encontrar el agua y llevarla lejos.*
She had to find the dress and wear it to the party.	*Tenía que encontrar* the dress *y llevarlo a la fiesta.*

Recall something we learned in Lesson 8: The reflexive phrase *se hace*, which literally means "it does itself", is usually used to say "it is done" or "it is being done".

This can apply to lots of verbs to make them <u>passive</u>. Let's use Llevar as our example: "Somebody took my things" is ***alguien llevó mis cosas***, but "my things were taken" (the passive voice) could be ***mis cosas se llevaron*** (literally "my things took themselves").

My car was taken!	*¡Se llevó mi auto!*
All my things were taken.	***Se llevaron todas mis cosas.***

Idiomatically, Llevar can also mean to bear the weight of having done something for a period of time. For example, to say "I've been living in Colombia for 3 years", you might change it to "I bear 3 years living in Colombia" (even if that's a positive thing, not a negative thing). That sounds a bit strange, but it makes sense if you get used to it. Here are some idiomatic examples:

I've been living in this city for 3 years.	*Llevo tres años viviendo en esta ciudad.*
I've been working in the city for 2 weeks.	*Llevo dos semanas trabajando en la ciudad.*
I've been here all my life.	*Llevo aquí toda mi vida.*

Preguntar and Desear

When using Desear and Preguntar, remember to use both an indirect object (usually something from the *le* crossroads scene) and a direct object (which is usually named specifically).

I wish you the best!	*¡Te deseo lo mejor!*
I wish them a very happy year.	*Les deseo un año muy feliz.*
I don't wish that for anyone!	*¡No le deseo eso a nadie!*

Admittedly, these sentences are a lot like something you'd read on a greeting card, not something you'd say in real life. However, Desear can also be used a lot like Querer:

I wish to do it well.	*Deseo hacerlo bien.*
They wish to speak with you.	*Desean hablar contigo.*
What do you desire?	*¿Qué desea usted?*

When using Preguntar, once again the simple structure is *le pregunto algo*, using an indirect object before the verb and a named direct object after the verb.

| She asked them something very important. | *Les preguntó algo muy importante.* |
| I'm asking you something very important! | *¡Te estoy preguntando algo muy importante!* |

However, very often, the "object" after the verb is actually an entire phrase that starts with *si*.

| He asked her if anyone knew. | *Le preguntó si alguien sabía.* |

This works, because a phrase starting with *si* can be used as a noun, just as a phrase starting with *que* can be used as a noun. Notice the similarity between Preguntar phrases and Decir phrases:

I told you that my sister was here.	*Te dije que mi hermana estaba aquí.*
I asked you if my sister was here.	*Te pregunté si mi hermana estaba aquí.*
I told you something important.	*Te dije algo importante.*
I asked you something important.	*Te pregunté algo importante.*

In each case, the verb is followed by a *que* phrase, a *si* phrase, or a noun.

As final practice, see how creatively you can customize this complex Preguntar example:

We're asking him if he has already arrived.	*Le preguntamos si ya ha llegado.*
They asked me if I'm always around here.	*Me preguntaron si siempre estoy por aquí.*
He asked him if he had already gone back over his steps.	*Le preguntó si ya había vuelto sobre sus pasos.*
I asked them if they had already told the story.	*Les pregunté si ya habían contado la historia.*

Gustar, Bastar, Importar, Preocupar, and Pasar

The verbs in the trees that "affect" something always get an indirect object.

I really like being here.	*Me gusta mucho estar aquí.*
It's very important to her to be here.	*Le importa mucho estar aquí.*
It worries me a lot to be here.	*Me preocupa mucho estar aquí.*
Being here is enough for them.	*Les basta estar aquí.*

Let's recall something we learned in Lesson 7: When we have indirect objects, such as those that use *le* ("to him"), we often mention the object twice: Once as a pronoun (such as *le*) and once again to be more specific. For example, "I gave my car to the girl" could be *le di mi auto a la muchacha* (literally "to her I gave my car to the girl").

This is still true when the verb is an "affective" verb, one of the verbs in the trees.

The car was pleasing to the girl.	*Le gustaba a la muchacha el auto.*

In this case, *el auto* is the subject of the sentence, but *la muchacha* gets more emphasis because she's the one "being pleased", so to speak.

So in general, when you use Gustar or any other affective verb, you're very likely to use the redundant indirect object, especially if a third person (such as *le*) is involved, rather than *me* or *te*.

The boy liked the food.	*Al niño le gustaba la comida.*
The boy liked playing with fire.	*Al niño le gustaba jugar con el fuego.*
The parents were worried about the fire.	*A los padres les preocupaba el fuego.*

The verb Pasar means several things related to "passing" or "happening". As an affective verb, it can work very much like Gustar; compare "something was pleasing to him" with "something happened to him".

Something happened to him.	*Le pasó algo.*
He liked something.	*Le gustó algo.*
Nothing was happening to him.	*No le pasaba nada.*
Nothing was pleasing to us.	*No nos gustaba nada.*

But Pasar can also simply mean "pass", as in "pass me the food". Idiomatically, it's often used as a question instead of an order: *¿Me pasas la comida?* (Literally, "You pass me the food?") You might notice that in these cases, it's being used as a dative-direct verb.

Can you pass me some food?	*¿Me pasas algo de comida?*
Can you pass me the water?	*¿Me pasas el agua?*
Can you guys pass me that thing?	*¿Me pasan esa cosa?*

When Pasar means "to happen", it's sometimes used to indicate that nothing is wrong. For example, if someone makes a mistake and says "I'm sorry", you can respond, "It's totally fine! Nothing really happened." The phrase *¡no pasa nada!* is often used to indicate that nothing is wrong.

It's totally fine!	*¡No pasa nada!*

Since Pasar has to do with the passing of time, or *tiempo*, the Tsar is often curiously interested in how people "pass" that time: Are they passing it well, or are they passing it badly? The idiom *pasarlo bien*, literally "to pass it well", is used to mean "to have a good time".

We had a good time.	*Lo pasamos bien.*
Did you all have a good time?	*¿Lo pasaron bien?*
May you have a good time!	*¡Que lo pases bien!*

In English we sometimes say "I'd like you to do this" or "I'd like it if you'd do this". But in Spanish, it's simply "I'd like it <u>that you do</u> this" (phrased as *me gustaría <u>que hagas</u> esto*).

I'd like that you stay.	*Me gustaría que te quedes.*
I'd like that you listen to me.	*Me gustaría que me escuches.*
I'd like them to eat this food.	*Me gustaría que coman esta comida.*

We have one idiom to learn for Preocupar. When it's used reflexively, it means "be worried" or simply "worry". For example, *me preocupo* means "I'm worried", even though it literally seems to say "I worry myself".

They're not worried.	*No se preocupan.*
Don't worry.	*No te preocupes.*
We're not worrying.	*No nos preocupamos.*

This reflexive version of Preocupar also can mean that someone "concerns himself/ herself" about something, meaning that they are concerned with taking care of something or making sure of something. This usually is followed by *de*. For example, "I'm taking care of that" is *me preocupo de eso*.

He always takes care of that.	*Siempre se preocupa de eso.*
He always takes care that that happens.	*Siempre se preocupa de que eso pase.*
He always makes sure that doesn't happen.	*Siempre se preocupa de que eso no pase.*

Very often, a verb's participle can be used as an adjective. For example, whereas *me ha preocupado* means "it has worried me", *estoy preocupado* means "I am worried".

That's why my brother is so worried.	*Por eso mi hermano está tan preocupado.*
That's why my sisters are worried.	*Por eso mis hermanas están preocupadas.*

Casarse, Quedarse, and Sentarse

I'll seat myself at some bar and wait.	*Me siento en algún bar y espero.*
I'll stay at some house and wait.	*Me quedo en alguna casa y espero.*
I'll get married in some country far away.	*Me caso en algún país muy lejos.*

To "get married" is Casarse (Casar, but reflexive). But to "get married to someone" is actually *casarse con alguien* (literally "to get married with someone").

His plan was to get married to the king's daughter.	*Su plan era casarse con la hija del rey.*
My idea is to get married to my friend.	*Mi idea es casarme con mi amiga.*

Idiomatically, Quedarse sometimes means "to end up" in a situation. For example, "I ended up without money" would be *me quedé sin dinero*.

I ended up without money.	*Me quedé sin dinero.*
They ended up really scared.	*Se quedaron con mucho miedo.*

That's it for our Ar verbs (in the woods)! Make sure you've solidified all of these before going on. Fortunately, most of our "beach" (Er/Ir) verbs are used in idiomatically similar ways to our "woods" (Ar) verbs, so if you can master all the woods verbs, you're ready to conquer the beach as well.

Seguir

Remember that the first neighborhood we encounter on the beeach has Deber and Seguir. These verbs tend to be followed by another verb, though in two different ways.

We saw in Lesson 10 that Deber tends to be followed by an infinitive, such as **debe estar por aquí** ("it must be around here").

However, Seguir tends to be followed by a <u>gerund</u>. The sense is to "keep", "stay", or "continue" doing something.

All right, let's continue eating.	*Bueno, sigamos comiendo.*
All right, let's keep talking.	*Bueno, sigamos hablando.*
All right, I'll continue being nice.	*Bueno, sigo siendo buena.*
All right, let's keep doing it.	*Bueno, sigamos haciéndolo.*

(As you can see from that last variation, gerunds can be contracted with object pronouns, which is fairly common after Seguir.)

Sometimes Seguir is followed instead by an <u>adjective</u>, typically from the Estar part of Joel's yard.

All right, let's continue together.	*Bueno, sigamos juntas.*
All right, let's stay happy.	*Bueno, sigamos felices.*
All right, I'll go on alone.	*Bueno, sigo solo.*
She's still crazy.	*Sigue loca.*

Other times Seguir is used by itself. In these cases, it simply means to "go on" or to "continue".

All right, let's continue.	*Bueno, sigamos.*
Life goes on.	*La vida sigue.*
They continued.	*Ellos siguieron.*

Here's a simple idiom: **seguir su camino** means "continue on their way".

He can continue his way.	*Puede seguir su camino.*
They were able to continue on their way.	*Pudieron seguir su camino.*

Salir

Salir is typically followed by *de*, like the verbs Hablar, Trabajar, etc.

He exits from the story when he wants.	*Sale de la historia cuando quiere.*
He speaks of the story when he wants.	*Habla de la historia cuando quiere.*

Creer and Vivir

They don't live in reality.	*No viven en la realidad.*
We don't believe in reality.	*No creemos en la realidad.*
We don't live in a house.	*No vivimos en una casa.*
They don't believe in God.	*No creen en Dios.*

Although it's common to believe "in" something, it's even more common to believe "that" something is the case. The simplest way is to "believe it", with the thing you believe in as a direct object (*lo*):

I can't believe it!	*¡No lo puedo creer!*
Can you believe it?	*¿Lo puedes creer?*
Now they believe it.	*Ya lo creen.*

But a more complex way is to describe the thing (or fact) that you believe, using a *que* phrase.

I think that he's here.	*Creo que está aquí.*
I think that I'm crazy.	*Creo que estoy loco.*
I think it's kind of difficult to do that.	*Creo que es medio difícil hacer eso.*

But what about when you <u>don't</u> believe something to be the case?

When you put *no* before a Creer conjugation, something odd happens: You get a subjunctive after the *que*. In other words, the phrase that you don't believe to be true becomes subjunctive. Practice switching out positives and negatives:

I believe that he's here.	*Creo que está aquí.*
I don't believe that he be here.	*No creo que esté aquí.*
I believe that it is difficult.	*Creo que es difícil.*
I don't believe that it be difficult.	*No creo que sea difícil.*
I believe that it is very strange.	*Creo que es muy extraño.*
I don't believe it to be so strange.	*No creo que sea tan extraño.*

Volver

I had to return.	*Tuve que volver.*
We had to return to the city.	*Tuvimos que volver a la ciudad.*

When he came back he was nice again.	*Cuando volvió era bueno otra vez.*
When I returned she was mean again.	*Cuando volví ella era mala otra vez.*

One of the most common uses of Volver is to indicate repetition. In English we usually say someone did something "again", but Joel likes to say that someone "returned to do something". The idiom is Volver + *a* + infinitive.

For example, "I'm searching for her again" could simply be *la busco otra vez*, but Spanish speakers often phrase it as "I'm going back to searching for her", which is *la vuelvo a buscar*.

He's doing it again.	*Lo vuelve a hacer.*
Today I did it again.	*Hoy lo volví a hacer.*
I never saw her again.	*Nunca la volví a ver.*

The Spanish idiom for "go crazy" uses the reflexive version of Volver. "To go crazy" is literally "to return oneself crazy", or *volverse loco*.

Everyone went crazy.	*Todos se volvieron locos.*
She's going crazy.	*Ella se vuelve loca.*

"Direct" Hill at the Beach

Let's quickly practice these short sentences using all of our beach verbs from the cliff scene, each in the present tense and with a simple direct object pronoun:

I'm eating it.	*Lo como.*
You're eating it.	*Lo comes.*
I'm reading it.	*Lo leo.*
She's reading it.	*Lo lee.*
I see them.	*Los veo.*
He sees them.	*Los ve.*
I hear it.	*La oigo.*
They hear it.	*La oyen.*
I know them.	*Las conozco.*
She knows them.	*Las conoce.*
I understand it.	*Lo entiendo.*
We understand it.	*Lo entendemos.*

Now let's practice this with more conjugations.

They ate it.	*Lo comieron.*
We'll eat it.	*Lo comeremos.*
You're reading it.	*Lo estás leyendo.*
You saw us.	*Nos viste.*
They heard them.	*Las oyeron.*
Do you hear it?	*¿Lo oyes?*
I heard it.	*Lo oí.*
We met each other.	*Nos conocimos.*
Do you understand it?	*¿Lo entiendes?*

The verb Conocer means "to know personally", "to meet", or "to get to know". This generally applies to persons, but it can also apply to places.

Remember that if a person is the direct object after a verb, you put an extra *a* before the human object. We can see that in the next example with the verb Conocer. Practice customizing the following sentence, but exchanging the <u>human</u> objects with <u>place</u> objects.

And do you know anyone like that?	*¿Y conoces a alguien así?*
And do you know this country?	*¿Y conoces este país?*
And do we see your friends?	*¿Y vemos a tus amigos?*
I know the president.	*Yo conozco al presidente.*
I know my city.	*Yo conozco mi ciudad.*

Remember that in many cases, you can replace a noun with a *que* phrase. For example, it's possible "to see the house" (*ver la casa*), but it's also possible to "see <u>that</u> the house is close" (*ver que la casa está cerca*).

Note also that although the verb Ver is considered "regular" for most purposes, it does have an irregular participle on the roof: *visto*. The next example will allow you to practice this while you also practice exchanging nouns with *que* phrases:

Haven't you seen the hospital?	*No has visto el hosipital?*
Haven't you seen that I'm eating?	*¿No has visto que estoy comiendo?*
Haven't you heard that I'm reading?	*¿No has oído que estoy leyendo?*
Haven't you understood these words?	*No has entendido estas palabras?*
Haven't you understood that he's here?	*No has entendido que está aquí?*
Haven't we seen that they're at home?	*No hemos visto que están en casa?*

Speaking of Ver, here's a common idiom that it uses.

In English, we have a funny idiom: When English speakers see that two things are related, they say that one thing "has to do with" the second thing. (For example, "this has to do with that".) But what do we mean by "has to do"? It can't be translated literally.

Spanish, instead, says that something "has to see with something", or *tiene que ver con algo*.

It has to do with the story.	*Tiene que ver con la historia.*
Does this have to do with your family?	*¿Esto tiene que ver con tu familia?*

One more Ver idiom. To say "let's see", Joel simply says *a ver*. Perhaps it's short for *vamos a ver* ("we're going to see"), but he hardly ever says it that way. *A ver* is often used when Joel is thinking or trying to figure something out.

Let's see... Where?	*A ver... ¿Dónde?*

Parecer

Parecer is a "dative-direct" verb, so it's used a lot like Preguntar or Desear. In the following example, the indirect object pronoun comes first, then the verb, then the direct object.

I wish you the best.	*Te deseo lo mejor.*
Does it seem the best to you?	*¿Te parece lo mejor?*
I asked him something important.	*Le pregunté algo importante.*
It seemed to her something important.	*Le pareció algo importante.*

Just like with Preguntar, you can use a *que* phrase instead of a noun as the direct object after the verb.

To me it seems like a house.	*Me parece una casa.*
To him it seemed not so.	*Le pareció que no era así.*
To her it seemed like good weather.	*Le pareció buen tiempo.*
Does it seem to you that I'm sick?	*¿Te parece que estoy mal?*
It seems to me that they love each other.	*Me parece que se aman.*
Does it look like a dog to you all?	*¿Te parecen un perro?*

Occasionally, *parece que* is used without an indirect object before it.

It seems that she took it.	*Parece que lo tomó.*

When Parecer is used reflexively, it means that multiple things look similar to each other, literally "appear themselves" or "appear each other".

I would say that they look like each other.	*Yo diría que se parecen.*
Many say that we look like each other.	*Muchos dicen que nos parecemos.*

Remember that some participles can be used as adjectives, such as *preocupado* for "worried". Another common participle-as-an-adjective is *parecido*, which means "similar" (the meaning is very much like that of *se parecen*).

I have many siblings, some very similar-looking.	*Tengo muchos hermanos, algunos muy parecidos.*
All the food here is pretty similar.	*Toda la comida aquí es bastante parecida.*

Sentir

The way that someone feels is normally reflexive. For example, "I feel happy" is *me siento feliz*.

Do you feel all right?	*¿Te sientes bien?*
We feel safe.	*Nos sentimos seguros.*

Note that you'll see a common but strange phrase in the next example, ***todo lo que***. It literally means "all what…" but it's just the most idiomatic way to say "all that…"

She feels happy because of all that she saw.	*Se siente feliz por todo lo que vio.*
She feels lonely because of all that happened to her.	*Se siente sola por todo lo que le pasó.*

Sentir can also be used to mean "I feel like something is the case", in which case it's not reflexive. Instead we get phrases such as ***siento que***, which is used a lot like ***supongo que*** or ***creo que***: When you think, feel, or suppose that something might be the case.

I feel like it's more than that.	*Siento que es más que eso.*
I guess the story has more than that.	*Supongo que la historia tiene más que eso.*
I feel like he's a better friend than that.	*Siento que es un mejor amigo que eso.*
I think that the position is better than that.	*Creo que el puesto es mejor que eso.*
I feel like death is better than that.	*Siento que la muerte es mejor que eso.*

Now for one VERY handy phrase: The idiom for "I'm sorry". (If you're like me, you'll find yourself having to use this one a lot!)

Joel rarely ever feels sorry for anything. Any time he actually feels remorse, it's a strange feeling for him. He isn't really sure how to respond to such a feeling, and he always blurts out, "I feel it!", which is ***lo siento***. This is the most common way that Spanish speakers say "I'm sorry".

I'm sorry!	*¡Lo siento!*
He's very sorry.	*Lo siente mucho.*
They told me that they were sorry.	*Me dijeron que lo sentían.*
I have to tell him that I'm sorry.	*Le tengo que decir que lo siento.*

Beach: Parking Lot

The verbs in the parking lot usually aren't followed by anything; they're just preceded by a subject noun. It's easy to put an adverb afterwards as well, such as *mucho* for "a lot".

This is worth a lot.	*Esto vale mucho.*
This thing is very valuable.	*Esta cosa vale mucho.*
That happens a lot.	*Eso sucede mucho.*
The parents were sleeping.	*Los papás dormían.*
My sisters are asleep.	*Mis hermanas duermen.*
His uncle died.	*Su tío murió**.*

For no explainable reason, Morir is often found reflexive. It isn't really supposed to be, but native speakers express it this way quite often.

Don't die!	*¡No te mueres!*
They died?	*¿Se murieron**?*
We're dying!	*¡Nos estamos muriendo**!*

*** In some verbs, there are a few strange cases where a letter O turns into a letter U. Native speakers have made this a habit for the sake of pronunciation; they seem to think that **morió** is hard to say, so it changes to **murió**. However, this difference is extremely subtle, so these verbs are basically "regular" for all practical purposes. (Most likely, very few people will even notice if you pronounce and spell it as a letter O, as it is theoretically supposed to be.)*

Immersion Time?

Lesson 12 rounds out the vocabulary that you need to begin immersing yourself in Spanish.

But before you dive in and lose yourself in Spanish conversation, I recommend reviewing the theory portions of each chapter of this book. Challenge yourself: What do you need to do to make your Spanish conversations as constructive and fruitful as possible?

As a next step, immerse yourself in the dialogues on the following pages. These will help you live and breathe in Spanish without jumping too far outside your comfort zone.

Afterwards, Volume 3 will help you push that comfort zone out further, step by step.

Appendix: Course Dialogues

Following are two dialogues that you should know by heart before immersing yourself in Spanish.

You'll find no English at all in these dialogues. Fortunately, however, their Spanish is entirely within the vocabulary taught by Accelerated Spanish Volumes 1 and 2, apart from these two words:

- *bar*: masculine noun meaning "bar" (cognate with English)

- *libro*: masculine noun meaning "book"

The sentences you'll find in **bold font** are sentences that you've been studying throughout this book.

If you want to hear recordings of these dialogues, as well as see the English and Spanish side by side, this is available at Spanishin1Month.com for free.

Juegos con Sofía y Laura

Sofía- Yo quiero jugar con la mujer de cara seria.

Laura- No la tengo. Estaba por ahí pero **nunca la volví a ver.**

Sofía- Eso siempre te pasa con todo lo que tienes.

Laura- Eso no es verdad.

Sofía- Sí, la última vez no pudiste encontrar el perro.

Laura- Bueno, eso sólo fue una vez.

Sofía- ¡Y ahora la mujer de cara seria!

Laura- Bueno, no importa, no está.

Sofía- Mejor juguemos en el cuarto de tu mamá.

Laura- No, mejor después de las cinco de la tarde. Para entonces se habrá ido y **podemos hacer lo que queramos.** Ahora juguemos acá, yo juego con esta y tú juegas con esta otra. ¿Sí? Eran amigas desde niñas, las dos son doctoras y policías y también juegan en equipos importantes.

Sofía- **¿Todas esas cosas a la vez?**

Laura- Sí. Entonces cuando la mía llama por teléfono a la tuya, la tuya no sabe quién es.

Sofía- Pero eran amigas desde niñas, ¿cómo no va a saber?

Laura- Es que se había ido por muchos años. Había estado en Argentina. Pero un día se quedó sin nada, gente mala se llevó todo y tuvo que irse. Cuando **llega al país** no tiene dinero entonces te llama para que la ayudes.

Sofía- ¿Todo se llevaron?

Laura- Sí, todo, hasta la casa.

Sofía- Bueno, dale.

Mujer 1- **¡Hola! ¿Qué tal tu día?**

Mujer 2-¿Quién es usted?

Mujer 1-¡Soy yo!

Mujer 2-¿María? ¡Qué bueno que seas tú!

Mujer 1- ¿Cómo has estado?

Mujer 2- ¡Estuve mejor que nunca!

Mujer 1-¡Qué bueno! ¿Y los niños?

Mujer 2- Están los dos muy bien. ¿Cómo estás tú? ¿Dónde estás?

Mujer 1- **Estoy en el país. Me tuve que ir de Argentina. Tuve un problema**, **se llevaron todas mis cosas** y **tuve que volver**. No es tan malo, era tiempo de estar en casa, pero ahora no tengo donde quedarme. ¿Puedo quedarme en tu casa?

Mujer 2- **Me fui a una nueva casa**, es pequeña, pero **tiene de todo, hasta una cama para ti**, claro que puedes quedarte. **Y te puedo dar dinero.**

Mujer 1- **¡Qué suerte! ¡Muchas gracias!** No me gusta que me hagan favores, sobre todo con este tipo de cosas, tú sabes, de dinero.

Mujer 2-No seas así, por suerte no tengo que preocuparme mucho por esas cosas. Bueno, me voy a trabajar, lo siento, pero **en casa nunca hay nadie por las mañanas**, llego a las siete, puedes venir a esa hora.

Mujer 1- Muy bien, **me siento en algún bar y espero**. Estaré feliz al estar en casa.

Mujer 2- ¡Hasta esta noche!

Sofía- Ya está. Juguemos a otra cosa. **Hagamos de cuenta que estos dos son amigos**, el mío le hizo cosas muy malas a su hermano. **Después se fue** y **cuando volvió era bueno otra vez**. Entonces su amigo, el que tienes tú, lo ayuda a encontrar a su hermano.

Laura- Bueno, dale. ¿Dónde está tu muchacho?

Sofía- No quiero que se vea aún, lo hago para que seas primera. Tú entras a este lugar, que es un bar, y crees que no hay nadie.

Hombre 1- ¿Hola? ¿Hola?

Hombre 2- ¿Quién es?

Hombre 1- ¡Soy yo!

Hombre 2- ¡Qué bueno verte después de tantos años!

Hombre 1- **Vine a buscar a mi amigo**, le tengo que decir que lo siento.

Hombre 2- ¿Y eso? ¿Qué es?

Hombre 1- Es de mi amigo… o sea, de mi hermano. Nos conocemos desde niños, es como si fuéramos hermanos, pero yo hice cosas muy malas. Después de muchos años entendí que había estado mal. Hace poco me supe que estaba en problemas. Entonces lo llamé, pero él me dijo no me quería volver a ver. De todas formas, lo vine a buscar. Le dije: "sea lo que sea, te ayudaré. Voy a estar ahí". No sé por qué lo llamé, supongo que para que supiera que venía, sería extraño si me viera por aquí de pronto. Tengo esto con cosas de cuando éramos niños, para que no olvide todo lo que vivimos.

Hombre 2- ¿Y todavía vive acá?

Hombre 1- Sí, **hace un mes hablé con Ignacio**, un amigo de los dos. Estaba con él hasta ese día, y **sé que su esposa está acá**, así que él va a estar aquí también. Tengo que ir a su casa, pero no sé dónde es.

Hombre 2- **No te preocupes, lo vas a encontrar.**

Hombre 1- Lo más difícil para mí es no preocuparme.

Hombre 2- Te ayudo con eso, ya que somos amigos. Tu amigo, ¿cómo es?

Hombre 1-Es alto, más alto que yo. **Muchos dicen que nos parecemos**, aunque yo creo que no tanto. **Es muy seguro de sí mismo**, pero yo no lo soy. Qué va a ser, soy lo que soy.

Hombre 2- **¿Tu amigo tiene un auto muy grande?**

Hombre 1- ¡Puede ser! Siempre quiso tener un auto grande, quizás lo hizo de una vez por todas.

Hombre 2- ¡Ya sé quién es! Trabaja con una amiga mía. Alguien, él o ella, está por ahí ahora. Te daré el nombre del lugar.

Hombre 1- Muchas gracias, has sido de mucha ayuda.

Hombre 2- No es nada.

Hombre 1- Bueno, y cuando lo veas le dices que yo te ayudé.

Hombre 2-Jaja. Ni bien eso pase, se lo diré. **Quizá sea muy tarde**, espero que no.

Laura- Bueno ahora hagamos de cuenta que pasaron unas horas y ya está hablando con el hermano.

Sofía –No, juguemos a otra cosa. Este no me gusta más.

Laura- ¡Siempre te pasa eso! Bueno. Juguemos a que una niña estaba en su casa, tenía una hermana y un hermano pero ni él ni ella estaban esa vez.

Sofía- ¿Dónde estaban?

Laura- **En la casa de unos amigos**, ella no había ido porque no estaba muy bien. Estaba con los papás pero **los papás dormían**. Entonces **se daba cuenta de que había alguien en la casa**, una cosa que da miedo. **Primero le daba mucho miedo** pero después **se dio cuenta de que la cosa era buena**. Esta es la niña y la mía, el tuyo es ese que está ahí, es la cosa.

Sofía- ¿Cuál?

Laura- El que está en la cama.

Sofía- ¡Pero es muy pequeño! Eso no da miedo, tiene que ser muy grande.

Laura- Bueno, busca el que está bajo la cama.

Sofía- Está bien, **espero que sea alto.**

Laura- ¿Listo?

Sofía- Listo.

Muñeca- ¿Cómo llegaste aquí?

Sofía- **¿No vamos a hacer la parte** en la que encuentra a la cosa?

Laura- No, ya están hablando y ya son amigos.

Sofía- Ah… bueno. Pero entró a la casa en medio de la noche… si él fuera bueno **no iría ahí, a su casa sin decirle**.

Laura- Es que no se da cuenta de que eso da miedo.

Sofía- **Bueno, sigamos.**

La cosa- Entré **por la puerta de atrás.**

Niña- ¡Qué extraño! Papá es el que **siempre se preocupa de que eso no pase.**

La cosa- No importa. Yo puedo pasar por cualquier lugar.

Niña- ¿Y por qué viniste?

La cosa- Siempre iba a ver a otra niña, pero se fue de la casa a otra muy lejos y estuve muy solo todo este tiempo.

Niña- **¡Pero podrías ser más bueno!** No deberías entrar así porque da miedo.

La cosa- Lo siento, **me gusta mucho estar aquí.** Y claro que **no me hubieras dejado entrar.**

Niña- No es así para nada. **Si lo hubieras hecho con cariño lo hubiera hecho.**

La cosa- Pero soy muy grande y extraño.

Niña- Bueno, sea lo que sea, eres bueno sí o sí. **Si hubieras querido hacer algo malo ya lo hubieras hecho.**

La cosa- Bueno, ¿y qué te pasa? ¿Por qué tienes esa cara?

Niña- Mi hermano hizo algo que no podía hacer. Nuestro padre no lo sabe aún, y **por eso mi hermano está tan preocupado.**

La cosa- Bueno, estoy seguro de que todo va a estar bien.

Niña- ¡Gracias!… ¿tú dónde vives?

La cosa- **¡En otro mundo!** ¿Quieres conocer mi casa?

Niña- ¡Claro! ¿Cómo es?

La cosa- **No lo puedo decir con palabras,** hay que ir, pero sólo se puede ir de noche y ya **casi es de día.**

Niña- Bueno, vamos antes de esta noche, te encuentro aquí mañana antes de que se haga de noche, ¿sí? Estaré con José en casa hasta que estés aquí.

La cosa- ¿Quién es José?

Niña- ¡Mi perro! Es mi mejor amigo, siempre nos entiende. **Antes teníamos una perrita, se llamaba Luna,** estaba muy sola y llegó José, pero Luna murió y ahora José está tan solo como ella. Ahora vete de aquí que papá y mamá llegan en cualquier momento.

Laura- ¡Listo! Se fue mamá, vamos a jugar a su cuarto.

Sofía- ¡Vamos!

Historias con Nicolás y Lucía

Lucía - **¿Qué hora es?**

Nicolás - Son las diez menos cuarto.

Lucía - **¿Y tú qué haces aquí sin hacer nada?**

Nicolás - ¡Ay! ¿Qué pregunta es esa? ¡Como si leer fuera hacer nada!

Lucía - ¿Por qué no vamos a jugar?

Nicolás - No, me gusta estar aquí.

Lucía: - Ustedes, los que leen todo el día, hacen cosas muy extrañas. Escucha, **hoy hablé con Miguel**, ¡**quiero que vayamos** a verlo! Vive en la otra parte de la ciudad, a **un par de casas de la escuela**, ¿fuiste?

Nicolás - No, no fui.

Lucía - **¡Deja de leer** y vamos!

Nicolás - Tienes que esperar. Después puede ser, ahora no, estoy leyendo así que no puedo.

Lucía - Pero nos está esperando.

Nicolás - ¿Por qué? Yo no dije que iba a ir. Pero bueno, ve tú y no sé, **dile que me disculpe.**

Lucía - Creí que ibas a querer venir conmigo…

Nicolás - **¿No has oído que estoy leyendo?**

Lucía - ¿Qué tiene que ver que estés leyendo? ¡Puedes leer después! Cuando lleguen mamá y papá será hora de comer y después de dormir y **no vamos a poder**. ¡Vamos! ¿Por qué no? **Extraño que hagamos cosas juntos.**

Nicolás - **Basta, ya te di suficientes razones. ¿Qué más quieres que te diga? No me hables** y déjame leer de una vez por todas este gran libro. Espera que llegue al final y puede ser que vaya contigo. **U otro día podemos ir**, a la casa de Miguel o **a cualquier lado**.

Lucía - Estás siendo malo. **¡Hace como mil horas que estás leyendo!** ¡No has hecho más nada hoy!

Nicolás - ¿Y a ti qué te importa lo que yo haga?

Lucía - Bueno, me voy.

Nicolás - **Bueno, hazlo.**

Lucía - No, mejor cuéntame, ¿el libro tiene juegos?

Nicolás - No, en vez de eso, tiene algo más.

Lucía - ¿Qué? **¿Un ser que no es de la tierra?**

Nicolás - Más o menos, algo así.

Lucía - Por favor, cuéntame de qué se trata.

Nicolás - ¿Cuándo? ¿Ahora?

Lucía - ¡Claro que ahora!

Nicolás - ¿Realmente quieres saber?

Lucía - ¡Sí! Si me lo dices ya mismo y me gusta quizás lo leo.

Nicolás - Bueno, **hagamos un trato**. Te cuento de que se trata y tú después me dejas leer en paz, ¿está bien?

Lucía - Está bien, ¡pero **trata de leer rápido**!

Nicolás - No, voy a leer como quiera.

Lucía - **Bueno, en fin**, cuéntame. ¿Es una historia de amor?

Nicolás - Pues… algunas, son muchas historias, todavía no lo he leído todo.

Lucía - ¿Por dónde estás?

Nicolás - Por la tercera parte y son diez. La historia general **se trata de un niño** quien entra en las historias que lee. Después, en cada historia pasan cosas, algunas parecidas, otras que no tienen nada que ver. ¿Alguna vez habías escuchado acerca de este libro?

Lucía - No, jamás oí algo así, pero parece una buena idea. ¿Entonces entra y sale cuando quiere?

Nicolás - Sí, por lo que vi, sí.

Lucía - ¿Cuántos años tiene el niño?

Nicolás - No lo sé, la verdad es que el libro no lo dice, pero **está claro** que no es un niño muy grande o al menos eso es lo que creo.

Lucía - ¿Y sus padres? ¿Dónde están?

Nicolás - ¡Ay! No sé, eso no importa, ¿quieres oír la historia o no?

Lucía - ¡Sí, claro!

Nicolás - **De acuerdo**, **la primera parte** habla de que el niño está leyendo un libro sobre reyes. El rey tiene un problema y necesita ayuda, entonces el chico entiende que él es el único que puede ayudarlo.

Lucía - ¿Y cuál es el problema del rey?

Nicolás - Un caballero quería ser rey. **En ese entonces el rey era joven** y el caballero viejo. Como iba a morir **antes quería matarlo**, pero el rey era más fuerte y **no era tan fácil hacerlo**, así que el caballero esperaba cada día por una oportunidad. **Su plan, una vez que el rey hubiera muerto, era casarse con su hija** para poder ser rey él mismo. Tuvo que salir del país para buscar algo que pudiera ayudarlo. **Pudo poner a todo el pueblo en su contra** porque les hizo tomar a todos un agua extraña, la cual encontró en un país **que estaba muy lejos**. El agua podía hacer que nadie quisiera trabajar, **entonces no había ni comida ni dinero.** Todo el mundo en el pueblo estaba como loco, quien más quien menos, pero todos trataban al caballero **como si fuera su amo**. El caballero sabía que una guerra bastaba para que el rey o estuviera muerto muy pronto o siguiera vivo, pero dejara su lugar y se fuera.

Lucía - ¿Y por qué sólo el muchacho podía ayudarlos?

Nicolás - Es que para que todo volviera a ser lo que era **había que encontrar el agua y llevarla lejos**. Pero el agua la tenía el caballero e iba a matar a quien quiera que la tomara. Pero, como el niño **estaba dentro de una historia**, no podía morir. Todo es seguro para él en esta historia.

Lucía - ¿De verdad? ¿Y cómo sabía?

Nicolás - **Al niño de vez en cuando le gustaba jugar con el fuego.** Como cuando uno pasa la mano rápido por arriba y **no se hace nada.** Bueno, cuando estaba hablando con el rey, había un pequeño fuego que daba luz. Dejó la mano sobre el fuego y se dio cuenta de que **no le pasaba nada.** Entonces le dijo al rey: "mire, yo puedo ayudarlo". Así que pudo entrar en la casa del caballero, tomar el agua, e irse de la historia. El rey creía que **no había forma de hacerlo**, pero, gracias a dios, el niño con su gran cabeza pudo encontrar la manera. ¿Qué tal? Bueno, ¿no?

Lucía - ¡Sí! ¿Y en la segunda parte qué pasa?

Nicolás - Pues, en la segunda parte está en una historia donde un policía está preocupado porque debe encontrar el dinero de un hombre muy importante y es muy difícil porque sólo tiene siete horas para hacerlo.

Lucía - ¿Por qué tiene tan poco tiempo?

Nicolás - Sucede que hacía seis días que estaba trabajando en ese caso, y el hombre, que tenía mucho poder, le había dicho que si no lo encontraba en una semana se olvidara de su trabajo.

Lucía - ¿Y le gustaba mucho su trabajo?

Nicolás - Mucho, **la historia cuenta que** desde que eran chicos él y su hermano **querían ser policías. Hablaban sobre eso desde la mañana hasta la noche**, todos los días. Aunque su hermano se hizo doctor **él hizo lo que siempre había querido.** En verdad, no sabría qué hacer si tuviera que dejar su trabajo. Y era de esas personas que hasta que no hacen las cosas **no pueden pensar en otras**. Y, como tal, casi se vuelve loco. Entonces, cuando llegó, el niño **le preguntó al policía si ya había vuelto sobre sus pasos** para ver si se había olvidado de algo. Al policía primero **le pareció que no**. Pero cuando se puso a pensar se dio cuenta de que se le había pasado algo muy importante. ¡Lo que sucedió fue que encontró el dinero atrás de la casa del tipo! ¡Del mismo que le decía que si no lo encontraba se quedaría sin trabajo! **Al final el niño tenía razón**, el policía había estado en la casa del hombre muchas veces y no había visto lo más importante. El tipo quería hacerle algo malo porque cuando eran niños habían tenido un problema y, como **estaba un poco loco**, no lo había podido olvidar.

Lucía - ¡Se debió sentir un idiota! ¿Y cómo supo eso el niño?

Nicolás - ¡Porque no era la primera historia de policías que leía! Ya había leído algunas y cada vez más veía que los policías se parecían: siempre se les olvida algo. Este policía podía ser igual a los otros, así que se lo dijo: quizá olvides algo que no parecía importante pero lo era, y cuanto más buscas más encuentras, así que siempre es mejor mirar bien por todas partes. **Con un poco de tiempo** todo el mundo puede encontrar lo que busca.

Lucía - ¡Al final era tal cual!

Nicolás - Sí, **de hecho**, antes de que el niño se fuera de la historia, **el policía le dijo que** si no hubiera sido por él **habría tenido que irse** a vivir a otro pueblo. No podía vivir sabiendo que no había podido con ese caso.

Lucía - ¿Y durante todo ese tiempo el policía supo que el niño era de otro mundo, afuera del libro?

Nicolás - No, **en ese sentido uno tiene que tener cuidado**, pues las personas de las historias no pueden saber que **no viven en la realidad** porque **pueden no tener control**, volverse locos. **Aunque sea verdad, puede que no sea seguro** y por tal razón hay que tener cuidado.

Lucía - **¿Y cómo sabes eso tú?**

Nicolás - Lo dice en la parte tres. En esa parte, el niño se encuentra con una chica. Se llama Olivia, **tiene diez años**, los ojos claros y **siempre lo sabe todo**, siempre tiene la razón. La niña está leyendo al mismo tiempo que él lee. Había entrado a esa historia muchas veces, primero entraba sólo de vez en cuando, pero le gustó tanto que quiso quedarse a vivir. Entonces lo lee una y otra vez. Pero le contó que hacía un tiempo, en el pasado, había vivido en otra historia. **Ella se había hecho muy amiga de cierto niño**, ya le había dicho **que pronto tendría que irse**, pero un día, cuando **fueron a dar una vuelta**, él le dijo "oye, **me gustaría que te quedes…** Quédate, estuve muy solo hasta que viniste". Entonces ella le dijo la verdad: "bueno, pero **vengo de otro mundo**", y también **habló de que lo quería mucho** y de que él estaba ahí, así que **ella iba a estar ahí también. Pero no pudo, porque hubo un problema y todos se volvieron locos.**

Lucía - **¿Quiénes son todos?**

Nicolás - **Las personas de esa historia, el niño, su familia, ¡el presidente y su mujer también!** Olivia tuvo que irse sí o sí porque, la historia ahora era otra y ya no estaba. Sin querer volvió a su casa.

Lucía - ¿Y qué pasó con esas personas?

Nicolás - No sabe, cuando quiso volver a leer la historia ya no estaba en el libro. La buscó por todas partes, pero pasaba de la historia número ocho a la historia número diez. **Entre ellas no había nada.** No había nada en el medio.

Lucía - **¡No lo puedo creer! ¿Se murieron?**

Nicolás - No sé. Olivia tampoco sabe. **En cuanto a eso**, hay quien dice que se vuelven nada… **siento que la muerte es mejor que eso**. **Ella estuvo muy mal por un tiempo**, sentía culpa y quería volver a estar con el niño, hasta que encontró la historia de la parte tres de este libro y fue feliz otra vez. En esta parte ella dice que **igual es un buen recuerdo**, y que **se siente feliz por todo lo que vio y vivió.** "La vida sigue", dijo en un momento. **Olivia vale mucho**, sabe muchas cosas.

Lucía - ¿Uno puede quedarse en cualquier momento?

Nicolás - En verdad, **no estoy seguro**. Parece que sí, todavía no entiendo bien porque no llegué al final. Igual, **si se puede**, creo que **puede haber problemas**.

Lucía - **¿Cuáles problemas?**

Nicolás - Creo que si uno se queda en la historia demasiado tiempo entonces todos se hacen viejos, pero uno no. Entonces los amigos se mueren.

Lucía - **¡No le deseo eso a nadie! Bajo ese punto de vista entonces es muy malo** vivir en una historia, mejor pasar por muchas sin quedarse en ninguna.

Nicolás - Claro, desde ya, yo pienso lo mismo. Mientras uno esté poco tiempo entonces no tiene nada de malo, es más, ¡es muy bueno! Uno puede conocer reyes y cosas extrañas, y después **seguir su camino. Es importante que uno sepa** cuando es momento de irse para no querer quedarse. Igual, al final, creo que es medio difícil quedarse tanto tiempo a la espera de que pasen cosas, **luego de un tiempo** seguro que **uno quiere irse.**

Lucía - **¿Y alguien más en la familia del niño sabe sobre esto?**

Nicolás - ¿Que entra en las historias? ¡No! Todos pensarían que está loco.

Lucía - Tienes razón, ¡este libro es lo más! **No le hace falta nada.**

Nicolás - ¿Viste? Te lo dije. Necesitamos más libros así de buenos.

Lucía - ¿Y cuando tú lees esas historias también entras a esos mundos?

Nicolás - **Supongo que sí...** Todavía no pude, ¡pero quisiera! A veces pienso que si los leo una y otra vez en algún momento voy a poder entrar. Cuando pueda entrar, espero ir al mejor lugar de todos.

Lucía - ¿Adónde?

Nicolás - ¡A donde está Olivia!

Lucía - ¿Siquiera sabes dónde está?

Nicolás - No, pero la voy a buscar.

Lucía - ¿Y **conoces a alguien** que sepa cómo entrar?

Nicolás - No, no conozco a nadie que haya entrado en un libro. Pero se tiene que poder, voy a leer hasta que pueda.

Lucía - **¿Y yo puedo ir?**

Nicolás - **¡Por supuesto!** ¿En serio quieres ir? Si entro, **alguien va a tener que darme una mano con muchas cosas**, puedes ser tú.

Lucía - ¡Claro que sí!

Nicolás - **Bueno, ¡ven!** Pero entonces tendrías que leer tú también.

Lucía - ¡Sería lo mejor de mi día, bah, de mi vida!

Nicolás - Bueno, dime, ¿qué quieres leer?

Lucía - **No sé, me da igual.** Dame algo y lo leo.

Nicolás - Mira, **allí hay muchos libros**, los cuales son todos muy buenos.

Lucía - **A ver... ¿Dónde?**

Nicolás - Allá, por la cama, ¿los ves?

Lucía - Sí, **los veo**, ¿cuál es mejor?

Nicolás - Me gustan todos, **puedes tomar el que sea**… a menos que quieras que leamos este juntos.

Lucía - **¿De veras? ¡Gracias!**

Nicolás - De nada. **Ponte aquí a mi lado**, así leemos. Quién sabe, **tal vez al final haya lugar** para que entremos los dos.

Lucía - **¿Y es seguro?**

Nicolás - Creo que sí.

Lucía - ¡Que sea lo que tenga que ser!

Nicolás - Sí… **¡Qué bueno que vengas conmigo!**

To get the other volumes in this series, or to access the free online course that accompanies this book, visit SpanishIn1Month.com.